AN OUTBURST OF FRANKNESS

COMMUNITY ARTS IN IRELAND – A READER

Sandy Fitzgerald has over thirty years' experience as a cultural practitioner and manager in Ireland and abroad. This experience includes founder member and director of City Arts Centre, 1973-2002; founder member of CAFE (Creative Activity for Everyone, now CREATE) and executive committee member of TEH (Trans Europe Halles – a European network of independent cultural centres).

Currently he is a board member of the Public Communications Institute and a partner in the international arts consultancy group Culture-Works.

He has contributed articles on arts and culture to a variety of publications including *The Irish Times*, *CIRCA*, *CAFE news* and *Kultur Risse*.

AN OUTBURST OF FRANKNESS

COMMUNITY ARTS IN IRELAND – A READER

Edited by
SANDY FITZGERALD

AN OUTBURST OF FRANKNESS

First published 2004

By tasc at New Island

an imprint of New Island

2 Brookside

Dundrum Road

Dublin 14

www.newisland.ie

ISBN 1 904301 64 9

British Library Cataloguing in Publication Data.
A CIP catalogue record for this book is available from the British Library.

Typeset by New Island
Cover design by PCC
Cover photograph: 'Burning the Demons – Embracing the Future' event in Fatima Mansions, Rialto, Dublin, 1994 (Enda O'Brien)
Printed in Ireland by ColourBooks

10 9 8 7 6 5 4 3 2 1

'All art is political'
Joseph Beúys

CONTENTS

Acknowledgements

A heartfelt thanks to all those who have helped with the publication of *An Outburst of Frankness*, in particular the contributors, who made this book possible by dedicating many hours of their time in the preparation and editing of their essays or through their participation in the fora: also Ed Carroll, Paula Clancy, Arthur Duignan, Kitty Farrell, Bill Harpe, Tara Hipwell, Nuala Hunt, Bill McAlister, Phill McCaughey, John Sutton and the staff of the arts office, Dundalk Town Council.

While three organisations came together to produce this publication, namely City Arts Centre, CREATE and Community Arts Forum (CAF), it could not have happened without the very important support of the following:

Introduction

Community arts first surfaced in Ireland in the late 1970s, ushering in something of a quiet revolution, which has since grown into a cultural phenomenon. While many might raise an eyebrow at community arts being either revolutionary or a phenomenon, it is worth pausing to consider the influence community arts has had on every aspect of cultural life on the island: from government departments to community projects; from funders to prestige art institutions. In fact, the unprecedented growth in creative activity and cultural development within the thirty-two counties of Ireland is heavily indebted to community arts, spanning, as it does, an exhausting array of activity including arts centres, festivals, youth projects, disability projects, community training programmes, artists in residence schemes, prison workshops and school programmes.

Yet, there is an anomaly here, because community arts go unrecognised and uncredited for such a flowering of cultural activity. It seemed that as the number of community arts projects and practitioners grew, far outnumbering the artists and audiences of the established arts world, a comparable level of support and recognition never manifested itself. Community arts remains a footnote to the fine arts, the latter promoted as the only real arbiter of artistic taste and cultured living. Indeed, arts commentators rarely mention community arts and, when they do, damn with faint praise, condescension or outright hostility. The reasons for this are many – it is still a very young practice, a percentage of its work is marginalised by definition, the radical and issue-based nature of some of the work excluded it from the mainstream, signature artists were and still are threatened by the communal approach, hundreds of years of cultural hierarchy is hard to overcome – but one singular fact has played a large part in dissipating the profile of community arts, namely the failure of community arts itself to secure its own memory or to articulate and distribute its values and work through dedicated printed texts.

This is never so stark as when confronted by racks of art publications in shops and libraries. While the shelves groan under the weight of art history tomes, following the line of western art from Grecian times to the present day, it is almost impossible to find anything written on community arts. This has been a key failure on the part of community arts and arises because people involved in community arts have largely been consumed with 'doing', hard pressed to find the time and the money for practice, never mind publishing its outcomes. But without the context of theory, analysis, recording and archiving, community arts has been easily relegated to the shadows of the establishment. As a result, the supporting dialectic is not there in the same way as the fine arts world manifestly has such support. *An Outburst of Frankness* is a response to the way community arts has been relegated to the sidelines of contemporary cultural history in Ireland and is a step towards redressing this imbalance.

By the same token, it is worth keeping in mind that *An Outburst of Frankness* is not definitive on the subject of community arts in Ireland and makes no such claim. Indeed the very nature of a reader is to create a debate, both within the texts and among the readership. The structure and layout of the book reflects this by counterpointing essays, quotes, visuals, recorded dialogues and historical references in the hope of creating a dynamic which informs and engages at the same time.

Not an academic book, the style here is accessible and open. Beginning and ending with the edited transcripts of two fora, which debate historic and contemporary issues around community arts, the body of the book is made up of fourteen essays and this material is grouped under three main headings. The first section traces the history of community arts and places this history in a wider cultural, social and political milieu. The second section examines community arts through a theoretical lens. And the last part has predominately a practitioner's voice. However, all these elements of discourse run throughout the book and this division must be recognised for the format device it is: there to assist the reader rather than create any artificial separations.

The editorial board had to make decisions as to who would be invited to contribute essays to the reader. Such decisions were not arrived at lightly and the process involved creating a matrix of intersecting themes and headings, such as practice, theory, art forms, north/south and gender. While there are many people who could have been included in the book, space was limited and we had to make our choices. Most of the commissioned contributors are not professional writers but the voices here are from people who passionately believe in creativity as a primary force for individual and communal change, empowerment and celebration. They were chosen for their experience and insight into cultural life in general and community arts in particular. Our sincere wish is that other voices appear on the shelves beside this book, complementing, or even questioning, our work.

We do believe, however, that the following content presents a wide range of views, which both illuminate and present a challenge to the reader on issues of community, culture and art in Ireland today. We are also excited by the opportunity to present our book in the context of the TASC imprint series with New Island. Placing the arts and culture debate within the framework of a cultural democracy initiative such as TASC introduces welcome and relevant connections, linking this book to wider social and political concerns.

Oh, and you may be wondering about the title. It comes from an off the cuff remark made by Michael D. Higgins when he was Minister for the Arts, Culture and the Gaeltacht at the launch of the Arts Council's first Arts Plan and seemed to suit our purpose admirably. Having read the book you may agree!

Editor: Sandy Fitzgerald

Editorial Board: Chris Ball, Alexa Coyne, Heather Floyd, Declan McGonagle, Ruairí Ó Cuív, Nicola Swanton, Wes Wilkie

COMMUNITY ARTS FORUM 1, CORK, 13 OCTOBER 2003

Two fora were held in Cork in October 2003, addressing the history and contemporary practice of community arts in an Irish context. These fora were chosen as a format for giving an insight into community arts because they offered an opportunity to hear a diversity of experience in a way which could not have otherwise been accommodated within the scope of this reader. They provided an opportunity for a range of views to be heard and also informed many of the points which arise elsewhere in the book. Both fora were recorded, and the edited versions of these transcripts appear here, 'book ending' the essays and other content, beginning with a historical perspective and ending with a discussion on contemporary practice.

FOOTSBARN perform on the Diamond in Dublin's north inner city as part of an NCCCAP festival, 1979. Photo: Derek Speirs/Report

Historical forum

Participants

Mowbray Bates, Ollie Breslin, Annie Kilmartin, James King, Tony Ó Dálaigh, Helen O'Donoghue, Sue Richardson, Peter Sheridan

Chairperson

Doireann Ní Bhriain (assisted by Susan Coughlan)

Participants' and Chairperson's biographies

Mowbray Bates' involvement with 'community arts' began in England in the early 1970s. Moving to Ireland, he co-founded Neighbourhood Open Workshops (NOW) in Belfast, piloted the use of theatre in a long-term substance-abuse project in Dublin and devised CAFE's first National Arts Worker development course. He has taught and lectured widely. Currently, with the Institute for Choreography and Dance, his interest is in the development of dance in specific contexts, from programmes for young people 'at risk' and the unemployed, to older people in dance (OPID).

Ollie Breslin is artistic director of Waterford Youth Drama, which is a youth arts resource in Waterford City providing workshops in drama, dance, film and creative writing for young people. He is also a founder member of the arts festival in Waterford. He became involved in youth and community arts through Ciotog Community Theatre, which was set up in the early eighties. He was a committee member of the Arts for All Project (Waterford) and CAFE for a number of years. He was very involved in the promotion of rock music through the music co-op Music Moves in Waterford. He worked for a number of years as a full-time youth worker in youth projects in Waterford and is presently a board member of the National Association of Youth Drama.

Susan Coughlan (see biography under essayists)

Annie Kilmartin began working in theatre as an actress in 1975, performing in *No Entry* and *Women at Work* (Project Arts Centre), *The Risen*

People (Project Arts Centre and ICA London), *Where All Your Dreams Come True* (ITC) and *The Liberty Suit* (Royal Court London). In 1979 Annie founded Moving Theatre and was artistic director until 1986. She was a director of the Project Arts Centre in the early eighties and a co-founder of CAFE (Chairperson 1988/89). Plays she directed include *Legs Eleven* (Dublin Theatre Festival), *We Can't Pay, We Won't Pay* (Project Arts Centre), *Heartstone* (TEAM) and *Accidental Death of an Anarchist* (Red Kettle). She was a writer and performer with the comedy twosome The Bawdy Beautifuls and worked in Fatima Mansions in the late eighties as part of the ACE programme. Annie trained in psychotherapy 1990–94 and is now a practising psychotherapist and writer.

James King is a lecturer in community drama at the University of Ulster, Magee College, Derry. His courses comprise a variety of community drama forms, including Playback Theatre, Theatre of the Oppressed, Action Theatre and drama therapy. His outreach work includes drama sessions in a local disability resource centre. He co-ordinates the Bag-a-Trix action group and regularly engages in spontaneous street art and performance experiments.

Tony Ó Dálaigh has been involved in arts administration since 1963 when he was appointed manager of An Damer, the Irish language theatre which premiered Brendan Behan's *An Giall* (*The Hostage*). He was co-founder and manager of Irish National Opera 1965–85; first General Administrator of Irish Theatre Company 1974–78; Director RHK (now IMMA) 1986–90; and Director Dublin Theatre Festival 1990–99. Now a freelance consultant, he has undertaken projects for the Arts Council, Draíocht, Mermaid Theatre and Tyrone Productions (Executive Director – Opening Ceremony of the Special Olympics World Games 2003 in Croke Park, June 2003).

Helen O'Donoghue qualified in Fine Art, Painting, from the National College of Art and Design, Dublin. In 1980, she initiated the first formal arts intervention at primary school level with artist Dervil Jordan. From 1983 to 1987 she piloted projects for the Arts Council as an artist working with community groups in counties Galway, Mayo and Dublin. In 1985 she formed a co-operative film and video company, City Vision, and was one of its directors until 1989. With this company she directed a series of video projects with and about children. The best known is Look at my Hands, a two-part documentary arising from two years action-based research with pre-school children. Currently, she is senior curator, Head of Education and Community Programmes, at the Irish Museum of Modern Art (IMMA).

Sue Richardson worked with Women's Community Press in the early eighties where she co-edited *Pure Murder*, the first Irish book on heroin use, and on *Write Up Your Street*, a collection of stories from community writers' groups. Concurrently she was a freelance typesetter and active in women's and prisoners' rights groups. She worked with CAFE from 1988 to 1999, when she left to become a student of painting, pottery and wood-work.

Peter Sheridan was born in Dublin in 1952, and has spent most of his life writing, directing and collaborating in the theatre. Recently he has extended into film (*Borstal Boy*), memoir (*44* and *Forty-Seven Roses*) and fiction (*Big Fat Love*). An early campaigner and practitioner in the field of community arts, Peter initiated one of the first recognised community arts programmes, City Workshop, in Dublin's north inner city in 1980. He was also instrumental in co-ordinating early efforts to formalise and strengthen the community arts sector in Ireland, notably as a founder member of CAFE where he organised the first community arts worker course.

Doireann Ní Bhriain is an arts consultant and broadcaster. She worked for many years with RTÉ radio and television, especially in arts programming. She was Irish Commissioner for l'Imaginaire Irlandais in Paris in 1996, director of the Celtic Film and Television Festival in 1998 and general manager of Millennium Festivals 1997–2001. Since then she has worked as an arts consultant with the Arts Council, Údarás na Gaeltachta, Fáilte Ireland and several local authorities. She continues to do some occasional broadcasting work for RTÉ and TG4.

Chairperson **Doireann Ní Bhriain** opened the discussion by asking how people originally became involved in community arts.

Mowbray Bates: I started in Belfast in 1978, at a juncture of political activity and politicised arts.

Doireann Ní Bhriain: My understanding is that the work being done by Neighbourhood Open Workshops [the organisation Mowbray Bates co-founded in Belfast] didn't go unnoticed in the Republic.

Annie Kilmartin: They were very influential in our work in Moving Theatre. Mo and the company came down and were very involved in initiating projects we did with the elderly in Drimnagh and this kind of kick started us working within a community context. They were our inspiration.

Doireann Ní Bhriain: Peter were you aware of Mo's work at the time?

Peter Sheridan: Yeah, but probably from a different base. In the late seventies many of us had been involved in left wing, agitational, drama. For me, the huge transition came about when you realised that the next stage is that of bringing theatre to a community and making it happen in a community context, of making the audience the performers. That in fact the audience had been disenfranchised. The thought that I have most, when I think back, is that inequality was endemic in the arts, it was actually enshrined in the whole organisation and infrastructure of the way the arts were organised in Ireland. Therefore the next stage was to actually make those communities the subject of the work itself. Suddenly you were legitimising and validating an experience that people had and you were doing it in an arts/cultural context, which was quite new, and there was a sense that something radical was taking place. Certainly that work was being mirrored by some of the work that James was doing in the north and Mo and other people and it was happening in Waterford Arts for All and Moving Theatre were doing it so one became aware that there were all these pockets of people who were basically on the same journey.

Doireann Ní Bhriain: James does that ring true with you, this need for legitimising and validating people's experience?

James King: Well that would have been the key underpinning of my work in the field.

Doireann Ní Bhriain: You referred there Peter to the deep inequality that there was in the arts. Maybe we should talk a bit about the context in which this was happening. Does anybody share Peter's view?

Ollie Breslin: Yes, I would be one of these people who got involved in the arts because of somebody like Peter. I was unemployed so I went to this workshop with this guy Ted O'Regan and Ted had us all 'feeling our space'. Anyway I eventually signed up for this theatre company [Ciotog community theatre] and it changed my life. I had no interest in theatre beforehand. I might have gone to see one play in my

'In order to understand this "poetics of the oppressed" one must keep in mind its main objective: to change the people – "spectators", passive beings in the theatrical phenomenon – into subjects, into actors, transformers of the dramatic action.' Augusto Boal from his book *Theatre of the Oppressed*, Pluto Classics, 1979

life before that. I was twenty-one and this was Arts for All, a project which came out of the work of Combat Poverty in Waterford. They were very influenced by developments in the UK. For example you have now in Waterford the Arts Centre [Garter Lane], Red Kettle Theatre Company, and ourselves in Waterford Youth Drama. All with direct links back to Waterford Arts for All Project. Unemployment to me is the key. At that time unemployment was huge and I think that that was really a big part of why a lot of these things happened because there was a radical side to the arts. I suppose people were fed up with the system and wanted to make a statement against the system and manifest it in some way. That was to me a very big backdrop to the whole thing.

James King: Unemployment links with our work on the streets in those days because, while there was a lot of political trouble going on we were involved in what was called Better Life for All, a campaign sponsored by the trades councils and trade unions. And a lot of our performance work would have been in relation to rallies that they were having.

Doireann Ní Bhriain: Mo, you said at the outset that it was political and that it involved politicised artists. Would other people share that view?

Table members: Yes, yes very much.

Mowbray Bates: There seems to be two broad strands in just hearing these stories that people are remembering. People who would be looking to push the boundaries of art, liberating art from museums and theatre spaces. Then there would be the direction of political activism and community development, the use of art in a creative way to further political campaigns, specific single issues. And I suppose then there would be people who would want to look at democratising culture. People who would see culture as defined very narrowly from within the terms of a strong left-wing socialist tradition.

Annie Kilmartin: And I think CAFE was born out of that idea of arts for all. We were all very passionate about the arts and wanted to make creative activity accessible to everyone and not just the privileged few. It was the politics that brought us together. We just found ourselves gravitating towards each other and then one day we were on the train to Cork twenty years ago this year.

Doireann Ní Bhriain: Why were you on the train to Cork?

Annie Kilmartin: I think it was to really make connections. We had contact with Neighbourhood Open Workshops, we had some contacts with Waterford and we wanted to broaden those contacts so we went to Cork, Galway and Belfast, and we held meetings in local venues to see who was interested and it drummed up enormous support. That was really the beginning and CAFE was born out of that subsequently.

Doireann Ní Bhriain: And when was that?

Annie Kilmartin: We went on our rounding up the troops expedition throughout '83 and then there was a seminar held out of those meetings.

Peter Sheridan: No, before those meetings.

Annie Kilmartin: No [table members laughing]. My memory is '83 was the meetings and '84 was the seminar in the North Star Hotel, it was actually April 1984.

Peter Sheridan: Oh yes, sorry, the seminar, but the first meeting was actually in the North Star Hotel in 1983.

Annie Kilmartin: The seminar [1984] is the landmark of CAFE's development.

Doireann Ní Bhriain: And what was that seminar called?

Annie Kilmartin: Creative Activity for Everyone and Michael D. Higgins chaired it and we had a number of guest speakers. We had Colm O'Briain, we had Peter Brinson, we had Jenny Harris from the Albany Empire [London]. A report on the seminar was then published which represented a diverse range of views but the key to the whole thing was that CAFE would be set up.

Doireann Ní Bhriain: Were the other art forms feeding into this process or was theatre the most accessible and immediate, the most appropriate to the needs at the time?

Helen O'Donoghue: This is my cue. I think I would pick up on a number of things that other people are saying. I found myself in the NCAD [National College of Art and Design]. As students we were aware that we were among a minority who were fortunate enough to have an awakening of aesthetic awareness through accessing third-level art college, something that I think our parents didn't have the luxury of. And we began to feel very strongly about the environment that we were living in, especially the city environment, and we began to link as a group of students with people who felt equally as strong from Trinity

Michael D. Higgins, Ted O'Regan and Ciarán Benson at the first community arts conference, North Star Hotel, Dublin, 28 April 1984. Photo: Michael Maher

[College, Dublin], so it was like a student movement really. I think access to education and access to arts were the key things that we wanted to advocate and access to people's voice and people's stories and the models that were being offered to us in NCAD were terribly limited. So we had to invent our own models of working and I worked with a fellow student, Dervil Jordan, and we went on to pilot the **Murals in Schools and Artist in the Community** schemes for the Arts Council. Other students who were engaged in any way in social commentary were doing it through photography at that time so after college we brought those skills to bear on the journalistic/sociological/community development skills of people from Trinity and we produced a magazine called *Strumpet*, a magazine of social comment, and circulated it ourselves out on the streets. *Strumpet* itself had a short life span but the connections between people stayed for a long time and what emerged out of that for a small number of us then was City Vision. Unemployment was a huge issue for all of us because we wanted to do what we wanted to do here in Ireland, we didn't want to emigrate. I think we were sort of this last wave of people who chose

Carnsore Point anti-nuclear festival 1979. Photo: Derek Speirs/Report

to stay; the generations immediately after us emigrated. In retrospect, I feel that we were very cocky and believed that we could make an impact on the society that we were growing up in. The eighties was the period when we wanted to work as artists in Ireland and connect with communities beyond the 'closed' arts community offered to us at college. I think our own voices needed to get out there.

Ollie Breslin: Just in relation to the influences and other art forms, I think one big influence, in the seventies particularly, was the whole anti-nuclear period. Waterford would be a strong socialist place, but what was very interesting during the anti-nuclear time was that all the new generation of young people got involved. What I'm saying is that it was the turning point for a lot of young people to get involved with the campaign. We went down to Wexford, to Carnsore anti-nuclear festivals, every year and we created a whole scene down there and that was very much creative.

Sue Richardson: It [Carnsore Point anti-nuclear festival] was a fantastic learning thing and because so many people worked on it all throughout the country, there were groups set up all over the place, and then the festivals which did have sort of playlets and music and drink and everything else, [table members laughing] but they were great and they had a purpose. It was just a wonderful feeling at those festivals.

Doireann Ní Bhriain: Is there anything else you can think of around that time which, like the anti-nuclear movement, would have influenced what happened?

James King: I suppose the hunger strikes. And while I was involved in things like the anti-nuclear movement and social issues, certainly there were these terrible, these awesome and awful dyings going on and I think those were so momentous that in itself it was sort of over-riding any performance.

Mowbray Bates: But there are particular occasions when the artwork does live beyond its time.

James King: We went to a village in Germany, a group of us. Joseph Beúys in the Free International University had invited artists from Belfast and the north. That was where there was sort of the blending of the community arts and the avant-garde.

Mowbray Bates: Yes, and a point I'm trying to draw out is maybe that this was a distinction between the north and south [of Ireland].

Sometimes the emphasis could be stronger, I think, on pushing the art forms than perhaps here [in the south] which, in my experience, would be coming from the more political, a more community action orientated direction.

Doireann Ní Bhriain: I have this image in my mind of you going off to a village to see Joseph Beúys and Annie on a bus going to Galway. Two images of two ways in which things were happening. Was there a pushing of the boundaries in the art forms as we described?

Peter Sheridan: The 'Inner City, Looking On' festival was a very important event in terms of the community arts movement, that you couldn't ignore if you were looking at that period, because it became a showcase for the drama work I had begun to do with City Workshop. Our first play was presented as part of that festival. But it was mainly a visual art exploration of the notion of tearing down the last remaining slum dwellings in the Sean McDermott Street area; it had a profound effect on the area. I mean, it was the first time I'd seen the river used as a source of visual art in the city. There were new flags designed. I always remember the Union Jack design in green, white and orange flying on the Liffey and this was at exactly the same time as the hunger strikes. All of these events had come together, so that in Dublin you had this incredible sense of a community marking a point of change, of a transition, and at the same time, you had this momentous political event taking place in the north, which in a way was the politicisation of Sinn Féin; it was out of that they learned politics because when [Bobby] Sands got elected [as an MP to the British Parliament] there just was a sudden shift, that 'my God, people are actually hearing us'. So it was this sense that something powerful was possible. I always remember that summer and Italy won the World Cup [table members laughing].

Doireann Ní Bhriain: Now, while all this was going on, Tony Ó Dálaigh, a civil servant, was sitting in an office in Dublin when along came people like Helen and Peter, kicking his door down looking for money for artistic projects ...

Tony Ó Dálaigh: Well I wouldn't have been aware of all that at all. I mean it's difficult to visualise say pre-1969. The government didn't give any cash to youth work or to sport. After the election of '69, for the first time, the Junior Minister for Education was given a hundred thousand quid. I became the first head of that [education fund] under

[Junior Minister] Bobby Molloy. The government was getting really worried about the whole level of youth unemployment and it was looking for proposals from different departments as to how that might be tackled. There was what they called the Youth Employment Scheme and then it was formalised as Teamwork and then they decided to brand it and to mark it and it was tremendously successful. I mean the take up! They suddenly were willing to put a lot of cash into that, and it was visualised mainly to help things like the GAA drain their pitches. They certainly weren't seen as arts schemes. It was the NCCCAP (North City Centre Community Action Programme) who came to us with the idea of doing a theatre project.

Doireann Ní Bhriain: Was that the first one?

Tony Ó Dálaigh: Yeah. I can well remember after we got it through, what year would that have been?

Peter Sheridan: February '82 we started, but we got the confirmation in November '81.

Tony Ó Dálaigh: I always remember taking one of my bosses up to a rehearsal, I think it was in Dublin Youth Theatre, and the incredulity on his face. But the reality was that the success of the first show and the reaction to it critically suddenly changed the minds of the Department [of Education]. One of the strangest things that time was that someone in the Department had the ability to give a grant of, say, a hundred thousand quid, to an arts organisation, and later ANCO then FÁS took this up in an even bigger way and supported the arts around the country. But the motivation from the government was to get unemployment figures down; there wasn't a policy 'let's promote community arts' or anything like that. The rules were supposed to be very strict, I mean six months only and nobody over twenty-five, but we had a grandmother, two grandmothers, very young grandmothers, in City Workshop and in reality the whole six month thing went by the board. With the success of City Workshop it went on for about two years with the same people basically. So you had that kind of flexibility then that you could either chop a scheme that wasn't working well or let something go and break all the rules. I don't mean just in the arts but in the general area.

Doireann Ní Bhriain: So, here's this hive of activity down in the Department of Education but meanwhile in the wider world there was an infrastructure, which was supposed to be dealing with the arts. Where does something like the Arts Council fit into the picture?

Tony Ó Dálaigh: There was a lot of frustration within the Arts Council. They were glad that money was going out, but at the same time there was a general feeling of 'we can't get cash'. Three million quid [Department of Education schemes] at the time. The Arts Council's budget was just under a million quid. To put it into perspective, three-quarters of that budget was going to the Abbey, the Gate, the ballet and the Dublin Theatre Festival. There was only 250 thousand pounds left in a year for all the administration and every other art form apart from those four. The government was doing this and the Arts Council kind of felt that it wouldn't have the criteria, that it was myself and a couple of people making decisions. That it wasn't going through a 'big committee'.

Sue Richardson: I just think as well, not only to do with money as far as the Arts Council goes, but really the Arts Council couldn't get their heads around the idea of community arts, they just couldn't understand it.

Helen O'Donoghue: I think the Arts Council didn't have any follow-through during the eighties. They wrote really good position papers but they didn't put the framework in place to support artists who were working in and with communities.

Ollie Breslin: Just a few things about the Teamwork scheme and that whole area of temporary employment schemes and then the Arts Council. I think that it was a whole mess, basically. I think that, OK, we got the opportunity to start off through schemes like Teamwork but what happened to people after two years? Or what happened to people after one year? There was no follow-on. A lot of people got disillusioned; a lot of people fell by the wayside. I found that a very difficult period, and the frustrating thing is that that's going on for twenty years, that people are on FÁS schemes now, at this particular moment, and they find that they are beginning to get expertise, beginning to get somewhere in our community and then what happens? After two years they are put back on to the live register and they don't have a follow-on system, and we've been saying this for twenty years, that there needed to be a follow-on system, somewhere where people go from A to B to C to D and eventually get up the ladder. And there

'Coherent structures should, as a matter of urgency, be put in place between FÁS and the Arts Council concerning the arts aspects of FÁS's training and community employment schemes.' Recommendation from *Poverty: Access and Participation in the Arts*, published by the Arts Council/ Combat Poverty Agency in 1997

has never been a proper structured system from the point of view of community arts, youth arts, whatever you want to call it, as regards supporting initiatives to move on. I think an awful lot of lip service is paid to community arts and the bottom line is that the only real support that we've received has been through the Department of Labour or through Combat Poverty or through the Department of Family and Social Affairs, but it hasn't been through the Arts Council, which should be where the responsibility is, and we've been told for years that they're going to phase out all these Community Employment schemes and the schemes are moving off to Greece because Greece needs Community Employment schemes and the Arts Council would come in and create real jobs in the industry and instead what happened last year was that the Arts Council got a big cut and you know the whole thing is back to square one.

Tony Ó Dálaigh: I think that's absolutely true because the Department [of Education] didn't have the resources or it wasn't their policy. And I suppose it's the same as now in a way with the building of all the arts centres in a much bigger picture: you put in the capital but nobody has thought ahead to what the ramifications are for staffing, for funding, for product and everything else.

Mowbray Bates: Just again from a northern experience, the structure was different from the south, and community arts funding predated the allocation towards community arts in the south. Again, it was a very small amount that was allocated. It was allocated through the Department of Education [in Northern Ireland]. So that generally the area that was supported was seen as education. It is interesting that the community arts committee funded community arts for deprived areas of Belfast and Derry only. That was the remit. And from 1978 it was a pilot project for ten years and, because it was a pilot project, its policy was therefore never fixed. So it went from year to year but inevitably there could be changes. It was always a difficulty for us, that. For example, I remember a huge difficulty when the Opera House [in Belfast] reopened after it was bombed. It reopened, and immediately around the province companies were cut and they just disappeared over night because the funding was needed to reopen the Opera House.

Doireann Ní Bhriain: Taking what Mo has said about the north and what Ollie said about the Republic, why was there that resistance to formulating some sort of policy that would embed it [community arts] firmly? Was it because it was threatening, or was it because there wasn't enough money?

Sue Richardson: I just think that a lot of it had to do with the fact that it was very radical. A lot of the people involved, a lot of the messages, if you want, from the plays, brilliant as they were as plays and enjoyable as they were to sit and watch, they were incredibly political. I mean, they actually analysed what was going on and there was a whole burgeoning of community development as well. But it was too political, it was questioning all sorts of things, it was saying 'why are so many people unemployed; why are people living in houses where there are no bathrooms?' It covered every aspect and that was scary. People were saying enough, we want changes.

Doireann Ní Bhriain: So is it a combination then of the fact that it was very radical and that there were no structures? And I don't mean just in the Arts Council, I mean in the arts establishment in general, that there were no structures to handle it?

Tony Ó Dálaigh: I think inside the Arts Council, if you look at the membership over the years, many, many of them come from the establishment who would see high art as being the important thing.

Doireann Ní Bhriain: Which does raise the question of standards and quality. I mean were they issues for those of you who were active in communities, or were they something for someone else?

Mowbray Bates: For writing applications, we all had to deal with these issues.

Helen O'Donoghue: People have talked about a really significant artwork that was made and I think that's where you get the fire in your belly from, when you know it's worked. You may forget how you got there sometimes, but you do know it has worked. I think perhaps when the partnership moneys came in [mid-nineties] there was a blurring of boundaries between the joint agendas of art and social gain and at times a dilution of quality in the actual artwork and I think that this offered a really good way out for the critics within the Arts Council to say that this was not art and they were not funding it any more. One of the turning points for me and why I have chosen to go and work in an institution like IMMA [Irish Museum of Modern Art] was seeing the work that emerged from the successful project 'A Woman's Place'.

Rita Fagan, Project Co-ordinator Family Resource Centre, describes the making of the exhibition 'Once Is Too Much' as a 'hard process because our subject, violence against women, is painful to deal with. During the period of making our work 30 women have been violently killed in Irish society, 19 in their homes. In some cases children witnessed the violence. We don't believe art can change the fundamental issue of violence against women and children. However, we do believe it can contribute to debates and discussions which raise awareness about the issue and to the changing of attitudes which could lead to the key issues of prevention, provision, protection and protest.'

There was no doubt that there was really good quality work done but it failed miserably in its exhibition. When it was finally brought to the public's eye, in my view, it failed the process. I couldn't judge as a person coming off the street whether it was good or bad work because I thought that it was really badly presented. It just didn't complete the process. And I think that a lot of work fails at the last post. Institutions, such as large ones like IMMA or smaller arts centres, needed to respect all artwork equally and when putting it into the public domain present it to the same high standards. We applied this principle to exhibitions such as 'Unspoken Truths' and 'Once Is Too Much' and the series of exhibitions by older people and children. Also IMMA offered me the opportunity to build on once-off projects and build that framework that I referred to earlier that would facilitate long-term engagement between art, artists and community.

Doireann Ní Bhriain: Does anybody else share that from their own experience? Sue?

Sue Richardson: I think there was an amazing sleight of hand that took place because I don't ever remember CAFE saying that the process was more important than the product but it was always put to us that that's what we said.

Helen O'Donoghue: Where did it come from then?

Sue Richardson: I'm not sure whether it came from the Arts Council, Combat Poverty or wherever. What CAFE always said was that the process was *as important* as the product. We realised that you don't get a high-quality product until you've been through a high-quality process. For people with no previous experience or skills, this can't be done in three to four months of one- or two-hour sessions a week. Much of the problem was that in order to get funding the group had to undertake to produce a product – no matter how little process or training they'd been through. Also, quite often the art form used was not the choice of the participants, but of their supervisor or even the artist. Now that I'm studying art myself, I believe that if I'd done the studying first I'd never have been able to do my job at CAFE. I would have known skills take time to learn and project participants can't put up with push, push, push and then goodbye, nice to have met you. Upskilling in creativity in itself was never recognised as a concrete benefit by most funders, showing a terrible lack of belief in people's potential achievements.

James King: Can I just come in? I would say that the process is what is important. It relates back to my original education in this field. In schools, there would be lip service paid to drama for development and what, in fact, they were doing was putting on a school play and somehow justifying that as of importance to the emotional health and psychological development of the children. Our aims were developmental so we would measure our success in terms of the quality of the process, the quality of the experience. It wasn't that we didn't have standards.

Peter Sheridan: Yes, this is a fascinating argument. It's such a core argument, this whole question of standards. It was the Arts Council response to me, 'you're not professional' – that was their response because they didn't have the wherewithal to respond. The work was highly professional; there was no question about that. It was different, it was breaking ground, it was all the things that a good piece of art should be. Beyond that, I'm not going to get into an argument about whether it's as good as the Abbey. That doesn't matter. That is not what the argument is about. I believe that there should have been at least one, and maybe more, educational models created in community arts, where people could come and study for two or three years with the best people around, inputting into that course, and that they would come out of it and then go out into a community context and do their thing. I think that was the biggest single failure that we had in the eighties, that we didn't create that.

Mowbray Bates: The National Arts Worker Course that I was instrumental in designing for CAFE – and something that Peter was involved in as well – I very much feel that it fed a particular version of community arts. If I was to think about this again, one of the problems I would see with community arts is this professionalisation of it. In becoming a profession in itself, a community artist, someone being a community artist is a problem for me. For one thing, it's very difficult to decide what a community artist is. It's not like a coalman or a teacher or whatever. It's a very nebulous concept, which none of us could begin to agree on. The interesting thing is that it's an approach towards making artwork, towards a piece of art. And I think that if I were thinking about training now, what would be needed is much more a mentor approach, much more awareness of a flexibility of practice, so that people are very much still back with their own group. But it's just a thought. When you're working in this area you're extremely isolated. You're so busy, you're so caught up. We did an enormous amount of work in Neighbourhood Open Workshops. There was no other group like us at the time. We felt very isolated and inevitably everyone would have shared their experience of being isolated with a mentor, the coach, the wise friend, someone who is maybe in the art form you are exploring, is maybe there as a sounding board or whatever. That would help enormously I think.

Helen O'Donoghue: I think the colleges have failed miserably in the south. I think that it is appalling. They give lip service. Until very recently it was the same experience that I had over twenty years ago. It depends on the individual tutor rather than being built in structurally. And in reference to the Arts Council, I think it would be its role to talk to the colleges about the professionalisation of artists, in the broadest sense.

Doireann Ní Bhriain: Could it be that the funders or the potential sources of funding would limit where things can go, and that your responses or the way you even design the whole thing from the start is heavily influenced by where you think you're going to get the money?

James King: It is all to do with evaluation as well. The funders might be quite happy if you're saying 'we're doing this scheme for personal growth'. And they say 'well that's great', but it's wherever you come to evaluate and show that that's happened. It's much simpler if you say here's a play or an artwork, there you see how much they've grown that they can do this. But I mean there are other ways of evaluating that.

Mowbray Bates: There's no question what you've just said is becoming true, especially with talk about 'investment' at the moment. It becomes more and more evident, if that's the case, that things are more and more frustrating. A large part of the impetus for this kind of work is very deeply personal. It's a rebellion against conditions and circumstances, of your upbringing, of your experience, of what you see around you. It's rebelling against 'them'. That certainly, in my case, was the feeling when I was young man. A young man's anger, I suppose, and then moving on from there.

Sue Richardson: But I think that that is a positive. I mean it is a rebellion obviously, but I don't see rebellions as being negative. It was for change, the most important thing: that's what we wanted, all of us were for change. And one of the things I would always say was, look, community development is great, but it's really tiring, it's exhausting, it's depressing at times, you don't seem to be getting anywhere and the great thing with using creativity is that it's fun, and your participants are going to have fun and you're still going to be doing work on whatever it is, whether it's single mothers or drug use or forestry. But you're really going to enjoy this and everybody's going to learn a huge amount. There is some sort of notion that if you're doing development work, you have to be terribly serious all the time and it can't be fun. Like revolution can't be fun, lefties are very unfunful. But when you bring the fun into it then all of a sudden, you know, it gives you strength, it gives you energy.

Ollie Breslin: Just in relation to the agencies. I think it's kind of strange in a sense that they haven't embraced community arts or youth arts, whatever you want to call it. Because I think that from what I can see, if you take established arts, I think a lot of it is dying and you know the audiences are getting that bit older. For the amount of money that is needed, what we're talking about is really Mickey Mouse money, in the whole area of community and youth, and a lot of things can emerge. I think that it's a very important investment and I know, for example, what I hear in America now is that even the corporate sector is coming around to look at youth neighbourhood drama projects as being a great model for education to follow, which is quite interesting as they've seen now that education in America hasn't produced the future. Whereas things like neighbourhood drama projects have.

Doireann Ní Bhriain: I deliberately didn't start with this, as we would probably be on the same subject two-and-a-half-hours later, but can we talk for a moment about the term community arts? I know that Annie, in particular, has had a discomfort about the term from way back, from the beginnings of CAFE.

Annie Kilmartin: In the early days of CAFE, the reason why we didn't use the term community arts was to do with funding. The Arts Council had a very small budget, for theatre, music, art and literature. They had a tiny budget for community arts and we didn't actually want to be labelled as community arts because we knew that it would become

'Criteria for funding cultural activities which began with a series of moral judgements about the place of certain activities within the "high arts" are not, and never can be, democratic. Whatever their apparent intention, they will always be oppressive.' Another Standard: Culture and Democracy – the Manifesto, 1986

marginalised and it would be undervalued and underfunded. We wanted to try and get funding from that larger pot so we defined the work as art in order to put it on an equal footing with mainstream produce and also to broaden its definition to include activities which promoted creative living. In our development of policies in those early days, our objectives were much more akin to the cultural objectives which were being developed in Europe at the time. But it never really went anywhere because when funding became available it was from within the community arts budget, but we had these aspirations to begin with.

Peter Sheridan: I had less of a problem with it than Annie had because I had a very clear concept of what it was, which was art happening in a community context.

Helen O'Donoghue: Was it that the term excluded people who would have gone through college? Imagine the other end with the title artist. I think there would have been a sense of being excluded from the inner circle of CAFE because it used terms like arts workers and cultural workers. You know it fell down on the term art worker.

Doireann Ní Bhriain: Are you saying that there wasn't the space to be an individual artist?

Helen O'Donoghue: Well I'd say there was a tension – I wouldn't say that there wasn't a space, but there was a tension.

Peter Sheridan: One of the big questions that came up was if community arts is simply arts happening in a community context, is amateur arts community arts? To which the answer must be yes. But it's not the same as what I do. It's a very different thing to what I do because, to be negative about it, it is like you're making a value judgement. I would criticise the Arts Council for the argument that they used to make to me that, you know, the work wasn't professional. That was just a convenient mantra for 'we don't have the wherewithal to fund you'.

Helen O'Donoghue: But I would challenge that as a different purpose. I think it's about your point of access to the arts. For a lot of people, it is an amateur arts group in some form or other that is the first point of contact.

Peter Sheridan: But very interestingly when after community arts had kind of established itself, and the kinds of things that we were talking about had established themselves, and the ACE committee was formed and then Ciarán Benson became the chair of the Arts Council proper so that it suddenly looked like this huge validation of everything we'd been talking about for the previous ten years and community arts became a buzz. The Arts Council very cleverly dragged loads of things out and called them community arts and so they were saying we give loads of help to community arts. It was the biggest turnaround I'd ever seen in the history of funding! Now everything is community arts because the politicians were all on this bandwagon of 'of course we support community arts'. So when it suits, it suits. It changed the goal posts.

Sue Richardson: I remember this argument about amateur drama and I remember what we said at the time. Well, amateur drama groups sometimes do really excellent stuff but they take their plays down off a shelf, and the whole difference with community drama was that people wrote their own plays with the help of their drama worker. And they were giving their own voice. I mean, I think that community arts is very much about telling your story. It didn't matter whether you did it with photography, dance, drama, visual arts, anything, but it was your voice and that was the major difference. And Helen is absolutely right about the artist. You were talking about the tension and there was tension because I don't know whether it's the way that artists were trained or whatever but artists had very much their own ideas and what they would tend to do would be to think up a project and then find a community group. They would be able to get funding through the community group, but it was their project. And I'm not saying that the people who did it didn't have fun, but it was the artist's project. It wasn't the choice of the participants. It may well have been the choice of the artist and the co-ordinator of the group, or the supervisor of the group or the manager of the community development project or whatever, but, for me, it always comes back to the participants.

Helen O'Donoghue: Can I ask you, when you say 'the artist' are you talking about the particular art form?

Sue Richardson: No. One of the things that struck me with amazement was to realise how few of the people that were on the CAFE database had actually received any professional training of any description. I mean, they came from all sorts of backgrounds and they had got into doing an art form, and maybe several, some of them were multi-skilled, but they hadn't gone through a college system.

'The mainstream cultural policy indicates that it's only some people's stories that are worth telling and that most people's role is to buy a ticket and listen quietly. And community arts is the antithesis of that. It [community arts] is to work with communities and neighbours to help people find their own stories and make them strong.' Jenny Harris

Helen O'Donoghue: I would agree with the problems with the training but I wouldn't blame the intentions of the artists. You know the scenario: an artist who is quite naïve in terms of experience, engaging with the community development worker who has got a really strong agenda, often what happens, when they try to work together, they are just repelled from each other and the result is that artists feel estranged. The current training initiatives with CREATE and NCAD aim to address this, which is a good thing, and what I'd be worried about now in terms of what's developing for the Percent For Arts Scheme is is that gap still there or is there an attempt at integration? I do believe that artists are members of community, are members of society. They share the same experiences; they share the same political views. But it's how to combine that artistically and creatively so that everybody wins as opposed to what you have described. And I think it does go back, unfortunately, to the failure of the college system to address these issues.

Doireann Ní Bhriain: Can I ask you all at this stage to look back a bit, and suggest what were the successes and what were the failures, what could you have done differently?

Mowbray Bates: If we had managed to extend individual art forms to a position of being more generous, more open and more accessible, more participatory so that we don't talk about community arts as such. That is a kind of red herring, arguing about community arts. We should talk about the theatre. We talk about painting. I would love to see much more energy and effort directed towards democratising specific arts practice and contexts than is put into creating institutions – though I can see that we had to create CAFE, an idea that was necessary for the time.

Annie Kilmartin: I'd really like to endorse that. I think it is very important. If I was to look back, this is what I think we were doing in CAFE in those early days, democratising certain art forms. Then suddenly it became about community arts and the focus was on that.

Peter Sheridan: I certainly think that at the time at which our energies as individuals came together as a kind of collective, we were all chipping away at the coalface in different ways but all towards vaguely the same notion that art has a social responsibility. We're not artists in a vacuum with no responsibility to where we live in our community and

I think that the arts in Ireland had become bereft of any kind of social responsibility. I think we were asking the question about people who had stopped asking the question. So I think that the main artistic institutions in the country had lost it and I don't think, for example, there'd be outreach and educational departments in IMMA or the Abbey Theatre today, only for the community arts movement. I think they followed on as a response to the notion that art is a social responsibility. Now I think that that needs to be pushed much further within those institutions, you know, that when you look at the kind of work that an outreach education department in the Abbey Theatre can do or in IMMA and that it doesn't happen in other institutions, and questions need to be asked when you receive funding, serious funding. What is your education policy? What is your community policy? Do you have a responsibility to the community you find yourself in? To embrace, to accommodate, to bring people in. These are really huge fundamental questions and I think that we've been partially responsible in creating that climate but that it needs to be pushed so much further.

Helen O'Donoghue: It does, I think it's more crucial now than it ever was. The pulling back of resources by government and the subsequent disempowerment of communities as a result. Communities that we have worked with at IMMA are currently fighting for their homes. I think things are very fragile at the moment. The strength of collective action was demonstrated in the early 1990s when community groups and arts institutions began to work together proving that artwork from all stands of society has a place in our national cultural institutions.

Doireann Ní Bhriain: And is there a missing building block there somewhere?

Helen O'Donoghue: Well the big one is the whole political vision for the country. That's probably what is the most difficult thing to work in.

Ollie Breslin: And it's kind of philosophical. For example, I walk through the streets of Waterford and people say 'well done, Ollie' about some Spraoi festival or about some Red Kettle show and I've never worked for any of these companies and I go 'thanks very much' and I walk on. So, as far as people are concerned Ollie is in the arts, right. We just have to realise the fact that we're all working together. Now we might be working on different types of organisations, different types of projects, but we're all in it together. But I think that is a big step for people to just make in their heads. That my corner is very precious and your corner is very precious, and there's somewhere where we all have to realise that we're all in the arts together. Now we've all different roles within the arts but all these are very important roles, we need to support each other.

'Balcony Belles' – Sheriff Street, 1996.
Photo:Derek Spiers/Report

Annie Kilmartin: My best memory is of the energy that we had together. I mean there was a very strong connection between us, way back in the eighties when we all met up to discuss the arts. There was tremendous energy and connection and commitment to each other. I don't know if that still exists today because I'm not involved in this whole area at the moment. But I think that was what was motivating, that's what made things happen: it was our actual commitment to each other, and our energy and the buzz.

Peter Sheridan: And that we had something to teach. One of the great things I think that we probably all shared is that the arts are predicated on the notion that you give in order to receive back, which is not how business works, it's not how finance works, so we're in a unique business, we're in a unique industry, and that some infra-structural things that have happened, like when [Charles] Haughey created that tax-free legislation he also created responsibility on the arts to share because if something is being given you have to give it back in some way. So there is a sense that the arts in Ireland are very different to other things. It's just very interesting to me the amateur arts thing because the Abbey Theatre was founded on an amateur company. The Fay Brothers were an amateur company. They crossed over because they obviously had a social/political agenda in terms of the whole question of Home Rule and what was going on at that time. But I'm just saying that the area that we work in is different to the thrust of the rest of how the thing works, especially of this aggressive Celtic-tiger-type economy where money doesn't talk, it screams! You know you only have to look at what's happening, it screams, it blows things away, like Sheriff Street is gone. Ballymun is going to be gone, you know, so these enormous developments are taking place within one kind of sector and we're in a different thing. We've got something to show the others that what we do is not predicated on that same level of financial aggression, that it's actually a shared thing.

Mowbray Bates: I just want to endorse that feeling. But how is it going to be resourced? I think that if you just simply see, to take Ollie's point, that it is a political decision that needs to be put in place … Peter's idea about opening up institutions … I think institutions, you know, following through examples like IMMA or the Abbey outreach programmes … It's simply a shift in existing resources. It's a political decision; it's a vision. It's not asking for a vast amount of money to be suddenly put in place for the arts, or for community arts, or whatever. It's just simply trying to re-orientate. Get back to the basic motivations for this kind of work and try to open up art institutions to make them more accessible and participatory.

SECTION 1

COMMUNITY ARTS IN CONTEXT

In this section we look at the history of community arts, what gave rise to this twentieth-century movement and how it has developed in Ireland over a thirty-year period. But to do this we must also look at the wider issue of art history itself, particularly the West's experience and how it has shaped our understanding of culture and the general perception of what art is. Anthony Grayling begins by articulating his view of art as a civilising force within society, a process that has evolved into the refined, some would say élite, practice that many people understand art to be today. Notwithstanding this distancing of fine art from everyday life, Grayling's essay champions the case for the western art tradition and points to it as a major source of cultural development. Fintan O'Toole counterpoints Anthony Grayling's essay with a perspective on the West's fine art tradition, which lays bear its darker side and how the model for perfection within our culture, derived from Grecian ideals, can lead to exclusion and oppression. Declan McGonagle takes up the question of the fine art/community arts relationship, addressing how and why the values of one have challenged the values of the other. It is then Martin Lynch's and Sandy Fitzgerald's task to set about tracing the recent history of community arts in Northern Ireland and the Republic of Ireland respectively, drawing on the historic and contemporary influences and milestones which gave rise to community arts on the island.

Macnas performing as part of the ICTU (Irish Congress of Trade Unions) centenary celebrations, 1994. Photo: Derek Speirs/Report

Art and Western civilisation

ANTHONY GRAYLING

(Originally a keynote address delivered at the symposium 'The Role of Art Centres in Civil Society' as part of the Civil Arts Enquiry, Dublin, February 2003.)

What is the role of the arts in civil society? There is a key assumption lying within this question – a hint contained in the word 'civil'. Perhaps the question should concern the role of the arts in civilising society, or in introducing civility into society, or even perhaps in enhancing citizenship in society. But putting the question in these terms, without careful qualification, carries too much freight: for it suggests a prescriptive view about what a 'good citizen' is, and we know that the arts have often done sterling service in showing that ideas about good citizenship entertained by absolute monarchs, ruling élites, church establishments and the like are not invariably good ones.

Still, it is a given that the arts are not just important but – more – essential, in complex and intriguing ways, to the civility of a society, which means: to the intelligence and flourishing of a society, and the possibility of fruitful relationships within it, and of possibilities for its individual members to live better lives – in the inner quality of those lives – because of their encounter with the arts. Of course, the claim that 'the arts are good for society' has the status of cliché, to the extent that we no longer have a clear grasp of what it truly means. To try to recover its significance, I adopt here the standard philosophical technique of re-scrutinising the familiar, of 'assembling reminders' as Wittgenstein put it, with the aim of seeing again what has been lost to view.

To talk about the arts in society, and in particular in civil society, raises questions of definition. What do we mean by the arts, what do we mean by society, and what do we mean in particular by 'civil' society? The questions need to be put because society was not always civil – indeed, the concept of civil society is a relatively recent one in history, for surprising reasons; and its emergence has much to do with the arts.

The idea of society is a simple enough one: humans are social animals, and like ants, dogs and other social creatures they live together in communities of various kinds, ranging embeddedly from couples to tribes, in villages, cities and nation-states. Being social is a defining human characteristic (in the strict sense of being part of the essence of what it is to be human), which in turn means that a large part of what we are is determined by our relationships. This observation alone ought immediately to alert us to simple but deep facts about why, for a central example, novels, films and plays – stories about people – are indispensable to us. Our bonds, our friends, families, workmates and neighbours help to create us, to make us the sort of people we are. We are familiar with the phenomenon of being slightly different people in each of our relationships: what we are with our spouses, friends and colleagues tends to vary slightly in each case.

The philosopher F. H. Bradley wrote an essay under the suggestive title 'My Station and Its Duties' to elaborate the idea of individuals identifying themselves morally by means of the role they play in their social relationships. Bradley was reprising an ancient idea, stemming from Aristotle, that thinking about the basis of ethics requires applying insights gleaned from the social nature of human existence – but without thereby losing sight of the fact of individuality, or of the fact that it is with the individual that moral and social responsibility stops. This latter point is equally essential to thinking properly about society, and especially civil society, because the values of individuality and autonomy, of freedom of choice and personal accountability, are fundamental to ethics too. And aspects of this – especially the autonomy, freedom and self-determination considerations – are indispensable to human flourishing.

Individuality and autonomy are not however inconsistent with community: far to the contrary, individuality and community need one another for their fullest expression. And here is precisely where questions of 'civility' arise. To see why it is necessary to note that the 'civil' in 'civil society' is not, as mentioned, a given. There have been many forms of society – they represent the historical majority, and they persist today – in which the individual is subordinate to society, exists only to serve it or its ruling caste, and is therefore, as a unit, dispensable. Such a society is not civil in any true sense.

'By taking decency as the paramount social value, a culture necessarily gains in importance. There is no decency without culture. And without culture there is no civil society nor any essential respect for human rights.'
Amishai Margalit, *The Decent Society*, Harvard University Press, 1996

A crucial moment in the development of civil society was the epoch of classical antiquity. A chief reason for its importance in the development of western civilisation is that it was the birthplace of ideas of civility. The philosophers of the classical period focused attention on questions of what it is to be human and to be in relationship to others – in short: it was the beginning of thought about ethics. The person with whom this first impetus is traditionally associated is Socrates. His contribution can be illustrated by noting the difference between the view of society and the 'good man' offered by Homer in the *Iliad*, on the one hand, and by the dramatists of the classical period on the other hand. For Homer the good man is 'the warrior'. The reason for this is obvious enough; warrior virtues are those of endurance, courage and strength, skill in fighting and ferocity with it, virtues needed for communities which lived in perilous times, where at any time people might be attacked by a neighbouring tribe or a neighbouring city and killed or carried away into slavery. People wanted their best and brightest to be those who can handle a spear and a sword to effect. The very word 'virtue', despite its Latin etymology, captures the Homeric conception in having as its stem the syllable 'vir', which denotes 'man' not in the generic sense of 'human being' but in the specifically masculine sense, as something powerful and brave, a fighter, a warrior. So in seeking to distil an ethical view from the Homeric poems, one finds in them a conception of society which is not based on civilian virtues, that is, virtues of community, tolerance, and co-operation, of trying to understand other people's points of view, and of trying to accommodate the competing interests of disparate groups. On the contrary, Homer's good man is the man of strength and everything that the good man did was by definition therefore right. In short: might was right. By the same token, a good society was one that was strongly protected against the depredations of neighbours.

But in the classical period in Athens, where Socrates and his pupil Plato (and in turn Plato's pupil Aristotle) lived, there occurred a fundamental shift in thought. Assent moved away from the belief that the great man is the warrior to the idea that the great man is the thinker, the statesman, the teacher, the person interested in politics (where 'politics' meant concern with the well-ordering of the community). Socrates was tireless in raising questions about the right relationships between people, and in particular therefore about justice. In the Greek outlook of the period more generally, the aesthetic dimension of the good life seemed deeply important, because aesthetic considerations, including the effect of those endeavours – the arts – which produced aesthetic responses, are intimately linked to the overall endeavour of living a good life and constructing a good society as its setting. So Socrates also tirelessly asked about the nature of truth, beauty, and the higher emotions, not least love.

In the dramas of Aeschylus one catches the moment at which the shift from the warrior to the civic virtues happened. In his *Oresteia* he tells the story of Orestes, son of Agamemnon, who was being pursued by the Furies because he had murdered his mother, Clytemnestra, in revenge for her murder of his father. He appealed to the oracle at Delphi to ask Apollo for help, and was told to go to Athens and throw himself on the mercy of its presiding goddess. When he did so, Athene summoned a thousand citizens to the Areopagus, the 'Hill of Mars', and invited them to sit in judgement on his case. This was the first ever jury. With Apollo as his defence counsel and with Athene's casting vote, Orestes was acquitted. The Furies were, as was their wont, furious; they said to Athene, 'You young gods have usurped the privileges of we old gods, and introduced new things that take away our purpose.' To placate them Athene offered them a home and honour in her city, which they accepted; and she gave them a new name, 'Eumenides', the Kindly Ones.

Thus the old law of revenge was replaced by something more like due process; thus the harsh old conception of right was replaced by a new, more thoughtful, more collegial ethics – or anyway, its beginning. It is easy both to underestimate the importance of the change, and also to overstate the virtue of the society in which it occurred; one has to remember that this was a slave-based society in which women were wholly disenfranchised, and in which the lingering imperatives of the warrior virtues remained alive (a fact amply testified by Sparta). Nevertheless, it was also the place where the new norms and attitudes began to emerge, and it is their origin and growth that matters now in our thinking about the basis of civil society.

Progress towards a full realisation of the values which the classical mind postulated has of course been painfully slow. Until modern times (from the seventeenth century onwards) the moral state of human beings was universally one of heteronomy, that is, a state of subjection to command from above or without, whether by God or king, priest or baron. The moral hierarchy of the world was, so to say, feudal. As a result of the Renaissance and Reformation, moral autonomy became increasingly possible. This is the state in which individuals are responsible for themselves, are free to make decisions, to act, and to accept the consequences on their own account.

Achieving moral autonomy – which is the same thing as achieving moral adulthood; hitherto people had been kept somewhat in the status of children relative to their rulers, dependent on them and subordinate to their authority – was a difficult process. The grip of religious world-views had to be prised off in a centuries-long struggle, during much of which people asserted moral independence at the peril of their lives. Part of the hegemony over thought and practice exercised by the Church in Europe included denigration of the body as a theatre of sin; the Gothic imagination of the medieval church encouraged the production of much *contemptus mundi* literature, describing the horrors of embodied existence – disease, pain, vulnerability to the devil's snares – and the beautiful hope of escape into the purely spiritual existence of life after death (if life before death was not too sinful). This major trope of religious thought stands in sharp contrast to the Renaissance's recovery of enjoyment in things of the flesh and the world, as its art, poetry, and philosophy show. The classical world, for example, had celebrated the beauty of the naked human form; joyfully, the Renaissance revived this celebration in its own art. The Greeks had enjoyed the human body as the measure of things; in returning the gaze of the intellect to the affairs of men, Renaissance humanists (the label is deeply significant) found the source of ethical inspiration in those features of human experience which promoted its flourishing, which made life good to live. The difference could not be greater between Gothic loathing of the flesh and Renaissance delight in its textures, tones and tints.

For present purposes, the significant thing about this change is the fact that the 'earthly city' came back into focus, having been occluded by focus on the Heavenly City. By this I mean that what had again come to matter centrally were the affairs of human beings (rather than souls and angels), and moreover human beings in the here and now (rather than their eschatological fate) – in their communities and families, in their education for life, their accumulation of wealth, their success in careers, their improvement of daily amenities, their development of skills and talents pertaining to the quality of their experience – experience, note, in the body, in the present, in the world, in society. And here the arts, from painting to literature, came into their own. No longer were they merely instruments of an ideological project for governing the faithful and converting the infidel. They had come to be part of the point of life itself. If he could afford it, a man commissioned portraits and landscapes, employed librarians, hired musicians and paid handsome fees to architects in furtherance of a project of living the good life here, in the world, in his own lifetime. Even if he could not afford to do these things, no man regarded himself as educated or reflective unless he acquired a capacity to appreciate these endeavours, and understand what they meant as interpretations of the world he was part of – the human world.

Already one glimpses, from what these remarks suggest, how the arts enter into the promotion of civility. Think of it this way: when there is conversation (in the inclusive sense of dialogue, of exchange of ideas and information) people get along with each other better, and their lives are enhanced accordingly. The arts, as the Renaissance princes and their people saw, are a part – typically a brilliant part – of the conversation a community has with itself. They are more than that, of course; but they are crucially that. And it is in growth, side by side, of ethical autonomy and the role of the arts in illuminating, commenting upon, gracing, entertaining and enriching the human scene, that we see the connection at stake: the juxtaposing of the word 'civil' with the word 'society'.

And now I turn to the most difficult part of the present discussion, which is the related matter of the nature of the arts, and of how, in more detail, they make their contribution to the civilising of society.

Familiarly, the term 'the arts' is a very elastic one. It embraces a range of activities and enterprises with very blurred outer boundaries – which is as it should be, for leaving those boundaries vague means that they are open, and we should not be restricted to thinking that art is only what you meet in a gallery of Renaissance painting or in an opera house. At the same time, there is something intrinsically unsatisfactory about any definition of the kind Andy Warhol offered ('art is what you can get away with'), which provides ready ammunition for those who

'The difference between the life of a skin-clad hunter leaving a cave with a spear over his shoulder to hunt mammoth, and a smartly dressed executive driving along a motorway in New York, London or Tokyo, to consult his computer print-out, is not due to any further physical development of body or brain during the long period that separates them, but to a completely new evolutionary factor ... we are the only creatures to have painted representational pictures and it is this talent which led to developments which ultimately transformed the life of mankind.' David Attenborough from his book *Life on Earth*, Collins, 1979

think that much of performance art, installation art, video art and other contemporary gestures is rubbish. No doubt most of it is; but it takes a lot of compost to grow a rose, and for that reason alone the plethora of forms has at least a use. The public, especially that sizeable portion of it which knows what it likes, is not as easily fooled as Warholians might hope, for they are capable of contrasting (say) modern dance, where there is no faking the basics, with a lot of what is said to be art by graduates of art colleges, for whom faking it is painfully easy.

One problem with grasping the nature of the arts now is the influence of Romantic conceptions of 'the artist'. Could one travel in a time machine to visit the studio of a Renaissance master, one would see teams of assistants at work, one painting the flowers in the background, another the horses and dogs, the master himself the faces of the Holy Family or whoever. The Romantics appropriated all of the inspiration and endeavour to themselves. The Romantic view is that the artist is the individual genius from whom everything flows, in whom everything starts, to whom all applause is due. To see how this is a change over earlier conceptions, consider the word 'inspiration'. It literally means 'breathing in'. In classical times artistic success was held to be a mark of the gods' favourable use of an individual as a conduit; they 'breathed in' the ideas, the talents, and he served them as their vehicle. A 'genius' was a little creature who sat on a person's shoulder and whispered into his ear. Poetry was, so to speak, dictated by the Muses; the genius guided the painter's hand. But the Romantic genius is the 'I', the author, the originator, the human creator of the work. The more the artist revised and improved, the more he worked and struggled, the more the work was truly and fully his own creation.

These thoughts must be put into perspective. Pliny the Elder, writing in the last volume of his *Natural History*, remarked that the great Apelles could 'command the wealth of a small town for a single painting'. Artists were not then, and have never been, mere artisans. But Apelles did not see himself in anything like the sense suggested, for example, by the words of Swinburne's 'Hertha': 'I am that which began/Out of me the years roll/Out of me god and man.'

Now whatever one makes of this dramatic shift of perception, one thing deserves remark: namely that whereas the pre-Romantic artist might accept a commission from, say, a church to depict some signal moment in the life of its patron saint, and therefore agrees to announce the church's view of the saint and the saint's ministry, post-Romantic artists have often and vehemently asserted that it is not their responsibility to cleave to a particular line, to express someone else's views, or to presume to lecture anyone on morals or indeed anything else. They are doing their own thing, prompted by their own imperatives; what consumers of their work make of it, what lessons they draw, what illumination (if any) they receive, is entirely a matter for the consumers themselves. This is a perfectly valid point. But note that although an artist might not seek to teach, a consumer of his or her work can still learn. Artists do not have to set up as prophets in order for people to get something from what they do. In so far as work offered as art is ever 'about' anything (and it might try hard not to be), it exists in relationship with people responding to it: and for some of these latter, the work might make a difference.

The arts are traditionally said to provide — even despite themselves — commentary, interpretation, perspectives on how the world can be seen and thought about. They can of course just be enjoyed — that is often enough — or offer some kind of escape. But in the process of doing even these modest things they might, again despite themselves, do more. Suppose, for example, you go with a friend to a gallery and discuss what you see. You will have shared something as users and consumers of the works seen, and might have opened one another's eyes to something that neither might have seen if each had gone on his own. Engaging with the arts in all their variety, in all their richness, can have consequences that were not sought or anticipated — whether by the artist, the consumer of art, or indeed the institution that conveys the art and makes it accessible for people who consume it.

And this leads to the argument that the arts, again even without wishing to or trying to, and certainly without having any responsibility to do so, can offer material to ethical reflection in society, to the ethical debate — perhaps, as often happens, by challenging its assumptions — and therefore to the nature of our community and to individuals. To the community it can offer seemingly disparate and contradictory things. It can offer the possibility of community identity by tapping into the rich, deep traditions lying in the history of a society, by whose means the society mapped its way into the present. It can also address the need for

The idea that artists and cultural workers are somehow more resistant to the stupidities and prejudices which breed in the junkyard of history is equal to the folly of the Marxist concept of communists as the avant-garde of the working class. The difference lies in the fact that this idea did not emerge from some ideological laboratory but was borne on the wings of a dream, the dream of the global rule of law and the civil society. Artists and intellectuals are not the avant-garde of the people, nor their conscience.' Velimir Curgus Kazimir from his essay 'Child of Europe', FREEB92/Cinema Rex, Belgrade/TEH, 2000

mutual understanding and tolerance now that communities are very multicultural, when the problem in hand is not one of asserting identity but of different identities allowing each other space to coexist.

It is almost needless to say what the arts can do for individuals, how the scales can fall from a person's eyes as a result of reading, hearing, seeing something which really strikes home, which really speaks to personal experience, really makes sense of something that one felt in the past. For anybody with any kind of sensitivity or interest in the arts this is an experience which is almost commonplace, and indeed is what one seeks when one goes to the theatre or a gallery. This is because being a consumer of the arts is in its way a creative process too. You might discover things as a result of your engagement with art which were not fully there in you until that engagement occurred. Making and responding are both parts of what the arts are for.

I want to end by illustrating the point about the contribution the arts make to ethics, however indirectly and sometimes even negatively (but thereby teaching us much). Consider a focal case of how this works in the narrative arts of literature, theatre, and film. What the narrative arts do among many other things is to make it possible for us to see into lives, situations and experiences which, if we did not have those narratives available to us, we might never otherwise encounter. Suppose you live an illiterate life in one cottage, in one village, in one part of the world, never going anywhere and never seeing anything other than the same familiar locality. You could be a wise and good person, and your relationships with those around you might be excellent relationships, for there is no suggestion that access to the narrative arts is necessary for being good or living a good life. But the supposed parochial life will, by its very definition, be a severely limited life. To be able to understand others, even those whose interests and choices you cannot agree with, and to get some insight into cultures you do not share, you need your horizons expanded, and your imagination fed, by an instrument with the power to generate such understanding and insight. That is what the narrative arts offer. By reading a novel or seeing a play or film you get to be a fly on the wall in many more lives than you could observe in your own one lifetime, and you get to live many more lives in narrative than you can possibly live in fact. Far from not mattering that the experience is vicarious, the very fact of bracketing, of distance, of knowing that it is narrative and not occurrent fact, helps to make salient the rich lessons to be gleaned. By this means, sympathies towards others have a chance of being broadened and enriched, at the same time as the same lessons are applied to oneself.

Sympathies; insight; understanding. This is where the work of the arts, intentionally or otherwise, connects with the notion of civil society. Sympathy, understanding and their hoped-for offspring of tolerance and mutuality, are not an automatic outcome of engagement with the arts – after all, some SS officers undoubtedly listened to Beethoven and read Goethe before going off to work in the gas ovens. But those virtues – sympathy, understanding, tolerance and mutuality – give society its best chance of being civil, just as the possibility of education offers an individual better prospects than being left in ignorance. Perhaps the point is best expressed in terms of its ideal. In the ideal, the arts offer those who engage with them attentively and responsively the chance to educate their sensibilities, to become more discriminating and thoughtful, and more alert to everything around them, not least to other people. It is not just Utopian but misguided to dream that the arts might thereby bring peace and enlightenment everywhere, as if it were a substitute for archangels; but it brings increments of these things, and in the course of history has brought enough of them to make the civility of civil society.

Unchaining from the chariot

FINTAN O'TOOLE

(This essay was first published in the exhibition catalogue 'Celebrating Difference', City Arts Centre, 1993)

The story of Plato's Cave is meant to be a story about truth. In it, Plato imagined that we human beings are chained up in a cave facing away from the entrance. Figures pass the entrance behind our backs and, as they do, their shadows are projected onto the walls in front of us. These shadows, because we don't know any better, we take to be the truth.

But the story is capable of another interpretation. Chained up as we are in ideals of truth and beauty, we are forced to watch an endless parade of shadows. Ideals of what we should be are projected onto the wall that keeps us imprisoned. And we forget that these chains and walls are of our own devising. They are human inventions, not manifestations of a divine truth. Byron, looking at the Medici Venus, imagined the viewer of this representation of the ideal body as 'chained to the chariot of triumphal Art', like a captured slave being paraded through the streets by an imperial conqueror. Though he meant it as a tribute, the image is in fact a reminder of the connection between artistic ideals of the naked body and naked displays of power.

Visual art has had a long struggle with these ideals. Classical art regarded real bodies as degraded versions of the Platonic ideal. Out there, somewhere, the perfect images of the body resided like dummies in the great window display of a heavenly department store. But we mere mortals were out on the streets with our far from perfect noses pressed up against the window. Our bodies were bad imaginations of the ideal. The job of art, therefore, was to make up the difference, 'to complete', as Aristotle put it, 'what nature cannot bring to finish'.

The art historian Kenneth Clarke expressed the notion perfectly when he wrote that 'it is widely supposed that the naked human body is in itself an object upon which the eye dwells with pleasure and which we are glad to see depicted. But anyone who has frequented art schools, and seen the shapeless, pitiful model which the students are industriously drawing will know that this is an illusion ... A mass of naked bodies does not move us to empathy, but to disillusion and dismay. We do not wish to imitate, we wish to perfect.'

And, indeed, if you are enraptured by the ideals of classical perfection, the mass of human bodies is disillusioning and dismaying. If you sit on a beach and expect it to be like *Baywatch*, the modern equivalent of the Greeks' Apollo and Venus, then the bits that don't match, the bits that don't work, will strike you as quite appalling. But then you yourself will appear pretty appalling to most people – a prig, a bore and a potentially dangerous bigot. Yet we are reluctant to say the same thing about the classical ideal in art: that it is priggish, boring and, in extreme forms, dangerous.

One of the confusions about classical ideals which still play a large part in our culture is that they appear to be a celebration of the body, of the sensuous, of the erotic. In fact they are no such thing. They mask, as the above quotation from Kenneth Clarke shows, a puritanical disgust at the human body. Real bodies are degraded forms of perfection. And the further they depart from the ideal, the more degraded they become.

There is, to be sure, an alternative tradition to the classical ideal in western visual art, one which shows bodies in more recognisable proportions and varieties. But it is a tradition of warnings about the evils of flesh – depictions of Adam and Eve, no longer 'beautiful', being expelled from the Garden, of tortured and distorted bodies in Hell, of pox-ridden prostitutes. And it is merely the other side of the coin. When the ideal is perfection, what's real is fear and shame. If you cut open all those Venuses and Apollos, you will find inside a puritan heart.

It is no accident that perhaps the greatest of painters, Rembrandt, an artist whose work still seems wonderfully immediate and human, was also one of the few to break out of this dichotomy of impossible ideals and shameful reality in depicting the human body. Rembrandt is great, not just because he has stunning skill, but because he has such a humane vision of the people he paints. He painted bodies that were wonderfully diverse and imperfect, old and young, firm and wizened, of every shape and stature. They are neither visions of beautiful perfection nor warnings of shame and death. They are human bodies, accepted and celebrated for their humanity. Yet the power of the old conventions was such that even Rembrandt could not change them. The

'I do not want my house to be walled in on all sides and my windows to be stuffed. I want the culture of all the lands to be blown about my house as freely as possible. But I refuse to be blown off my feet by any.'
Mahatma Gandhi

images of the body, particularly the images of women's bodies that we are still presented with today, are still shaped by the old ideals.

If this were only about art, it would be regrettable. But it is much more than regrettable because it is also about power and the abuse of power. Real people are and always have been chained to the chariot of that triumphal art. For implicit in the classical ideal is not merely a notion of beauty, but an assumption that this beauty is the same thing as truth and moral worth. The Good, the True and the Beautiful are one and the same thing. And if you have power to define beauty, then you also have power to define what is true and what is good. You have, in other words, the right to rule.

Women, like rich men's suits, have been made to measure — to measure up to an abstract (and of course changing) ideal which keeps them static and subject. Conquered peoples have been caricatured and distorted, categorised by physiognomy or colour, in accordance with their descent from a physical ideal embodied, of course, by the master race. The lower orders have been depicted as physically different, lumpen, ugly, uncouth. And people with disabilities have been at the furthest extreme of this continuum of using the body as a marker for exclusion from power. Their bodies declare their fall from grace, their distance from the ideal. And since the ideal is an ideal not merely of beauty but also of truth and goodness, then it is a short step to exclude all these 'lower' classes from the power that only those who are good and true have a right to wield.

The neo-Fascist on the streets of Germany, London, Dublin or Belfast who refuses to practise discrimination and will happily beat up blacks, Jews, Turks, Chinese and people with disabilities expresses the ideal perfectly. They are all different in his eyes, not from each other, but from a wider world. It is a cruder and more direct form of something that is subtly present in more respectable forms of art and politics.

All sorts of bad art continue to give a pseudo-moral meaning to the appearance of the body. The bad guys seldom wear black hats any more, but they still look bad. Limps, twitches, bald heads, thick eyebrows, wheelchairs, heavy jaws, club feet, false hands — the medieval association of departures from the supposed physical norm with the disapproval of God is alive and well and living in Hollywood. People with disabilities are as likely as anyone else to be dirty rotten scoundrels, but if they are, it is because they are human, not because they are physically different. Yet the associations continue, not least because they save all the work of having to invent histories and personalities for fictional characters.

One of the effects of the images that we consume every day in films, television, advertising and newspaper photographs is that they make the usual appear unusual. They reverse the actual order of things. They give us a world populated essentially by idealised human forms, from which the 99 per cent who do not conform to whatever the ideal happens to be at the time seem to represent a departure. Everything that is summed up in the phrase 'the beautiful people' reinforces a manufactured association between money, sex, power, intelligence and physical appearance.

But all sorts of bad politics continue with the same basic associations, too. In the late 1970s and the 1980s, social Darwinism became respectable again. For the neo-liberals, the world was a great primeval jungle in which people competed for survival. Some people were rich and others poor, because some were naturally more competitive, naturally stronger. The fittest survive. Nature has created differences that had nothing to do with fairness. 'There's nothing fair', wrote Milton Friedman, guru of Reagan and Thatcher, 'about Marlene Dietrich's having been born with beautiful legs that we all want to look at; or about Muhammad Ali's having been born with the skill that made him a great fighter.'

In this formulation, a celebration of human difference becomes a celebration of social inequality and unfairness. 'Different' becomes synonymous with 'better' and therefore with a fundamental challenge to the democratic notion of human equality. Marlene Dietrich's legs are used to kick the poor in the teeth. Muhammad Ali's fists used to beat those who have no right to power. When Margaret Thatcher spoke of those who were always 'drooling and dribbling about compassion', she was merely expressing more clearly the same notion. The classical ideal had become explicitly political. If you don't have legs like Venus (or Marlene Dietrich), if you don't have arms like Apollo (or Muhammad Ali), if you dribble and drool, then – tough. Only those who approach the ideal have the right to success. Nature decreed it, life's unfair, so go and drool somewhere else.

How do we unchain ourselves from the chariot of this triumphal art? For a start, by remembering that equality and sameness are not synonymous. If we were all the same, we wouldn't need democracy at all. If we all looked alike, acted alike, felt alike, thought alike and had the same interests and desires, democracy would be unnecessary, because societies would function automatically in the way that we all wanted them to. It is difference which creates the very notion of equality. We are equal because what underlies difference is an essential similarity, a similarity that we all call humanity. To celebrate difference without also celebrating equality is a dangerous fallacy.

There is after all a stratum of continuity in all human bodies. But it is not the frozen ideal of the classicists from which all real bodies are more or less of a departure. It is humanity itself, in all its perverse, funny, odd, vital, graceful, but always irreducibly individual, manifestations. To celebrate difference is to celebrate, not 'The Body', but bodies. To reject the tyrannous ideals of classical form or of the beauty industry is not to reject human bodies, but to do the opposite: to reject the puritanism and fear of the flesh that are the inevitable consequence of the ideals. It is not surprising to find that, when people with disabilities paint or sculpt, they gain access to the sensuous, sometimes to the erotic. To demand acceptance of the body as it is, is also to cancel out the disgust and disillusion at finding that real bodies are not much like their supposed ideal models.

If celebrating difference is also celebrating bodies, it is equally true that the cost of not celebrating difference is borne by bodies. Stereotypes kill and maim. The habit of seeing difference as a departure from what should be ends up on this island with bodies shredded and pierced by bombs and bullets. It ends up with bodies malnourished and weakened because they belong to people such as travellers who are not 'normal'. It ends up with bodies violated and abused because women, once frozen into symbols, are available for possession. And it ends up with bodies unnecessarily limited and confined because people with disabilities are denied access to power in supposedly 'normal' society.

Disability, like inequality, is a function of society, not of nature. The actual capacities of the human body may differ naturally. But what makes those differences into disabilities is the shape of the world around the person who has them. People may be born different, but they are made unequal. A society that does not see itself as an amalgam of differences creates disabilities by pretending to a norm which is then set up as a test to be passed before access to full participation is allowed.

Art forms which are unrespectable, which don't pretend to be governed by classical ideals, are often better at picking up on this than the forms of high art are. Think of the way, for instance, that circus celebrates the diversity of human form, the way it actively seeks strange and new shapes of the human body and applauds them: men and women hanging upside down from the roof, contortionists with their legs bent over their shoulders and their feet sticking out from their chests, a whole body that is balanced, not on a leg but on a fingertip. Or think of comic books where the line between the mutant and the hero is erased, where the superhero is a normal person who became disfigured in an accident or a genetic mutation. In these forms of so called low art, being different from the norm is a source of wonder and awe, not of contempt and exclusion. Such art reminds us that physical difference, like any other form of difference, is not just to be accepted but to be embraced as a source of new perspectives, new visions and new hopes. And if art does not lead us to those new visions, then it merely leads us, tied to its chariot, in abject procession through the streets as part of somebody else's triumphal march.

From community arts to civil culture, and back again

DECLAN McGONAGLE

It may seem curious to begin a text focusing on contemporary community arts by looking through a lens provided by a work of art which qualifies as an historical masterpiece of 'high' western European art, a work which appears to confirm the values of exclusive 'signature' culture, which defines artist as genius, as opposed to the participatory and inclusive nature of community arts. The artwork I want to consider, in order to open up this issue of signature and participatory culture, is a painting in the collection of the National Gallery in London, *The Ambassadors* by Hans Holbein. Clearly Holbein was not a community artist, within our working definition, but I begin with this work because elsewhere in this publication, and generally, when the characteristics and capacities of community arts are discussed, certain ideas of quality, excellence, high and low art are brought into play in particular disempowering ways. Certain capacities and characteristics in art are projected as central to our civilisation – a civilisation deemed to be the product of an inevitable, linear chronology – and others as marginal. Happily for some, this told us we were/are central to the universe – that is, that a white, western and male modernist mind-set is central to the universe.

Modernism of this kind was not just a product of the mid-twentieth century. The modernist mind-set has crystallised at different moments in human history when a belief formed, and was then supported and exported, that things happen as a result of the actions of man (literally man) rather than the action of nature (God?). And, by definition, this linear chronology could only be recognised, developed and articulated by certain men, and the resulting culture could only be made and read by certain men. This is a self-serving and exclusive model of arts, culture, human experience and development. The nature and meaning of human experience, which the arts have always tried to represent, with varying degrees of simplicity or complexity, is wider, more diverse, richer and, definitely, more coloured than that which is held and described within the modernist frame. It really is time we began to examine, test and value what lies in the shadows of modernism – outside the frame – in terms of arts/cultural and social experience, of practice, production and distribution.

While I would argue that a particular model of community arts has also run its course and is in need of revisioning and restrategising, it is also true that community arts did succeed in reclaiming the means of production, albeit within areas of experience, in social space beyond the modernist field. However community arts never claimed, and it has to be said never tried to claim, the means of distribution in cultural space. To have done so would have meant breaching those barriers between the 'centre' and the 'edge' in socio-economic as well as cultural terms and ultimately between power and powerlessness. As a result this remains to be done. At the very centre of this debate must be the issue of power because at the centre of our idea of civilisation is the idea of power – after all it is the 'winners' who write the histories.

Essentially there is arts/cultural activity which is connected to power, and there is arts/cultural activity which is not connected to power – whether that power is articulated in terms of human, financial or institutional resourcing, or simply in terms of validation. And community arts has, historically, not been connected to power. In fact at its best community arts has embodied a practice-based critique of power.

The idea of the artist as genius may seem a typical product of late modernism in the twentieth century but this particular characterisation of modernism developed in the early nineteenth century and held a dominant, defining position in our society up to the end of the twentieth century. Not only did that model exclude and invalidate whole areas of human social and cultural experience, it also excluded and invalidated whole contexts, such as Ireland, which were seen as sites of retarded modernity. Yet, historically, Ireland's problem with modernity was, in fact, a problem with modernism. These two concepts are constantly presented as synonymous, when in fact modern simply means of the present and recent past and modernism means an ideological state of mind, which works very hard to pretend to be ideology free – that is, which pretends to be natural rather than cultural

The Ambassadors by Hans Holbein.
The Bridgeman Art Library

– and not socially conditioned, when, in reality, it is a construct and, as such, could be remade.

And nothing could seem less 'natural' and more man-made than a painting of the high Renaissance – the painting of *The Ambassadors*, to which I have already referred. Produced in the mid-sixteenth century *The Ambassadors* is not a modern painting but it is modernist. It is a complex work, operating on many levels at the same time. The use of lenses and its formal and ideological content predicts more recent articulations of the modernist mind-set, here cast in the form of two worldly, powerful and wealthy men, French ambassadors to the court of Henry VIII of England. This artwork has a clear social and political purpose which is bound to its aesthetic properties, and that is to describe in great detail the wealth and power which allowed these men, for instance, to dress in expensive furs and silk. The painting's surfaces therefore had to trick the eye into believing that the painted surfaces actually could be fur or silk and this, the painter's skill, was part of what the collector owned. Holbein's particular aesthetic language – high realism – was not developed innocently, for aesthetic reasons alone, but to be able to fulfil an ideological function, the requirement to represent, and also embody in its own preciousness, wealth and power. *The Ambassadors* is firstly a political painting about power and, like many historical portraits, intended to confirm the self-image of the collector as deservedly powerful. The work was made at the very beginning of what we, in the west, refer to as the Age of Discovery, the period when western-European countries developed the means to navigate the globe relatively safely and begin the process of trying to dominate the planet. The painting depicts many of the navigational instruments which would be used to travel across the globe. These 'secular' references were woven into a complex mix of imagery with religious references – to the crucifixion in particular. But the device at the very centre of this work, at the centre of the two-dimensional object and at the centre of the meaning of the work, is significant in this context because it insists that the viewer becomes a participant in the creation of its meaning, and not just the consumer of its apparently single, authoritative message.

The strange shape in front of the ambassadors – strange, that is, when viewed frontally from a fixed position – only becomes clear as an out-of-scale skull when the viewer shifts position a few metres to the right of the painting. The skull has been painted anamorphically and, optically, only reads from a position to the right of the painting. This is not simply a trick played by Holbein to show off or to tease his 'client'. As is well known it was very common for portraits of powerful people, in that era, to include a skull or some other *memento mori* (memory of death). Had Holbein simply wanted to provide that information which a *memento mori* represents – that even the rich and powerful have to die also – he could quite easily have painted in a convincing skull. The question is this, and this is the key to my larger point, why did the artist deliberately use a different optic in representing the skull? The orthodox statement, the modernist statement of man's power, was made and is legible frontally, but the different optic of the anamorphic skull problematises that frontal reading, not by destroying it but by adding another reading, in a way which empowers the 'reader'. That, in my view, is the key to participatory practice. The two readings here are simultaneously available. The modernist statement is left intact but is challenged and problematised in the mind of the viewer/reader – or, now, participant – in the process of negotiating the meaning and value of the work, facilitated by the imagination of the artist. In this model, taking it as a powerful example of signature culture – a high Renaissance painting – the idea of participation is central to, not a contradiction of, its real function. The artist is exploring with his 'readers' the nature and meaning of human experience and facilitating a new negotiation. From that basic act of physically shifting position in front of this work, a new negotiation is created which is inclusive of the viewer, in fact redefines the viewer as a participant, not in the manufacture of the artefact but in the creation of meaning. What is going on in this work is actually how art has functioned over millennia – with the idea of participation at its centre. To argue for reconnection to that idea is not eccentric, nor is it sentimental. It is to argue for art that is centred on empowering negotiation and to seek the new practice, new art(s) forms that will articulate those values and, further, to argue for the new organisational forms that will support those negotiations. We need a different 'optic'.

In a way community arts did provide a different optic in relation to contemporary art production by creating the opportunities for participation at the level of manufacture. Participation has been central to the very long process of image-making of self and 'other' and the negotiation of that relationship in human history. Yet it was this very process, the idea of direct participation, which was first eroded and then stolen outright by nineteenth- and twentieth-century modernism, certainly in the visual arts. When you consider that imperialism and colonialism were also aspects of that modernist mind-set in this period, it is no surprise that metaphorical theft within western society echoed actual economic and cultural theft outside it. The task now facing those who claim allegiance to the idea of participatory practice is to reposition those values of participation and negotiation at the centre of our culture, not to replace but to co-exist and dialogue with the existing armature of signature values and practice. And it is in dialogue, in that dialectic, that entry points will be negotiated on new terms for much wider ranges of people.

Of course a key difference between now and the period in art history which I am using as a jumping-off point is that most people lived within a universal belief system, of which art was an articulation and therefore accessible and legible to a wide range of people. Religious art is a very powerful model of participation, even if we may be uneasy about the purpose of the participation. But we do not now inhabit an equivalent universal belief system that is concerned with the nature and meaning of human experience. Instead we inhabit consumerism. The dialogue or dialectic I mentioned above must be developed self-consciously in the face of global consumerism, which cannot be wished away, and maybe should not be wished away. What cultural practitioners now negotiate with consumerism will be crucial in determining the health of the social body and the health of specific communities, of place and of interest. While I argue that the codes used by Holbein were legible because they were part of a common currency, I am fully aware that neither Holbein, nor the man who commissioned the painting, would have had any sense of its eventual availability to a mass audience in a free National Gallery in London – in fact the painting only came into public ownership at the end of the nineteenth century. But although Holbein operated within a commercial commissioning process so central was the idea in mainstream art of participation/negotiation of meaning by the viewer that the capacity was built in to the work, giving it a use value. The ultimate 'offer' of modernism – consumerism – works by appearing to give us what we want rather than what we

'The history which comprises "our heritage" is not in any way objective. It has been written by those groups occupying the positions of power which enable them to shape public knowledge. These are also the groups with most to protect.' Another Standard: Culture and Democracy – the Manifesto, 1986

need, but it also works, of necessity, by making us a slave to exchange value rather than use value

People often, and sometimes deliberately, confuse the art business – the exchange value of the artefact – with the business of art – its moral and social purpose – and, by the mid-twentieth century, nineteenth-century modernism had succeeded in separating the aesthetic responsibilities of art from its moral and social responsibilities. This is the space we are inhabiting now and a 'new' community arts, or, as I would prefer, a new civil culture, has to be negotiated consciously in this space. The reconnection has to be made in art practice – in new art-forms and forms of production – and in new organisational/ institutional practice – in new forms of distribution to support practice. For distribution is actually the classification process in the arts. The mechanisms of distribution – galleries, museums, theatres and so on – are the means we use to classify what we make and do in culture.

If there is a shorthand for the task in this period, for use value over exchange value, then it is to create an armature of memory, language, supports and practice which reconnect those responsibilities again. They connect in *The Ambassadors*, which identifies the art process and the idea of participation in the art process at the centre of our civilisation. The idea of participation, of negotiation, be that political or cultural, therefore, is consistent with the idea of civilisation, not a contradiction. It can, and must, be made central again, rather than marginal.

The history of community arts in Northern Ireland

according to MARTIN LYNCH

I have a confession to make. I was involved in writing and producing community theatre in the mid-seventies, before I ever heard the terms 'community theatre' or 'community arts'. Of course, I quickly cottoned on after reading a few books and seeing a few particular productions. Consequently, we changed the name of our group from Turf Lodge Fellowship Theatre Company to Turf Lodge Fellowship Community Theatre Company. Since those days I've been privileged (we'll leave the word 'traumatised' until another article) to have been associated with very many of the important community theatre and community arts developments in Northern Ireland, and particularly in Belfast, for nearly thirty years now.

I think it's important to take a moment to reflect here on why, where and how the community arts movement arrived into our lives, or at least my take on things. I also hope you will pardon me for concentrating on theatre, as that has been my main area of experience. Furthermore, as the title suggests, this is not an academically researched blow-by-blow history of community arts in Northern Ireland. It's merely what I can remember. I apologise in advance if I have omitted the important work of any individual or any group.

The Historical Context

In order to understand how remarkable current community arts developments are, they have to be placed in the context of what went before. It is important that we appreciate and know that production of the arts worked in an entirely different way for probably three hundred years before community arts emerged in its various guises across the world in the 1960s. In that three-hundred-year period, the production of what we will call the 'professional arts' was carried out almost exclusively by people from 'educated' and materially well-off backgrounds. It was also – and this is just as crucial – watched and consumed by, that is, its audience was, the same social bracket of people. If you take theatre for example: it was written exclusively by people (men) who came from wealthy or at least middle-class backgrounds and who had the economic means to go to university. In Irish terms, Oscar Wilde, George Bernard Shaw, Boucicault, Yeats, Synge and so on spring to mind. For the most part, their plays were performed in specially constructed theatres that were patronised only by people who could afford to pay to see them, i.e., people from the upper and middle classes. This scenario can be translated to any theatre-producing country in the world at that time, i.e., England, France, Germany, Italy, Russia, USA and so on. The millions of people from those countries who grew up in poorer backgrounds were in no position to partake in these activities. They had no education about the theatre and most couldn't read or write, so they didn't even have the basic tools to begin to make theatre. By the time the twentieth century got into its stride, however, playwrights from poorer backgrounds began to emerge. In Ireland we had, for example, Seán O'Casey and Brendan Behan.

It wasn't until the 1960s, and the emergence of individuals from a society where education was no longer the privilege of the middle and upper classes, that access to partaking in the arts began to change. In the theatre arena, independent theatre companies emerged in the UK who broke from the old convention of relying on a playwright to write a play for production in a specially constructed theatre – they wrote the plays themselves and put them on wherever they liked. The core subjects of plays began to change as well. Many of these plays were written by more than one person. Often they were written in collaboration with communities or interest groups. Instead of plays about 'self' and personal concerns, plays began to emerge that dealt primarily with social, communal and community issues. By the 1970s the face of theatre in England had been changed forever.

In Ireland developments took a little longer. When community theatre began to develop in England, we were still sleeping in 1960s Ireland, north and south. Similarly, when community theatre was in full swing in England in the 1970s, we were just beginning to stir.

Northern Ireland in the 1970s.

My first experience of theatre of any kind was going along to a play in early 1972 at the Vere Foster Primary School in the Moyard estate, near Ballymurphy in west Belfast. The Troubles had erupted, and bombings and shootings were the daily norm. I don't mean the daily norm downtown or somewhere else or on the TV: I mean right outside our front door, out on the streets of our estate, Turf Lodge, and anywhere else I called my world at that time.

I had seen a hand-written poster on a wall in a social club advertising a play. I can't remember the title of the play, but when I went along it was packed. It turned out to be a play written by Fr Des Wilson and it was all about the injustices of internment without trial. Local people acted in it. I remember a scene where a group of women were banging bin lids on the floor. It was quite good, certainly authentic, and I enjoyed it.

Around the early 1970s also, a visual arts group called Media Workshop was set up. They organised exhibitions at various venues, on subjects (among other things) associated with the political unrest, and later established premises in downtown Belfast. As I remember it, a lot of posters that adorned the walls of Belfast promoting the causes of various radical organisations were designed and printed from within this group.

In 1976, as mentioned above, myself and a group of people from Turf Lodge set up the Fellowship Community Theatre, Turf Lodge. Between 1976 and 1982, we performed about six plays and three million sketches at various clubs, community centres and theatres, mostly in Belfast but also in other parts of Northern Ireland. Some of my best memories and funniest times are from the days touring with the Fellowship.

In 1978, a radical new development occurred when Lord Melchett, a Labour Party Minister for the direct rule administration at Stormont, gave the Arts Council of Northern Ireland £100,000 to set up a community arts fund. This money was used to stimulate a range of activities, including support for a community arts collective called Neighbourhood Open Workshops (NOW) and support for a new professional theatre touring group called PLAYZONE, which included in its ranks Stephen Rea, Marie Jones and Andy Hinds.

'Culture has been called the visible expression of the health of the community. Whether celebration or critique, culture is essentially about communication. Communication, in turn, is dialogue, debating difference through rational conflict resolution. Violence breeds when dialogue fails. Violence has been called the last realm of the inarticulate. To restore the health of our communities, we need to encourage the expression of their unique voices through their respective cultures. And community arts can help communities do this.' Tom Magill, Community Arts Forum (CAF) Chair, 1996

The most significant of these turned out to be NOW. It lasted into the early nineties. Some people were sceptical of its work, as it was perceived by some as being made up of a collection of do-gooder English people assisted by an eternally passing raggle-taggle of students and other adventurers. Whilst it put on some fairly radical work, particularly in the Moyard area of west Belfast, the perceived wisdom was that it never really rooted itself in the community and could therefore have no lasting impact.

The 1980s

The first half of the 1980s saw community arts activity continue to grow in a very haphazard, patchy way. The Arts Council of Northern Ireland, whilst continuing to support sporadic work, had no real policy on community arts and certainly no systematic development policy. This effectively meant that energy emerged here and there but faded as the energy associated with individuals was exhausted.

A very exciting development on the professional theatre front happened with the formation of Charabanc Theatre Company. Whilst not directly a community arts product, this company's first couple of plays were widely performed in every available community centre, club and day centre in working-class Belfast. The production of *Lay up Your Ends* played to over thirty venues in both Catholic and Protestant areas. No significant working-class area of Belfast didn't host the play. In my understanding, this record remains unsurpassed to this day. This was what you called bringing theatre to the people.

Perhaps the most significant development in the mid-1980s occurred when Peter Sheridan and Sandy Fitzgerald arrived north, contacting myself and the few others that were active at that time, to help set up a northern branch/arm of Creative Activity for Everyone (CAFE). In spite of our best efforts, the north wasn't ready for it. Myself and a few others joined CAFE's executive but there simply wasn't enough of what we understand as community arts activity in the north to sustain a supporting network organisation. But it planted the seed.

Also in the 1980s, three key community arts organisations were formed in the Belfast area: Belfast Exposed, a community photography facility; Northern Visions, a video and film facility; and Belfast Community Circus School. These three organisations have been bulwarks of the community arts sector in Belfast ever since.

Supported by the Arts Council of Northern Ireland, Belfast's first community theatre group, Tongue 'n Cheek, based in Ardoyne, was formed around this time and is still going strong to this day. West Belfast Community Theatre, formed by Jim McGlade, Joe Reid and Fr Des Wilson, did some great work in the second half of the eighties but faded by the early nineties.

In Derry/Londonderry a number of initiatives took place that reflected a growing awareness of community arts. The following groups made their first impact in the 1980s: Frontline Community Drama, Pilot's Row Community Centre's community arts programme, North West Musicians Collective and Camera Work.

In 1998, Northern Ireland's first ever large-scale community play, *Fair Day*, took place in Warrenpoint, Co. Down. It was the brainchild of Warrenpoint-born but English-based actor and writer Patch Connolly and drew huge audiences to its short run of performances. This was followed a year later by *The Stone Chair*, written by myself and directed by John Haswell. It was based in the small Short Strand area of east Belfast but broke new ground by putting in place a unique combination of professional and community participation. It broke further ground by coming out of 'the ghetto' and performing for nine nights at the Belfast Grand Opera House to packed houses.

The 1990s

It wasn't until the 1990s that anyone could truly say that community arts in Northern Ireland took off. And by God did it take off! In Derry/Londonderry and Belfast groups, projects and events took place that had a lasting impact.

By 1992, around half a dozen community theatre groups had been formed in Belfast that were to form the basis for perhaps the most prolific and sustained community theatre explosion in these islands. In Derry/Londonderry The Playhouse and the Verbal Arts Centre were new bases where community arts activity was encouraged and could thrive.

To my mind the most significant event to take place for community arts in Northern Ireland happened on a cold day at the Golden Thread Theatre in January 1993, when the Belfast community theatre groups came together to discuss issues of mutual concern.

The result of the meeting was the formation of the Community Arts Forum (CAF). And the key to its significance was its remit to lobby and advocate for something called 'community arts'. CAF became a membership organisation and very soon represented over two hundred groups. Over the next six years, it literally went on the offensive. Its main target was the Arts Council of Northern Ireland. The reasoning was that most Arts Council funding at that time went to support mainstream arts activity, for example Ulster Orchestra (£1.2 million), Lyric Theatre (£500,000), Grand Opera House (£600,000) and so on, whilst less than £300,000 went to the entire community arts sector. This was patently unfair. And if the sector was ever to get decent resources it would have to come from the main funder of the arts in Northern Ireland – the Arts Council.

For four years CAF battered at the Arts Council of Northern Ireland's door. It had little or no effect. Instead, the burgeoning community arts sector in the Belfast area was given huge financial support by a government social-regeneration quango, Making Belfast Work (MBW) – later to become Belfast Regeneration Office (BRO). MBW effectively started the community arts sector as we know it in Belfast today. It funded CAF to get it off the ground. It then went on to plough over £3 million into the community arts sector over the following six or seven years, giving many organisations their first serious funding – an astonishing amount of money and an incredible development, largely due to the foresight and vision of MBW chiefs such as Tony McCusker.

Still, the Arts Council of Northern Ireland was digging its heels in. Their chief executive at that time, Brian Ferran, declared in a workshop he and I were both attending that community arts was 'social engineering' and that he didn't have any new money for such activities. By the end of the four-year lobbying process he refused even to meet us. We were desperate. We felt we were getting nowhere. We had to change tack and try something radically different. After a particularly soul-searching CAF executive meeting, we decided to go straight to the Department of Education for Northern Ireland (DENI), the government department which gave the Arts Council its money. We

Community arts demonstration, Belfast, 2000

lobbied DENI like we'd never lobbied before. I have to admit to a strong dollop of luck at this point.

First, a new deputy Permanent Secretary had recently been appointed at DENI who immediately understood our argument and the injustice taking place. He grasped the nettle and went for the throat of the Arts Council of Northern Ireland (ACNI). Second, the Labour government came into power in Britain and very soon we were sitting back with some satisfaction as the Arts Council was sent down one new government policy instruction after another – identical to the issues we had been campaigning for over the previous four years. Third, a devolved administration arrived at Stormont and, lo and behold, our old ally in DENI was appointed to an even more powerful position in the newly created Department of Culture, Arts and Leisure (DCAL).

Within eighteen months, Mr Ferran resigned and for the first time ever, instead of being appointed by a government minister, places on the next board of the Arts Council were to be advertised publicly. I can't say there wasn't a good deal of joyous celebration when the Arts Council of Northern Ireland got a new chief executive and a brand new board with at least six community arts representatives onboard. One year later, the next funding round of the new Arts Council produced a radical uplift. Their spending on community arts jumped from around £500,000 to over £1 million.

We entered the new millennium with the community arts sector in Northern Ireland at last getting some official recognition and standing at its strongest ever.

Things are not perfect. They never are or never will be. Both Belfast City Council and Derry City Council have recently taken funding decisions that have seriously impaired the community arts sectors in those cities. At the time of writing, BCC is trying to repair the damage in its next budget. The last couple of years have been difficult in that many organisations in the Belfast area who had achieved relatively potent expansion and growth via MBW and other non-arts sourced funding have now lost that short-term funding. The slack – the long-term sustainability – can only be filled by ACNI. That's where the slack belongs. There are, in my opinion, still individuals well placed at the Arts Council of Northern Ireland, who would, given half a chance, reverse everything to the bad old days. The sector and its friends need to be on constant guard.

The most important fact we have to keep in our sights is that the vast majority of people in Northern Ireland (or people in any other part of the world) still do not participate in the arts, either as makers or audience. This is a challenge to all of us. Funding for the community arts sector could triple in the next twelve months but it would still only be scraping the surface of what needs to be done.

Nevertheless, the legacy of the last thirty years of community arts development is clear. The notion that access to the arts is a human right to all, irrespective of where or into what circumstances you were born, is undisputed. The notion of 'community arts' as a way of working that gives a voice via the arts to huge sections of our society that previously had none is well established. The term 'community arts' is now truly understood. It has an impact throughout society in Northern Ireland. It is understood and utilised in government departments, statutory agencies, local councils, the voluntary and community sectors and, most especially, it is clearly understood in communities. People who previously wouldn't have touched something called 'the arts' have no problem getting involved up to their neck in community arts.

It gives me great satisfaction when, by chance, I might see a job advertisement in the *Belfast Telegraph* from some local council or community group seeking a community arts officer. It wouldn't have happened ten years ago. That is real change.

And finally … I have often been asked – indeed we often ask ourselves – what impact, if any, the community arts movement has had on political developments in Northern Ireland and, specifically, the peace process. The straight answer is I don't know what impact we have had. But I'm fairly certain the troubles have had a big impact on us. Some of those active in the last ten years are convinced that the turmoil, the upheaval, the searching of consciences, the unwanted confrontations, the closeness to death and tragedy, the political uncertainty – have acted as a powerful incentive for unusually large numbers of people to look for answers, to go in search of something better than what we have – through the medium of the arts. It's been an extraordinary journey.

The beginnings of community arts and the Irish Republic

SANDY FITZGERALD

My aim with this essay is not to attempt any detailed history of community arts, as that would be impossible in the limited space available. I have set myself the task here of sketching out the historical context of and reasons why community arts evolved as it did, visiting some of the key moments for the sector along the way. Like its counterparts in other countries, the Irish experience of community arts has its own unique character, but whatever the geographical location, all have similar influences and values. In the first part of my essay I endeavour to outline these influences and values in a more global context before moving on to the Irish experience and its recent history. And, obviously, the story is open-ended because the community arts' momentum continues to evolve, even as I write.

Genesis

In 1926 one Edina Savage established a community arts centre in New York as part of the Harlem Renaissance. Is this the first recorded use of the term community arts?

The community arts centre of 1926 was not familiar to the early advocates of community arts in Ireland but the Great Georges Street Project, better known as the Blackie, in Liverpool, much to their surprise, discovered its existence some months after believing they had coined the term 'community arts centre'. The Blackie, who still operate from their original base, an old church in Great Georges Street, came up with their descriptive subtitle in 1968. While laying a gentle claim to being one of the first to use the term 'community arts', the Blackie also recognise that many similar ventures were emerging all around England and the world, at and before that time, as the Harlem centre attests.

There are a thousand starting points and hundreds of locations across the globe that could join the community arts genesis list. The concept of cultural democracy and the liberating of individual creativity surfaced as the twentieth century progressed. For instance, the Marxist view of 'social' art and artists as workers; Roosevelt's 'New Deal' and $46 million spent on commissioning work from unemployed artists (1935–1939) in the US; the Committee for the Encouragement of Music and the Arts (CEMA) established under the United Kingdom's 'emergency government' at the outbreak of the Second World War and a forerunner of the Arts Council of Great Britain (the latter established in 1945). However, it wasn't until the countercultural explosion that was the 1960s gave rise to what could be termed a community arts movement that our contemporary understanding of that term comes into focus. While America pursued a cultural democracy agenda, England witnessed the birth of community arts when a number of radical initiatives intersected and combined. These initiatives can be broadly divided into two camps: the counter-culture rebellion – a predominantly middle-class phenomenon – and a working-class revolt. Both were forged on the post-Second World War, post-industrial anvil.

All you need is love

Counterculturalism was a complex phenomenon whose adherents were dismissively labelled 'hippies' by an alarmed older generation. 'Hippie' was a term used to trivialise this teenage uprising but the cultural tidal wave was unstoppable. 'Hippies' were only part of a counter-culture revolution that was in direct conflict with the social, economic and political *status quo* of the time. The broad church of counterculturalism embraced a wide spectrum of activists from Cuban revolutionaries and American Black Panthers to naturalists and flower children. What united these disparate groups was a passion for change arising from the view that a corrupt and conservative establishment had to be challenged and, ultimately, subverted.

Such radical talk was not new, in so much as anarchists, socialists and even artistic movements such as Dadaism and Surrealism had voiced similar manifestos earlier in the century. But the difference when it came to the counterculturalists was the populist nature of the movement and the fact that it arose from within the heart of the western system. These rebels were the sons and daughters of the middle class: educated and privileged. Suddenly this motley shambles of teenage angst was a mass movement. The best universities, suburbs and upper-crust bedrooms found a *coup d'état* occurring in their midst.

This insurgence drew its inspiration from a range of sources. In America young people were reacting to immediate realities such as the Vietnam War and brutal racism, while in France the movement's *raison d'être* came more from left-wing radicals and philosophers. What they all had in common was a desire to shape a new world based on equality, peace, love and understanding, qualities that the establishment singularly lacked when it came to reacting to this new challenge.

Many initiatives by this loose, world-wide, alternative family were met by force. Thousands and thousands of small skirmishes took place as police raided clubs and battled with squatters. There was a genuine fear on behalf of the establishment that their order was in danger as protests flared in many world capitals on issues ranging from nuclear weapons to human rights. (In August 1963 a quarter of a million people gathered in Washington to demand equality for black people; riots broke out at an anti-Vietnam War protest in London in June 1966; May 1968 saw ten thousand students and workers battle with police on the streets of Paris; a peaceful 1969 civil rights march in Derry ended in violence when confronted by an aggressive police force, ushering in over forty years of bloodshed in Northern Ireland.)

The tools used to symbolise and achieve these new 'contra' ideals were, in the main, cultural: instead of a suit you wore a caftan and beads; instead of a modest dress you wore a mini-skirt; instead of regulation short back and sides you wore shoulder-length locks; instead of a dry martini you rolled up a spliff. And the leaders of this revolution were not politicians or soldiers: they were artists. They played guitars and wrote poems.

These outward signs of individuality and difference also represented a new creative freedom. Art institutions, such as galleries, opera houses and art schools, were treated with contempt or ignored altogether. While these old houses of culture were shunned, the counterculturalists needed new places to make and display and this happened naturally – on the street, in communes and squats and in the American titled 'arts lab'.

Shortly after the emergence of the counterculturalists in America, Europe saw the lights and heard the chanting from its own dilapidated

Paris, 7th May 1968. Students and police battle in the Rue St Jacques. Hulton Archive

buildings. In London the Drury Lane Arts Lab (1967) was among the vanguard, witnessing the birth of the original 'The People Show'. The Birmingham Arts Lab, The Roundhouse, Battersea Arts Lab and many more soon followed. Amsterdam was a virtual city-wide arts lab and became the European Mecca for hippies because of Holland's liberal drugs laws.

Some of these early labs survive to this day, such as the Melkweg in the aforementioned Amsterdam, Traverse in Scotland and Project in Dublin, and the opening out of creativity as a means of personal expression and liberation changed the social and cultural landscape irreversibly.

Working-class heros

While the youth of the middle class was confidently proclaiming revolution, the working class found itself increasingly marginalised. The economy was post-industrial and entering a new era of technology. The market for labour was shrinking and whole communities found their way of life changing. Where a production line or port once supported thousands of people, now there was nothing but empty factories and rusting machinery. In the midst of a brave new world, the newly non-working class were forgotten.

Under pressure from unemployment, poor housing, minimal services and a distinct lack of political interest, many communities went into a downward spiral. Most noticeable in their deterioration were the inner-city and dock-land communities. Traditionally ports were the hub of industry. Factories were built in close proximity to the docks to avail of both import and export possibilities. Large communities of workers settled around these facilities. But by the sixties the industrial world was changing. Services and new technology were fast taking over from the labour-intensive industries of the earlier part of the century. A second and even more devastating blow came in the form of roll on, roll off ferries. Loading and unloading of cargo was no longer necessary. The great ports of London, Liverpool, Glasgow, Belfast and Tyneside virtually shut down. Many of the smaller docks followed suit, including Dublin. While the hippies were animated and enthused by their vision of a new future, enabled by education and their families' wealth, the

'The Dadaists wanted to get rid of all the West's political, social, cultural and artistic traditions, which they held responsible for the carnage of World War 1.' *Dada* by Serge Lemoine, Art Data, 1987

Cover of the Greater London Council's (GLC) report, A Record of Struggle and Achievement, on their community arts programme 1981–1986. The radical Labour GLC, led by Ken Livingston, supported and developed community arts projects in London as never before, until its dissolution by Margaret Thatcher in 1986.

working-class vision was crumbling, and from London's Bermondsey to Dublin's Sheriff Street the future looked pretty bleak.

As the reality of their abandonment began to sink in, some people among these disenfranchised communities decided to take matters into their own hands. Action groups were formed and priority issues were tackled from the ground up. Housing, education and health all became a focus to mobilise around. And culture too became an issue. Some of the agitators realised that modern communication tools could be very advantageous to their cause. Obtaining support from a wider public and embarrassing the government into doing something would take more than a few local marches. Poster-making, leafleting, pageantry, theatre, photography and film-making were all pressed into service, usually drawing on the expertise of 'radical' artists and creative types. Communities also began to realise that they needed to discover their own cultural voice, different in tone and resonance to their original 'masters'. And this is the point where the counter-culture movement and the working-class struggle formed an uneasy alliance out of which grew 'community arts', circa 1970.

In England this new movement spread rapidly, galvanising around issues of local agitation and based on left-wing principles.

And in 1978, ten years after the Blackie had a eureka moment, the name 'community arts' had floated on the breeze to Ireland.

Thank God we're surrounded by water

The Republic of Ireland in the late 1970s was still emerging from a history of conflict, isolationism, crippling poverty and the overshadowing of civil-war politics. There is no escaping the fact that the country was conservative in the extreme, driven by nationalism, crass in its articulation and dangerous in its fundamentalism. Artists were tolerated once they promoted a good, wholesome recipe of Irish mythology sanitised by a strict Catholic doctrine.

By adopting this vision for the newly formed Irish Republic, the leadership basically dispensed with art in any contemporary sense and defined the country as one large heritage centre where the past would become the model for the present. This was a safe course to pursue for the politicians and a comforting idea for the populace.

The only problem was that it flew in the face of any cultural, social or economic development. It was, of course, an emotional and historical reaction to our neighbour, England, and served to define us as what we were not, rather than what we were. Trying to go it alone culturally (as well as economically) was an impossibility and, while there is a certain heroic nobility about declaring your total independence, the reality is quite different.

This defensive position led to enormous amounts of time and energy being spent on schemes to place Gaelic games, music and dance and the Irish language at the centre of people's lives. By definition, it also meant keeping foreign influences out. Censorship became a means to this end. The laws for censoring films and books come into force in 1923 and 1929 respectively. Radio was state owned and, as such, was closely monitored for undesirable content. Television, when it arrived in 1962, was similarly policed.

In 1951 the first Arts Council was formed in the Republic. Before this the responsibility for arts lay with nobody in particular and with the government of the day in general. The thinking behind forming an Arts Council derived from the British model of fostering post-war modernism. While the complex and ever-present trend of following Britain's lead while, at the same time, seeming to reject it at every turn cries out for a book in itself, the particular issue of forming an Arts Council in the Republic had more to do with a small coterie of contemporary-art enthusiasts than of presenting ourselves to the world as modern and cultured. But it did represent a modest attempt to break out from the 'fortress island', a policy that had begun to create embarrassing anomalies and public-image disasters. While the economic argument for opening up was of prime importance to the country's leaders as the 1950s progressed, the cultural case was also gaining momentum. The body of exiled artists and banned works was growing and the ever-increasing traffic between Ireland and the rest of the world was encountering a fair share of sniggering and pointed questions. If the Lemass era of modernising the country was to triumph, Ireland had to be seen as a forward-looking place and fertile for new ideas and investment. Having the artistic community sniping from at home and abroad was not helpful.

But as the island's population struggled through dark years of poverty and emigration, the arts were not much on anybody's minds. The hermetically sealed world of the fine arts was of little interest to the wider public. Working-class communities of 1970s Ireland were barely surviving, struggling under layer upon layer of bad decisions. Very real community actions, such as the housing movement of the time, gave people some strength and confidence to move forward. Again, as had happened in England, the intersection of small groups of people who had artistic skills with community groups led to the realisation that being creative was also about having a voice and effecting change. The particular issue in question, be it health or housing, was important but so too was the bigger picture of cultural identity. More opportunities to explore alternatives to traditional employment, education and personal expression were sought by the community activists because there was nothing much else. People became politicised and informed but they also became witnesses for themselves and their communities. They wanted to tell their story and they began to feel the power of these stories. Every step was a learning process, including creating the means of informing others of this experience because there were no established avenues to do this. The education system, if children from depressed areas even attended schools, merely imparted irrelevant facts and very circumscribed ones at that. The artistic community performed for their own little band of critics. A small élite had all the venues, stages, printing presses, cameras and wall space tightly controlled for a particular type of art, a particular type of voice. Working-class communities had to reinvent and acquire the means of expressing themselves. This turned out to be community arts.

The early years of community arts in Ireland

During the 1970s, pockets of arts practice began to emerge around Ireland that drew more on local circumstance then on any notion of formal art history or tradition. And these local groups were informed by the *realpolitik* of the community in question, combined with new techniques in creative participation and driven by idealism. Examples of such groups are Neighbourhood Open Workshops in Belfast, Waterford Arts for All, and Grapevine and Moving Theatre in Dublin, all operating by the end of the 1970s.

By the early 1980s the number of such groups had grown from a handful to something more substantial and they began to gravitate towards the ideas of community arts. One such group was City Workshop in Dublin's inner city.

The moment where community arts in Ireland formally recognised itself and looked to the outside world for recognition and support can be pinpointed to a meeting, a seminar, in the North Star Hotel, Dublin, called by City Workshop in the summer of 1983. At this meeting no more than fifteen organisations were represented – the majority of community arts groups working in the thirty-two counties at the time.

City Workshop was a drama project initiated by the NCCCAP and run by Peter Sheridan. Both the NCCCAP and City Workshop are worth looking at in some detail because they were the forerunners of much that was to follow.

The North City Centre Community Action Programme, or N-treble C-A-P as it was known, arose from the socially deprived and ghettoised communities of the north inner city of Dublin. By the early seventies the authorities had all but abandoned this community, unable or unwilling to tackle the issues of poor housing, unemployment, social deprivation and all the attendant problems that went with such a combination of social ills. The unstated but understood answer was to slowly dismantle the community, scattering the population to the suburbs, and to bulldoze what was left. The NCCCAP was formed to resist any such destruction of the community and to fight for amenities within the area. In 1982 they succeeded in getting a local man elected to the Dáil on an independent ticket. Tony Gregory was one of the youngest politicians ever to be elected as a TD and also one of the most unconventional. What seems quaint now was then front-page news, such as not wearing a tie into the chamber. But Gregory was no fool and, in the same year he was elected, forged the famous Gregory deal with then Taoiseach Charles Haughey, which gave substantial benefits to the north inner city and, as importantly, highlighted the issues of such a working-class community. But the high profile of the NCCCAP and its representative in Dáil Éireann hid an even more impressive list of local achievements and local activists. A whole range of training programmes, community information services and cultural activities were initiated which both inspired and created models of practice for other communities around the country. The latter was an important development because it recognised the necessity of identifying and exploring your roots and of finding ways to develop your community and then securing the means and expertise to actively engage in positive change. The result of this position was a wide range of community activities, including the groundbreaking refusal to 'import' a received culture or to only see art as the preserve of the privileged.

This led to a continuous and expanding flow of arts initiatives, resulting in some memorable achievements. The 'Inner City, Looking On' festival of 1982 focused attention on this part of the capital and attracted nervous spectators and journalists into The Diamond and its surrounds, many for the first time. The programme was comprehensive and exciting. In a staid world of wine receptions and first nights there was a realisation that something else was going on – and with a programme that was hard to ignore. The festival was also a forerunner of and a role model for many subsequent local festivals.

The NCCCAP also initiated a unique drama experiment. City Workshop brought together local men and women under the newly established Department of Education Teamwork Scheme (the first of many art projects funded under this scheme) to work on researching and devising drama pieces arising from their own experiences. Over a three-year period, participants produced three pieces of theatre. Housewives, unemployed dockers and kids out of school found skills and voices they never knew were there and produced riveting entertainment that not only appealed to their neighbours (many of whom had never set foot in a theatre before) but also impressed critics and others of the 'theatre world'.

City Workshop was very successful but its funding under the Teamwork scheme was coming to an end and the group was looking for alternative grant aid to stay alive. As part of its campaign, City Workshop organised the North Star Hotel seminar of 1983 to discuss the wider issues related to the funding and development of the type of work City Workshop was engaged in. It was also the first time that such a group of people had the opportunity to sit around a table and discuss community arts. The meeting included representation from Waterford Arts for All, Neighbourhood Open Workshops, Moving Theatre and Grapevine Arts Centre.

The Kips, the Digs and the Village by City Workshop, performed in O'Neill's pub, Summerhill, Dublin, 31 July 1982. Photo: Derek Speirs/Report

Following on from the North Star a second meeting was organised and this loose collective began to coalesce into what would become CAFE (Creative Activity for Everyone), the umbrella group for community arts in Ireland. (It is interesting to note that the discussions around the formation of an organisation contained the elements of what continues to be a debate in the Republic. That is, should it be a representative organisation, a lobbying group or an advocacy group?)

Outside of the capital, things were stirring too. Action groups were forming around new ideas for more contemporary, participatory arts activities, for example, Waterford Arts for All, Theatre Omnibus in Limerick, Macnas in Galway and the arts centres Triskel in Cork and Cornmarket in Wexford. Immediately after the two Dublin meetings, four regional meetings took place – in Cork, Waterford, Galway and Belfast – resulting in a series of action points and the election of an *ad hoc* national committee to address these points. The main issues for the *ad hoc* committee were policy, funding, communication, database, solidarity and establishing an administrative office.

Out of these meetings came the fledging CAFE organisation, based in the Grapevine Arts Centre, Dublin (the latter a forerunner of City Arts Centre), and, shortly afterward, the first conference on community arts took place, again in the North Star Hotel, organised by CAFE in the spring of 1984.

This first conference agreed a number of important steps, including:

- CAFE should accept the broadest possible definition of creativity
- CAFE should negotiate with the Youth Employment Agency with regard to funding
- a sub-committee of CAFE concerned with education should be formed
- regional practitioners should hold meetings and contribute to a CAFE policy document

From the beginning, CAFE was anxious to include its Northern Ireland counterparts in its activities and development plans. At this early stage it was envisaged that CAFE might be an Ireland-wide organisation. As a result, the conference organised after the North Star gathering of 1984 was in Belfast. This conference, which took place in the Central Hall, Rosemary Street, in March 1985, was called Art and Social Change in Ireland. The organising partners were ARE (Art and Research Exchange), NOW (Neighbourhood Open Workshops), WEA (Workers' Educational Association) and CAFE. At this meeting it became clear that the differences between north and south of the border were too great an obstacle to overcome and the idea of an Ireland-wide organisation was abandoned. CAFE would establish itself in the twenty-six counties and northern colleagues could affiliate if they so wished. (In 1993 the Community Arts Forum [CAF] was founded in Northern Ireland to represent the interests of community arts in the six counties.)

CAFE moved into permanent offices in the Grapevine Arts Centre in 1984 with an administrator (funded under a Teamwork scheme). The idea of CAFE was to give a focus and a co-ordinated approach to community arts in the Republic, strengthening and building the movement. Besides organising the Dublin and Belfast conferences, CAFE set about creating a database for the sector and operating an advice service. Early projects also included the first community arts worker course and the publishing of a funding handbook. But probably the most important role it played at this time was giving community

Jungle Bullion: a Midsummer carnival (1983). Neighbourhood Open Workshops commissioned UK-based Welfare State International to help recreate a Victorian garden party in Belfast's Botanic Gardens. The project successfully combined NOW's network of contacts in communities and groups in Ireland, north and south, and WSI's spectacular theatre skills and expertise

arts a profile and creating a rallying point for isolated and struggling groups working in far-flung corners of the state. But CAFE itself suffered from chronic under-resourcing from day one and the pressure from all sides, including the Arts Council (which was keen to have one single community arts voice to deal with), meant that its capacity to deliver was constantly strained and pulled in all directions. In fact, CAFE was a mirror image of many of its clients in its struggle for survival and it can only be marvelled at that the organisation achieved as much as it did, never mind survived at all.

As the number of projects under the banner of community arts grew in the early eighties, fuelled, to a large extent, by ever more grants under Department of Labour 'back to work' schemes and from European structural and other funds, the Arts Council decided to respond to the increasing demand.

The southern Arts Council initiated an action research programme in 1985 that it hoped might help to both map and define community arts and it turned to the Gulbenkian Foundation for funding. The Gulbenkian responded positively and ACE was set up. ACE stood for Arts Community Education (not to be confused with Northern Ireland's ACE schemes, which were similar to FÁS's back-to-work schemes). The Arts Council established an ACE committee, chaired by Ciarán Benson, and it set about advertising for participants for its three-year programme. One hundred and four applications were received, which is an indication of how many groups had sprung up or decamped to the community arts' flag in the short year since the first meeting in the North Star Hotel. By 1989, when the ACE report was published, the activities taking place under the banner of community arts were so many and so varied that it was almost impossible to quantify. Ciarán Benson, in his essay for the ACE publication *Art and the Ordinary* mentions just some of the activities described as community arts: 'festivals and classes, arts centres and canal renovations, community theatre workshops and local publishing ventures, heritage parks and video projects, skills exchange workshops and artists residencies'.

Although Ciarán Benson sees this as a good thing, it also showed that community arts had become indefinable. This view was confirmed at the 'Arts and the Community' conference (Maynooth, June 1995), where the extent, range and diversity of topics and views expressed confounded any notion of a 'sectoral' view or position. In fact, many different sectors were represented at the conference, from health to disability, youth services to local authority provision, education to employment projects, prison art workshops to multi-cultural projects. Indeed, one of the main issues arising from the conference but left unanswered was how to define community arts in the face of such diversity. The seeking of a definition had also been at the heart of the North Star conference some ten years previously and had come up time and time again in various fora over the years.

At this point it is worth remembering that the original momentum for community arts grew from a very radical philosophy whereby the activists of the sixties wanted to overthrow the establishment in favour of a new utopia. In England in the 1970s this hardened into community arts as informed by Marxism and articulated in the manifesto (published in 1986) of Another Standard, a cultural activist group that became highly influential within the community arts scene of the time. It is fair to say that while a number of the Irish community arts adherents were likewise political, the main motivating factor of seeking to gather under the community arts heading in Ireland was one of solidarity. In fact, there was quite a lot of opposition to the term community arts from practitioners in Ireland for two main reasons.

First, they did not want their work associated with any political creed. There was a natural suspicion among the Irish arts practitioners of orthodoxy. Keeping in mind the divisiveness of mainstream politics in Ireland over many years, the idea of aligning your work to a political doctrine, left wing or otherwise, was anathema to many who were trying to work in new and collaborative ways. And community arts as a movement arrived with some political baggage attached.

Second, practitioners became alarmed at the Arts Council's move to create a community arts heading within their funding portfolio, particularly because it had a small budgetary line yet an ever-increasing list of clients. It looked to many like an expedient move by the Council to shunt this new activity off to one side with a few crumbs and lots of lip service. Better to stay under one of the traditional headings, such as theatre, with a much more generous wad of money, than be shoved out to the Arts Council Siberia of community arts.

Notwithstanding these reservations, people did align themselves to community arts and became very creative and successful in attracting grants outside of the Arts Council structure. Community arts received relatively large sums of money throughout the eighties and nineties from Europe (Structural Funds, ERDF, Horizon and Kaleidoscope grants, Youth Exchange grants), Department of Labour Schemes (Social Employment Schemes, Enterprise Grants, Community Employment), disability and health funding and local authority funding. For instance, there was a time when the FÁS grants to the arts far outweighed the total Arts Council budget and these grants were almost exclusively for community arts projects because of their intrinsic social and community perspective.

In addition to, or maybe because of, all this well-funded activity, it is now the norm for mainstream organisations to have a community arts dimension within their policy, often called 'outreach' or 'education'. Community arts became a necessary part of mainstream arts validating their funding or support for the more traditional work.

While all these projects and impressive funding levels are an amazing achievement for a sector that began with a handful of participants only thirty years ago, it could also be argued that the temporary nature and non-art aim of the work under employment and other funding has deflected the central role of creating art within a cultural advocacy context, keeping community arts outside of the established arts sector and, conversely, hiding its central artistic role from the social and civic sector because it was fulfilling other agendas, such as creating employment. Consequently, it fell into a limbo of frenzied activity.

In the early years it was easy to group anything that was participatory or developmental under the term community arts because the number of such projects was small. And most of the projects were art-form based, led by artists and/or community workers who were politicised or who had a social conscience, so the continuity was to do more with practice than apostrophising. The leaders of this early movement in community arts were invariably artists who had come from disadvantaged communities, people who had broken through the system, despite all the obstacles, to emerge as actors, directors, writers, photographers, film-makers and musicians.

Of the group that gathered for the initial meeting in the North Star Hotel in 1983, the majority were involved with theatre. Perhaps this reflected the tradition of story-telling in Ireland, which resulted in a love of language and all its outlets – novels, poetry, song and plays. Indeed,

Ireland had one of the largest amateur drama movements in the world per head of population. This, along with Ireland's vibrant music tradition, sometimes offered a door through which people from disadvantaged or working-class backgrounds could shift into the mainstream arts world. But these cases were extremely rare and usually ended up as parodies of their background, witness Brendan Behan. But a new generation used their artistic skills to try and liberate a new creative voice that they knew lay oppressed within themselves and their neighbourhoods. It was a feeding back of tradition and skills that was more comfortable with the verbal tradition than the visual sensibility. And anyway, the élitism of the arts was epitomised by the visual arts and visual artists.

But, after the early initiatives, every art form was accommodated under community arts. However, as the number of projects and practitioners grew with ever-increasing funding, so too did the separation of artistic practice from necessary outcomes. Most of the funding did not look for an artistic outcome. They needed employment indicators and EU integration; addiction, poverty and crime reduction; the learning of job skills – in fact, anything but an artistic output. The long list of projects, as community arts entered the 1990s, tells its own story. The North Star conference participant list for 1984 shows twenty-five groups represented, with twenty-one of this number having the practice of art as their primary activity. The participant list of the 1995 community arts conference in Maynooth shows one hundred and six groups with only thirty having art as their primary activity.

And now …

Accepting the fact that the creation of jobs and the social integration of people are important, the necessity to prioritise such goals for community arts organisations to receive funding must be questioned. Particularly as the net result seems to be a weakening of the activity called community arts through a separation of the work from cultural advocacy, a confusion around direction and purpose and, in the end, diminished support by funders, in particular the Arts Council. As the EU and other funding slips away, we see that the established arts, while having adopted certain elements of community arts such as outreach (often seen as a marketing tool), has not changed its core values and remains firmly entrenched in the notion of a cultural hierarchy based on a very selective tradition.

Whether inappropriate funding is the cause or not, it is certain that support for community arts by the establishment, which reached its height somewhere around 1993, has waned considerably in recent years. For instance, there was a time in the Republic when access to the President (Mary Robinson), Minister (Michael D. Higgins), Chair of the Arts Council (Ciarán Benson) and American Ambassador (Jean Kennedy Smith) was an open door for community arts. In fact, these individuals and their various organisations during this period adopted much of the community arts ethos as policy. It is now the case that community arts hardly features in any of these establishments.

In recent times, in the twenty-six counties, the term community arts itself has come into question. There is a view that the term has outlived its usefulness and new definitions should be found that are more relevant to the work and the practices currently bunched together uncomfortably under community arts. Whatever about the practitioners, the Arts Council dropped the term altogether from its Arts Plans and began to refer to participatory arts. This change went unnoticed and unchallenged by the community arts sector itself. (However, it should also be noted that the Northern Ireland community arts sector has strengthened its endorsement of the term community arts and is very positive about both the name and the nature of the activities that happen under this name.)

Besides the politics, the rhetoric and the debates, there are values around this activity called community arts that are as relevant today as they were forty or four hundred years ago. At the core of these values is the question of power and the right of people to contribute to and participate fully in culture, the right to have a voice and the right to give voice. As Ariel Dorfman said, 'People aren't voiceless: we're deaf – we don't hear them.' From this point of view, arts and culture should be at the centre of all political, social, educational, individual and communal activity, particularly in this time of dangerous change, for Ireland and the world.

SECTION 2

FUNDING, ETHICS AND QUALITY

Because community arts deals with issues of cultural democracy such as access, participation and power, the debate touches on every level of activity within society. In this section the essayists turn their attention to some of these issues. Paula Clancy undertakes a review of the position of community arts in the Irish Republic's cultural policy. Susan Coughlan investigates how funding in the Republic has been allocated, while Jo Egan and Gerri Moriarty speak about ethics and quality issues around community arts.

'Once Is Too Much', an exhibition initiated by women and friends of the Family Resource Centre, St Michael's Estate, Inchicore, in collaboration with the Irish Museum of Modern Art, 1997

Rhetoric and reality

A review of the position of community arts in state cultural policy in the Irish Republic

PAULA CLANCY

Introduction

This review[1] was commissioned by the City Arts Centre as part of its Civil Arts Inquiry to test ideas and ways of working in support of wider participation in cultural production and experience. The brief was to provide an assessment of the evolution of cultural policy in Ireland with particular reference to the treatment of community arts and the importance given to the idea of greater equality of participation in the arts through access to both the production of art and its outputs.

The assessment covers three time periods. The first, which takes us to the 1970s, is a necessarily cursory glance to set the historical context for the emergence of the debate on cultural democracy at its broadest and the approach to community arts within that. The second is a more detailed treatment of the decades from the mid-seventies to the mid-nineties. This was a period not only of debate and discussion but also of a variety of actions, projects and institution building. The mid-nineties to the present was a period of more sophisticated evidence-gathering, as well as one of more confident and trenchant demand from the arts sector. It is also one which acknowledges not only the relative failure of previous endeavours to effect significant change in the conceptualisation of culture, but also the complexity and intractability of the issues.

Early development

Until the 1970s there was little perceived conflict between the twin ideas of encouraging excellence and creating access for all, in much the same way as there was little critique of wider social and economic structures. To the extent that arts and culture excited interest among policy makers and key influencers in Irish society since its foundation, it was as an expression of the values and ideas shaping modern Ireland. The emphasis was on 'grand gestures' as signifiers of a civilised and cultured Ireland. Those with control of expenditure on the arts reflected the views of the élite, urban middle-class male and any measures taken to increase arts activity were spent almost entirely to further the values and ideas of that group. Notions of a differentiated approach to different groups – either those living in marginalised urban areas or those in rural areas, geographically distant from centres of cultural activity – were not part of the discourse. Thus, in a society where the ascription of value to an art product and, indeed, the very definition of what constituted a piece of art was unproblematically in the gift of an élite few, the concepts of 'excellence' and 'access' were easy bedfellows; the only issue was how to make this excellent art accessible to the interested citizen.

A 1949 study of the condition of the arts resulted in a damning report that stated that no other country in western Europe cared less or gave less for the cultivation of the arts than Ireland.[2] It also highlighted the fact that there was no instruction in art in our schools, primary, secondary or university. These criticisms were to be repeated in successive waves of debate and discussion about the arts in Ireland to the present day.

Thus, for much of the early history of independent Ireland, the arts and culture were of marginal interest in the shaping of an overall policy framework for the state. As detailed in Brian Kennedy's comprehensive analysis of Irish cultural policy (1990), the arts did attract greater attention from the Irish government in post-Second World War Ireland. At that time there were a number of significant developments, including rapid industrialisation, urbanisation, the arrival of a consumer-orientated society and increased leisure time, which gave rise to significant developments of structure and resource allocation to the arts. Principal among these was the 1951 Arts Act, which established the Arts Council.

Excellence and Access: Twin Policy Objectives
Early references in government documentation justifying expenditure on arts and cultural activity emphasise two imperatives. One of the most frequently cited drivers is the principle of equal access for all to a

cultural environment that enhances the quality of life. The first articulated function of the Arts Council as given in the 1951 Act is to stimulate public interest in the arts; the second is to promote the knowledge, appreciation and practice of the arts. The idea of excellence was also to the fore. The third and fourth functions of the Arts Council, as cited in the 1951 Act, are directly concerned with standards, namely to 'assist in improving the standards of the arts and organise or assist in the organisation of exhibitions (within or without the State) of works of art or artistic craftsmanship'. In 1956 the then director of the Arts Council, Seán Ó Faoláin, stated that in future, policy should reflect an Arts Council concentration 'on fewer things of the very first rank in order to establish standards of excellence' (Kennedy, 1990: 119), while at the same time the original statement of intent from the Arts Council in 1957 read: 'Future policy, while not failing to encourage local enterprise, would insist on high standards.' In 1960 this was altered to read: 'The Council's main function is to maintain and encourage high standards in the arts.'

As described by Declan McGonagle in a different context (1997:17) the institutional or value-making structures in Irish society were understood and accepted as natural (given) rather than cultural (made). He characterises the mind-set which shaped these structures as one which: 'defines the artist as the provider of cultural products reducing the viewer/visitor to consumer' (ibid:19).

Thus the debate between excellence and access rested on a narrowly conceived concept of state support for access to and participation in the arts, limited to the removal of obstacles to the 'consumption' of arts and culture by the ordinary citizen. The Arts Council's actual focus was on the promotion of 'excellence', mostly in the form of the 'high' arts, while government and civil servants, responding to the demands of a newly industrialising and urbanising country, concentrated their activities on increasing the grant-in aid for a variety of flagship cultural institutions.[3]

Emergence of a counter-discourse
The first signs of challenge can be detected in the mid-sixties.[4] An early signal of the conflict emerging between theories of art by the people (community arts) as against art for the people was the establishment of Project 67 (eventually to become the Project Arts Centre), whose

stated aim was 'to allow ideas to interact freely between artists and their public who have become separated from the arts'. At the same time the Arts Council became the subject of critical comment. Kennedy quotes one government official of the time as describing the Arts Council as a 'coterie' or 'clique', which was too 'in-grown and in-bred'. Those involved with the Project Gallery felt especially aggrieved that the Arts Council had not publicly supported their policies and activities, aimed at broadening the accepted definitions of 'good' art and artists deserving of state support. The Independent Artists, marking what Kennedy regards as a 'new self-awareness among the artistic community', published a radical manifesto, which accused the Dublin art world of 'symptoms of class bigotry, racial prejudice and pernicious art snobbery' and among other things suggested building art centres throughout the country.

These criticisms found resonance among liberal or left-leaning politicians. For example, Mary Robinson in a senate speech suggested that the Project Gallery provided a good example of how the community approach could work while Senator James Dooge commented:

> In regard to artistic matters we are an unhealthy nation … I think more than any other country we tend to separate art and artists from the other sectors of our national life … We tend to deny to the members of the community their full humanity because we tend to separate our art as something which belongs only to one group of people in the community.

The introduction of the 1973 Arts Act was the state's response to these pressures. According to Liam Cosgrave (Taoiseach):

> There is a danger that many people may regard the arts as the preserve of a privileged coterie. We must actively promote and encourage a wider approach than this: a philosophy that art in all its forms, is a means by which a fuller and more satisfying life may be achieved by the people at large.

Against this background, the 1973 Arts Act was regarded by commentators as ushering in a period of vigour and expansion for the arts in Ireland.

Challenging and broadening the definition of arts: 1975–1995

The appointment as director in 1975 of Colm O'Briain, a voluble exponent of ideas of cultural democracy, was important in bringing about a shift in emphasis of Arts Council policy. His sense of obligation 'to both artists and public to see that adequate facilities exist, especially at regional level, to enable all to participate meaningfully in the arts' (Kennedy, 1990:185) heralded the new era. The stewardship of Colm O'Briain ushered in a new and greater awareness of the wider environment as well as a more democratic approach to the functioning of the Arts Council.[5] The discourse around the idea of community and access began to emerge as a coherent set of propositions culminating in a sophisticated discussion of the underlying concepts as articulated in the ACE Report of 1989.

Participation and access: the role of the Arts Council

From the 1970s the Arts Council has continuously renewed its commitment to developing and implementing policies concerned with making arts accessible to all sections of Irish society, and in particular to those who have been 'culturally disenfranchised'. Indeed, by the mid-1980s access had become the touchstone of policy-making. However, interrogation of what is meant by participation and access reveals a relatively narrow conceptualisation (O'Hagan and Duffy, 1987; Arts Council Annual Report, 1987).

In 1987, testimony to the Council's success in driving the policy agenda towards increasing access and participation is the state's first White Paper on cultural policy, which was given the title 'Access and Opportunity'. In its submission to the government on the White Paper, the Arts Council underlined the necessity to concentrate on developing greater access to and participation in the arts. Thus it became a central goal of the emerging cultural policy to enable the general public to benefit from cultural affairs. However, the Arts Council's interpretation of its statutory responsibility to promote and develop the arts was confined in the main to its grant-aiding function: the focus was on the professional arts to the virtual exclusion of the amateur sector (*Dublin Arts Report*, 1992). The concept of access was confined to ideas of facilitating access to art institutions and making art objects more accessible by moving them out through touring programmes to where people lived. This kind of approach is most aptly reflected in a report dealing with the issue of resource allocation. *The Performing Arts and the Public Purse* differentiated between two kinds of access, vertical and

Members of the Grapevine team gathered outside of their North Frederick Street building in the 1970s. Grapevine, a forerunner of City Arts Centre, was one of the early challengers of the artistic *status quo* in Ireland

horizontal: horizontal referring to the geographic spread of population and vertical to the need to integrate the multiple layers and strata of society. The report identified the key development decisions as the choice between art forms, for example drama or music; the choice between whether to give all to one major company or distribute evenly among many small companies; the choice as to geographic location, that is whether to centralise expenditure in the capital city or disperse funds evenly throughout the country (O'Hagan and Duffy, 1987:11).

Regional development

The grant-aiding by the Arts Council of four arts centres and five arts festivals in 1977 marked a shift in stated policy, acknowledging the need to encourage regional development of the arts as a matter of urgency. Regional arts policy moved into a new phase in 1985 when the first local authority Arts Officer was appointed jointly with Clare Co. Council and a policy of co-operation and partnership with local government was articulated. This single Arts Officer was soon joined by a number of others. It was intended that a network of local authority Arts Officers would eventually cover every county in Ireland.[6] Arts Council policy also encouraged the development of relationships with other institutions such as libraries, museums and existing local arts centres.

By 1985 also, there were fourteen arts centres throughout the country, encouraged and funded by the Arts Council. A new and more direct relationship with local authorities was initiated with the Partnership Conference in Galway in 1986 where the notion of cultural agreements with various local authorities and city corporations was floated.

This commitment to development of the arts in the context of other local authority activity led to the establishment of a network of facilities, chiefly arts centres but also locally based theatre companies and annual arts festivals. This was matched by a commitment to touring including, for example, Opera Theatre Company and Music Network in music, and theatre-in-education with TEAM and Graffiti. The Irish Theatre Company (ITC) operated for roughly ten years until the early 1980s as the National Touring Theatre Company. Subsequently such centralised initiatives gave way to increased support for a number of locally based theatre companies around the country.

Participation and access: critical voices

The establishment of Creative Activity for Everyone (CAFE)[7] following its first national conference in the North Star Hotel, 1984, marked a key moment in the project of integrating arts and culture into the wider society. Its founding aim was to co-ordinate and strengthen the efforts of all groups and individuals to the idea of creative activity for everyone. It represented an important radical counterpoint to the essentially conservative tendencies of the state and its main development agency, the Arts Council. As Colm O'Briain remarked in an address to the conference, 'The Arts Council is not integral to this society. It is cast in the model of medieval patron. Community arts must not be dependent on this patronage as community arts must be integral' (O'Briain, 1984). The conference was attended by groups and individuals working in community arts in areas throughout and outside Ireland and included key figures in the ongoing debate and discussion. Michael D. Higgins, subsequently the first Minister for the Arts under a coalition government, was the chairperson for the weekend. Ciarán Benson, subsequently chair of the ACE Project, author of *The Place of the Arts in Irish Education* and chair of the Arts Council in the early 1990s, was one of the speakers.

A number of universal characteristics of community arts projects were identified:

- Encouragement of critical thought and action amongst both the people participating and the observer
- Validation of the idea that ordinary people can take an active role in building culture
- Building culture as a dynamic ongoing enterprise, which rejects a perspective on non-artists as people who are consigned to the role of consumers consuming the mass media or the professional arts
- The role of the artist to be seen in an economic, political and social context

In an essay, 'Art and the Ordinary', included as Section One of the ACE Report, Benson (1989) rehearses the arguments for and against state support for community arts.[8] He comments first that up to this point little has been published debating the values and beliefs underpinning the concept. In his view community arts is explicitly political:[9] it opposes hierarchical control of the many by the few and is in favour of democratic collective action over individualistic action. The arts constitute a means for changing society in the direction of greater equality and democracy. But, problematically, Benson is also concerned that preoccupation with the political role of art in society meant marginalising the personal and social experiences of art, with the unintended consequence that community arts had itself become marginalised.

Benson identifies the types of misunderstanding that usually arise around the concept of community arts. First, he argues, members of the Arts Council and members of Aosdána will naturally tend to approach questions of art and society from the viewpoint of the artists, because the majority are artists. A second and related source of difficulty revolves around the distinction made between the execution and the implementation of artworks. Recognition of the artist's need for a properly receptive public was a major stimulus to Arts Council interest in improving access to the arts: attention was paid to the public because the needs of artists required it. This mind-set was consistent with the conventional definition of an artist as someone who practices one of the fine arts. It is exemplified in Anthony Cronin's collection of essays *Art for the People*. The logical corollary to this perspective is the belief that only a small number of people have the capacity to experience artistically (productively) rather than aesthetically (receptively) to any significant degree. Benson forcefully makes the argument that such a definition belongs to a particular historical period and contests the notion that artists are 'special people'. Instead he argues that fully committed artists are different from people whose work lies in other fields: not so much for what they are as for what they do.

The ACE Report

Arts Council policy and behaviour come under strong challenge and critique in the report of the ACE project, published in 1989. The project was an initiative of the Arts Council in partnership with the Gulbenkian Foundation and is perhaps the seminal work on community arts in Ireland. It has defined the parameters of the discussion since then. Initiated in the mid-eighties, ACE aimed at 'developing model work from exemplary projects in community arts and arts education throughout the country'. The methodology employed by the project committee, chaired by Ciarán Benson, was itself a departure from the traditional approach of developing the arts. The project has been described as one of path-breaking co-operation by two bodies involved in different ways in the arts: in a community and an educational context. In his review of the report Michael D. Higgins (1990) applauds what he describes as an approach to the arts based on 'a theory of interaction', that is, one of initiating and developing rather than waiting to patronise projects, and where a high value is placed on the integration of such projects into community life. Presumably in recognition of its shortcomings in this arena, the purpose of the project for the Arts Council had to do 'with establishing an attitude to a sector that was clearly burgeoning but which did not present itself in the conventional discipline-based models of arts practice familiar to the Arts Council and for which Council procedures had been designed' (Benson, ed., 1989).

The report critically interrogated the notion of access and its translation into cultural policy. It asked the question, 'Access to what, access by whom and for what purpose?' The report concluded 'access as an end, is still a concept belonging to a version of cultural practice defined from a position of possessing the centre and of certainty about the nature of art. Indeed so deep are those certainties that the "possessed" can be generous enough to lend out the keys to the tabernacle where art resides or indeed to provide funds for the tabernacle to be taken on tour from the centre to the margins.'

The focus of the report is on the sense of cultural disenfranchisement that many individuals and communities experience in Ireland, although it is anxious to acknowledge what it refers to as the 'honest efforts of the Arts Council personnel to create "access"'.

Accurately pinpointing inconsistencies in the Arts Council's own discussion and policy documents, it argues that such inconsistencies are an outcome either of 'deliberate institutional double-think or it is that the policies of the Arts Council have failed to engage with the enormous implications of the statements made in the documents'. The ACE Report provides support for its accusation. The White Paper demonstrated how influential the Council's submission to it had been

Detail from *Art and the Ordinary – the ACE Report*, ACE Committee, 1989

and how current its ideas were: in that submission it emphasised that it did not see itself as 'a paternalistic foundation, repository of artistic wisdom, embarking on a crusade to bring culture to a benighted country'. Lar Cassidy, one of the Arts Council's influential officers during this period, underlines this perspective in an interview with Brian Kennedy. He describes community arts as 'the process of creation in concert with one's audience as opposed to the traditional view that the work of art is an end in itself, divorced from the social context of its making'. Despite this laudable rhetoric, the authors of the ACE Report discern a far more circumscribed understanding of participation in the Council's next document, 'The Artist and the Public'. In this later document the Council made reference to 'the two complementary traditions of the arts' and described the first tradition as 'providing the resources whereby the artist's work can be experienced by the public'. The second tradition is defined as arising 'from the evolving role of the artist which now includes an engagement in a framework that is more participative' and 'which acknowledges the creative resources of his or her community'. In summing up the position the ACE Report states:

> It is clear that two traditions are acknowledged and provided for. The conventional artist – art object – spectator model which forms the backbone of Arts Council policy and programming, is provided for. More recently the notion of artists' work in non-arts contexts like schools, libraries, workplaces and public spaces has received attention and funds. The third tradition is acknowledged, though ill-defined and totally unprovided for. It is the tradition whereby so called 'ordinary' people are individually and collectively retrieving their own creative selves and making images in art, drama literature, video, music and dance, of their own lives.

The Arts Council: between a rock and a hard place?

The ACE Report, while critical of the Arts Council, was also forgiving in tone, perhaps in recognition of the honesty of the efforts of the Arts Council to engage head-on with the issues while working within its own political constraints. For example, the report comments:

> In particular the area of community arts was deeply problematic for the Arts Council because the issues it raised were fundamental ones concerning the nature and purpose of art, sharpened by an awareness that the Council's resources were public money and therefore carrying certain obligations with them. It is also the case that community arts is to an extent

a social and political movement, albeit that that term suggests a coherence which is spurious, and that the Arts Council is perceived as part of the Establishment bent upon supporting conventional arts practice in galleries theatres and concert halls.

The report later states:

> There is little doubt that there is an, at times barely disguised, resentment between the world of community arts and the world represented by the Arts Council. It is possible to characterise the resentment as follows: one party resents the other because of its monochromatic vision of what constitutes art and its virtual monopoly of public moneys for the arts; the second resents the first because of its monopolisation of the word 'community' when it believes that much of what it supports is for the good of the community in ways that are obvious and in ways that are hidden.

It was also acknowledged that the Arts Council was itself operating within a broader social structure and that its efforts to give effect to a programme of implementation that was consistent with its emerging perspective on the role of the arts was often impeded or at least diluted by other impulses. 'It should be remembered that these developments did not occur easily and were often obstructed and delayed by "high arts" prejudice, by civil service resistance to expansionist policies, or by local objections to manifestations of contemporary cultural practice.'

Though community-oriented and community-situated arts activity in Ireland was validated by its base in public and popular demand, its proponents as well as its opponents expressed concern about standards. Thus the ACE Report called for more and better training at all levels; development of the infrastructure of arts centres on a national scale; development of more organically related arts policies to allow for effective collaboration between organisations, public and private, which have an interest in aspects of this work.

Arts and education

The provision of arts education is a vital precursor to the development of a capacity to participate in and have meaningful access to arts. How it has been treated by the state is a necessary part of the discussion of community arts policy.

The Arts Council has consistently held the view that the education system holds the key to future cultural and artistic development in

Ireland. This perspective is shared with community arts protagonists who hold that there is an integral relationship between community arts and arts in education.

> The best relation between the education system and its arts responsibilities and community arts and its responsibilities is a temporal one. Community arts should take up where the schools leave off. (Ciarán Benson, speaking at the first CAFE conference, 1984)

During the 1980s the Arts Council initiated a discussion of arts in Irish education. The importance given to this policy area is illustrated by the number of reports, submissions, documents and public statements that emanated from the Council at that time.

In 1979 the Arts Council had targeted education as a 'primary area for policy development' and published *The Place of the Arts in Irish Education* (Benson, 1979). In doing so, the Council made a commitment that the arts in education would be a major concern for the future. This report described a more active role for the Council.

Role of the Department of Education in arts education: a catalogue of neglect
The response of the Department of Education was contained in a brief chapter in its *White Paper on Educational Development* in December 1980. The department proposed to implement only one of the recommendations of *The Place of the Arts in Irish Education* (Benson, 1979), that is, that a committee would be established to examine the extent to which artistic and creative activities are being catered for in second-level schools (Kennedy, 1990:196). The Arts Council endorsed the paper but complained that the Department of Education had ignored its recommendations.

A revised education policy was agreed by the Arts Council in 1985, when it made an important distinction between arts-in-education activities and arts education. The former are strategic interventions into schools by the arts community while the latter is concerned with the ongoing artistic and cultural development of the young person, in or out of school.

In this way the Department of Education, as the institution responsible for the education system, came under sustained pressure from the Arts Council and other notable public figures to seriously address the issue of arts in education. Michael D Higgins, in a review of the ACE Report, provides the flavour when he describes his experience with the Department of Education as 'one of despair': 'From buildings with fixed walls, concrete floors without one suitable for dance, to inflation of insurance difficulties, cuts in arts education in the training colleges, no in-service release or provision, and voluntary cake-sales to purchase tin whistles I came to know at first hand the philistinism of the Department' (Higgins, 1990: 432).

The institutional uncertainty as to where responsibility lay for the development of arts and culture in the educational system had led to what in 1989 the then chair of the Council described as 'a cultural dysfunction of significant proportions' (*The Arts Council and Education 1979–1989*, 1989). In 1993 in its submission to the White Paper on education, the Arts Council was trenchant in its criticism of education policy in relation to the arts. Responding to the Green Paper *Education for a Changing World*, the Council expressed 'the utmost concern at the almost total neglect of the arts in every aspect of the document, but in particular, in its treatment of curricular and related issues.'[10] The Arts Council case was again publicly represented at the National Education Convention in October 1993: an emphasis was laid, not just on the educational significance of the arts, but also on the contribution which the arts can make to economic development and, therefore, to employment. A number of strategies were proposed as a means to bring about some of the changes needed in the educational system. These strategies included a suggestion that the question of resources be addressed and that there be some discrimination in favour of the arts.[11]

The 1994 report on participation in the arts entitled 'The Public and the Arts' summarised the position as follows.

> The debate engendered by the publication in 1979 of the Benson report on the arts in Irish education has been sustained and has been informed by further Arts Council research and practice in this area; the deficit in the school system has been acknowledged by government itself; the educational arguments have been made both carefully and often in the past decade; the detailed curricular planning has been done by a range of bodies, chiefly under the auspices of the National Council for Curriculum and Assessment; and the need for special attention to the arts has been underlined for many years by the three teacher unions. What the present survey indicates is that all of these developments are underpinned by a

clear public mandate to provide well for the arts within the Irish education system. Here then is an immensely significant agenda for action in the coming years. (Clancy et al., 1994: 92)

The Arts Plans: lost opportunity

Since the mid-nineties we have entered the era of the 'Arts Plans' – prepared by the Arts Council and adopted by government. These plans outline not only the Arts Council's aims but also the strategies and budgetary resources by which these will be given effect. The plans are instructive in setting out Arts Council thinking on the various competing issues that it seeks to address and are probably the most revealing source of the establishment mind-set during this time. Interestingly, fifty years following the establishment of the Arts Council, its primary concern continues to be with the effort to make the case for an adequate funding level. The Council continues to set itself the twin objectives of excellence and access, but without significantly developing the conceptualisation of these two issues, notwithstanding the radical language used in many of the reports which it itself has been responsible for commissioning.

The aim of the first Arts Plan (1995–1998) was to seek an overall increase in the arts budget. In the period 1995 to 1998 the total amount of Exchequer/National lottery funding to give effect to the plan amounted to €103.463 million (£81.484 million).[12] This increased budget was to be used to achieve strategic objectives of quality, creativity, greater access and participation in the arts, and in that order. Thus, reordered, the twin objectives are restated. Of nine areas of activity, those relating to community arts are covered under just one – multidisciplinary arts – and represent just 15.3 per cent of the total arts council budget in 1997, albeit that multidisciplinary arts received a 90 per cent increase in actual budget since 1994.

First Arts Plan: 1995–1997

This first plan provided the fullest and most direct statement of commitment to access of all three plans. It proposed an area-based approach that was primarily focused on achieving access. In its statement of intent it declares that 'everyone in Ireland has an entitlement to meaningful access to and participation in the arts', while one of the six

'Our problems in education are exacerbated by educational systems and philosophies that stress verbal facility at the expenses of other important parts of man's mind, which are either ignored or downgraded. The result is enormous waste of talent and dreadful damage to an unknown but significant portion of our population.' Edward T, Hall, *Beyond Culture*, Anchor Books, 1976

strategic objectives of the plan was to 'encourage real participation in the arts in terms of availability and access … taking account of social as well as geographical barriers'. The plan explicitly acknowledged that, despite efforts up to this point, 'penetration beyond the middle-classes is yet minimal and little impact has been made on the urban/rural divide. The Arts Council as a public body entrusted and concerned with equity of provision must take full account of these factors.'

Disappointingly but not surprisingly, the analysis conducted by the plan's official evaluators – Indecon International Economic Consultants in association with PricewaterhouseCoopers – suggests that 'real participation' in the arts was at the end of the plan's period still largely limited to certain socio-economic groups. While there was some progress in providing regional access for the arts, in many cases local authority involvement is still fairly modest (*Succeeding Better*, 1998: xix).

Even in the post-ACE Report era, the more narrowly conceived definition of access was the one applied: reviewing the effectiveness of Arts Council strategies for furthering this objective, the reviewers commented as follows:

> The objective of access has various dimensions to it; those stressed in the Arts Plan related to regional access and demographic access. Even in relation to this more limited definition the efforts to implement met with mixed success. (*Succeeding Better*, 1998)

A comment in the review refers to the problems created by the lack of clear articulation of objectives, probably an outcome of an inability (or unwillingness) to confront the contradictions between the rhetoric of inclusivity and the actual failure to allocate sufficient resources to achieve access. According to the reviewers, the 'main difficulty with the objectives, while similar to virtually all government-supported arts plans, is that they are specified in a manner which is open to different interpretations and the issue of how to resolve potential conflicts in objectives was not addressed'.

Further indications of the lack of seriousness given to using the arts planning process to bring about real change can be deduced as much by what is not examined in this review as what is. None of the eleven conclusions of the review dealing with the barriers to development facing the sector address the issue of cultural disenfranchisement of certain groups in our society. Of the fifteen recommendations just two deal with the question of access, in itself undefined, one of which concerns the need to give greater priority in the education system to 'arts appreciation'.

The only explicit assessment of the plan in relation to community arts is the following:

> With respect to community arts there has been a dramatic increase in the demand for community arts programmes. The artist-in-the-community scheme has expanded significantly though the proposed transfer of the scheme to CAFE has not been implemented as yet. (*Succeeding Better*, 1998: xvii)

Second Arts Plan: 1999–2001

The second Arts Plan maintains the focus on the twin objectives of promoting 'excellence and innovation' in the arts and developing 'participation in and audiences for the arts'. The plan adds a third objective focused on the requirement to 'build capacity in the arts sector': this objective addresses what is perceived to be a requirement for greater professionalisation of the sector.

The three central objectives referred to above were to be implemented through twelve specific strategies aimed at increasing the Arts Council's capacity to become a development agency for the arts. Total funding to be provided by the exchequer under the plan was to be €127 million.

At the conclusion of the period of the second plan and in preparation for the third, the Arts Council conducted an extensive consultation process with representatives of the arts sector, assessing the condition of the sector. The outcome of the process as published on the Council's web site under the title 'Composite Output of Consultative Meetings' summarises the widespread belief in the sector of the ongoing marginalised position of community arts: 'There is a need for community arts to be explicitly named and discussed within the [third] Plan.'

The continuing struggle for adequate resources and sustainability is summarised as follows:

> The Arts Council should place a higher value on community arts, offering a wider variety of grants and supporting long-term projects ... and facilitating higher standards of practice.

There is a section on participation that is noteworthy for both its brevity and vagueness and is worth reproducing in full.

> The tenor of the participation strategy seemed to suggest that the arts constitutes a sphere of activity from which people are excluded – in actual fact what is needed is a means of linking arts activity to the broader range of cultural activities with which the people are already engaged.

> The assumption that participation in the arts is invariably a collective experience is a mistaken one.

On arts in education, an essential complementary policy area to an effective strategy for achieving broad participation in both access to and making of art, there is a real sense of disappointment. The language used in the commentary is instructive. 'Lack of progress' indicates 'fundamental failure' and there is an 'urgent' need for various reforms and actions.

> The lack of progress in advancing the Department of Education/ Department of Arts, Heritage, Gaeltacht and the Islands partnership is a fundamental failure of the last Arts Plan. An advocacy campaign to raise the priority of the arts in the education agenda is crucial.

Third Arts Plan: 2002–2006

The context for the third Arts Plan, to run from 2002 to 2006, was to be one of expansion. According to the chair of the Arts Council: 'Local involvement in arts provision is at last beginning to grow. The role of the arts in education is gaining recognition with curriculum reform. Major international festivals and other emblematic events promote international recognition of Ireland's contemporary culture. The move towards multiple sources of policy intervention enriches recognition and support for the arts' (www.artscouncil.ie/artsplan/context).

In a less than upbeat description in the plan on the condition of the arts as we face into the first decade of the new millennium, it is worth noting that the list of concerns given about the state of the arts contains no mention of the disparity in access and participation between different groupings. Thus:

> Looking at the arts in Ireland today, we see low living standards, with many artists and companies too often battling against the odds. There is

'When it comes to asking what it is that artistic and aesthetic education can contribute to a quality contemporary education that nothing else can, I would say that they develop capacities which are evident in very young children, intrinsically human capacities, which would not be legitimated nor encouraged by any other dimension of the curriculum, and which would, without such encouragement, atrophy and die at a great cost to the quality of individual and social life. And we must remind ourselves that it is quality of life that we live for: all the rest is endurance or survival or mere existence.' Ciarán Benson in his keynote address to the sixth annual delegate conference of the National Parents Council (Primary), 1992

little or no investment in audience development. Organisationally, we see skills shortages and under-resourced managers and artistic directors. The transition from emergent young company to stable maturity defeats too many. The contributions of remarkable individuals are too often dissipated where no provision has been made for succession planning at management or board levels. (www.artscouncil.ie/artsplan/context)

That said, the constraints and obstacles to broadening and enriching participation are listed and reflect the input of the work of organisations such as CAFE and Combat Poverty Agency. These include a number that have long been recognised as problematic, for example the poor provision for the arts in formal and informal education. Others address the complexity of the task: examples include the scarcity of opportunities for high quality artistic experience and the short-term nature of much of the financial support.

Inconsistencies revealed: what the figures show
In this section we look, necessarily briefly, at the quantitative indicators of the way in which the arts in Ireland have been developed. Two measures are useful here. First, as an indicator of the willingness and ability to follow through on commitments, and thus as a kind of proxy measure of seriousness of intent, the financial resources actually allocated by the state to support its policy aims are instructive. Second, public-behaviour surveys are useful as a means of providing us with some kind of indicators of the impact of policy on the arts and culture landscape.[13] The findings of two studies conducted by the Arts Council in 1981 and 1994 respectively are helpful here: the second was designed to be directly comparable with the first. In addition, the survey of a sample drawn from a marginalised community as part of the 1997 report *Poverty: Access and Participation in the Arts* provides more recent valuable data.

Funding of community arts: the Cinderella factor
Establishing an adequate funding base for the arts has been a central if not the central preoccupation of the Arts Council and those politicians and civil servants in favour of such provision.

Direct public funding of the arts is channelled through the Arts Council, the Department of Arts, Tourism and Sport (from 1993 the

Department of Arts, Heritage, Gaeltacht and the Islands, and previously directly through the Department of Finance, prior to this, the Department of the Taoiseach) and the Local Authorities. Other sources of public funding to the arts include the National Lottery, FÁS, the Department of Education, Vocational Education Committees (VECs), Combat Poverty Agency, the Department of Social Welfare, County Enterprises, Local Area Partnerships, Leader Programme and Local Development Boards, Ireland Funds, PETRA, other EU funding, tax concessions and import and export controls.

The bulk of expenditure on arts, culture and film is given to institutions funded directly by the department and include the National Museum, the National Library, the National Archives, the Irish Museum of Modern Art, the National Concert Hall and the Irish Film Board.

It can be argued that there are various means of providing budgetary support to state policies to improve access and participation in the arts. Nonetheless, the actual dedication of budget lines to this aspect of the arts is a good indicator of the level of importance and priority given to the state's commitments to ensuring that all citizens have 'meaningful' opportunities for participation in the arts, as is the allocation of staff resources specifically to this area of activity.

In 1977, when the heading of community arts and regional development was first used, the expenditure figure was £15,039, which represented a minuscule proportion of just over 1 per cent of the overall budget of £1.2 million. Nearly ten years later, in 1985, the proportionate spend (1.7 per cent) had hardly improved, although the actual sum allocated had reached £98,000 under the specific heading of community arts.

By 1996, more than ten years later again, the allocation to community arts and related activities, while significantly improved, still reflected its continued Cinderella status. Although the Arts Council had experienced an almost doubling of budget allocation over the previous five years, most of the money continued to be allocated to fine-arts expenditure and in particular to the performing arts. Community arts was by then largely funded under what is termed the multidisciplinary arts budget, which also includes expenditure on festivals, arts centres and programmes for children and young people not included under individual art forms. The proportion of the Arts Council budget spent on all these activities, together with funding under Local Authority Partnerships had by 1997 reached 15 per cent. This increase is attributed to the Arts Council's developing emphasis on community arts and participation arts.

The third Arts Plan sets out its approach to categorising its expenditure in ways that are not directly comparable with what has gone before. However, what is clear is that adequate budgetary support for efforts to ensure 'the fundamental right of all citizens to have full access to and participation in the cultural life of the community' has still a long way to go.

The relative short-term and often *ad hoc* nature of the sector's funding is an ongoing source of frustration and difficulty in the sector. This is not helped by the complexity created by the expansion of the number of state and quasi-state agencies involved in the area of community arts. These include Area Development Management Ltd, the Arts Council, the local authorities, Department of Social Welfare, the Combat Poverty Agency, the Department of Education and the VECs. Thus it is not surprising that demands for more coherent funding mechanisms to be put in place for the more long-term development of community arts practice are to the forefront: 'Such mechanisms should provide for consultation with local communities, the establishment of links with arts institutions/venues in the area and the artforms, and the development of models of good practice' (*Poverty: Access and Participation in the Arts*, 1997: 11).

Patterns of attendance and involvement

From a survey conducted by the Arts Council, published in 1983 under the title *Audiences, Acquisitions and Amateurs*, it became clear that rates of audience participation in art and cultural activities in Ireland had remained static despite policies to increase participation in arts events. The survey commentators concluded that support for arts events was 'relatively low' and did not 'suggest a healthy situation'. Roughly, this audience consisted of those who earned the most money, had the highest education and were located in Dublin. In their commentary on the survey findings, Sinnott and Kavanagh (1983: 3) implicitly identified an absence of clear strategy when they pointed out that 'Although the question of audiences is integral to many of the Council's plans and policies it has never yet been examined by the Council in isolation from its other policies.'

Neither were the increasingly targeted and sophisticated strategies of the 1980s to provide any cause for complacency. The 1994 study *The Public and the Arts* (Clancy et al., 1994) found that there was a welcome and impressive increase in attendance figures across all art forms. However, less welcome were the findings that showed that the urban/rural gap described in the 1981 study continued to be in evidence as were the contrasts between regions. The starkest finding was that of the failure to close the social class divide. In relation to certain types of events, and particularly those that form the focus of the publicly funded arts, there was found to be a widening of the class differential, particularly in relation to the semi-skilled/unskilled working class. These events included plays, performances of classical music and exhibitions of paintings or sculptures – art forms that traditionally attracted a middle-class audience. These findings were also reflected in patterns of purchasing. The social-class differences in proportions purchasing arts goods widened in the thirteen-year period between the two surveys in favour of the higher occupational classes. This pattern was most notable in respect of purchase of records/tapes of classical music, novels, poetry and plays and paintings/sculptures by living Irish artists.

Measurement of participation in arts activities was confined in both studies to what was described as 'amateur arts activity'. It showed low levels of active participation, such that it was difficult to provide comparisons between different social classes or geographic regions. In the brief provided to the researchers who conducted the 1994 study only a slightly broadened definition of what constituted amateur arts activity was provided, thus effectively ignoring all that had taken place in the development of community arts as a legitimate arts practice. There is little option but to infer a relative failure to internalise and move the community arts agenda into the mainstream of policy development. As might have been anticipated, the desired effects did not transpire and despite energetic efforts only the usual well-educated and well-to-do classes participated in these activities.

As recently as 1997 the gap between rhetoric and reality was starkly noted in the report *Poverty: Access and Participation in the Arts*. The chair of the working group responsible for the report states in his foreword, 'the main concern in my opinion with the uneven distribution of attendance at the so-called fine arts events is that the bulk of public money goes to these art forms. It is inevitable then … that there will be considerable unease about the fact that so much of public money goes to art forms the consumption of which is effectively the reserve of the well-educated and the rich.' The report states that while 'many thousand of people living on low incomes are engaged in activities at a local level … this is little reflected either in policy or provision'. The report goes on to comment, 'Part of the reluctance seems to be based on uncertainty as to whether arts at a local level is a legitimate area of practice worthy of investment by funding agencies' (1997: 10–11).

The persistence of barriers to attending and participating in the arts was confirmed by the research conducted for the 1997 report. These encompassed financial, physical, practical, social and cultural obstacles. More specifically, besides the practical barriers such as cost, transport, childcare facilities, a lack of company and a lack of information, people referred to the cultural barriers they experienced, such as feeling out of place, a lack of interest in what they thought was available to them and a feeling that the arts were not relevant to their lives. Travellers experienced the additional barrier of a lack of physical access, including being denied access to basic services such as entry to pubs and other music and art venues.

Closely reflecting surveys of political participation and attitudes to same, a survey of a sample on low incomes revealed that there is a not unsurprising consistency in views on the relevance of art and culture on the one hand and on political participation on the other. 'The view most frequently given was that the arts were for other people and not for them. The arts were not considered to be an important part of daily life, and held less importance on a given list of priorities than access to education. In addition, the general perception of the "arts" was limited' (1997: 13).

Into the new millennium: dissonance between rhetoric and reality

> [I]t's time to stop the destructive divisions between high and low art and look at the similarities and strengths. It's a time to question what we consider art and what it can do. Never before have we had such an incredible opportunity to redefine and reinvent. (Duffy, 2001: 3)

Following the debate chronologically as I have done in this review shows that translation of new thinking into real change is a much slower process than might be apparent from a snapshot view taken at a given point. There are certainly changing fashions in thinking about the arts, different interests and confusion on objectives reflected in shifting and sometimes contradictory strategies. What is revealed is a continuously shifting interplay between what can be characterised as an 'integrationist' approach to the role of arts and culture in Irish society in contrast to a 'separate but equal' apartheid between 'high arts' and 'community arts'. Fundamentally, however, little attention has been paid to the 'creative instincts of the Irish people', described as the state's approach to arts policy since its foundation in a recent document of the Department of Arts, Heritage, Gaeltacht and the Islands (*Towards a New Framework for the Arts*, 2000).

We have seen how policy inconsistencies arise from the interplay between evolving trends and developments and apparently immutable constants – the pre-eminence of the position of the individual 'artist' and professional arts organisations – which have persisted over time. We have seen that the early years of Irish cultural development were marked by a uniformity of perspective and an absence of critical discussion about the arts or the state's responsibilities towards them. Ideas of access and participation were narrowly conceived as the removal of obstacles to 'consumption' of arts and culture by the ordinary citizen. From the late sixties/early seventies we traced the emergence of a counter-discourse that shattered the cosy consensus on what constitutes desirable cultural policy. Key players included a revitalised Arts Council under the leadership of Colm O'Briain, which from then evinced an uncomfortable ambivalence in relation to the emerging community arts sector, initiating and supporting initiatives while at the same time maintaining its traditional preoccupations with the concept of excellence.

The Arts Council emerges as an organisation grappling with the demands of community arts protagonists informed by a radical social and political movement, while itself being part of the establishment constrained by powerful champions of 'high arts' prejudice and by civil service resistance for demands for increased expenditure. Thus, over the years, there is plenty of evidence of a clear attempt by the Arts Council

A group of young men from 'Fatima Freedom Fighters' work on a mural, part of the 'Art in the Beloved Community' event, Rialto, Dublin, August 2004

to engage in a meaningful way with the drive towards greater cultural participation and democracy. A notable example of its efforts is the submission to the White Paper on the arts published in 1987. It also supported the emergence in 1984 of CAFE as a strong advocacy lobbying and support group on behalf of community arts: CAFE ensured that the essentially political project of integrating arts and culture into the wider society would be kept to the fore. The report of the 1989 ACE project, an Arts Council initiative, identified the 'cultural disenfranchisement' of whole communities as well as individuals in Ireland. In the 1990s other key players promoting the cultural democracy agenda were present: both the language of the Arts Plans and indeed the allocation of increased resources are positive developments.

Despite these efforts the Arts Council must be held accountable for much of the failure to realise equality in levels of participation and access, even while the difficulty of its position is acknowledged. The effect of policy ambivalence in practical terms has been to treat the project of increasing access and participation in a fragmented manner. Most successful were the strategies to increase geographic access. Almost wholly unsuccessful, despite a huge array of community arts activity and increased recognition of its important role, have been the efforts to increase participation and access by those living in poverty and in marginalised communities. A persuasive rationale for this failure is that by segregating 'high' arts from 'community' arts and relegating its participation strategies to the sphere of 'community' arts, the Arts Council in effect wasted already limited resources in fragmented and *ad hoc* support and ensured that the discussion of participation was incorrectly framed.

Thus it is fair to say that while there has been real progress in terms of at least bringing the discussion and language of cultural democracy into the heart of policy statements, with some advances in terms of allocation of real resources, the conclusion that those changes that have taken place are still at the margins remains inescapable.

> Community arts was established as a function of the Arts Council ... in compensation for the failure of the centralised model to reach the widest range of people. But the effect of this structurally was and is to hold 'community arts' in a position outside the real power structure and to absorb energies, which might otherwise have been towards real change, at the centre. (MacGonagle, 2001: 3)

An Outburst of Frankness Community Arts in Ireland – A Reader

Contradictory or opposing impulses gave rise to a lack of clarity in relation to objectives and strategies, which in turn results in at best limited progress and at worst outright failure in achieving stated goals. There is relatively little development in the way in which the term 'excellence' in art is defined or in the value ascribed to it compared with the set of activities and arts practices which are included in the term 'community art'. Community arts is still a residual category, underlining how these activities, while worthy and valuable, are not considered art and further that art must be protected from the possibility of being adulterated by unworthy practices. This has been described by one practitioner as keeping ideas of community and access at 'arm's length from the centre rather than as part of a strategy of change in the cultural/social or the economic/political power relationships'. Furthermore, it is argued that community arts is now seen as something only necessary for poor or marginalised groups and as a result standards of practice are influenced by the low self-esteem or marginal status of the community arts sector (Cocking, 2002: 51).

It is worth noting, however, that the discussion of art and community arts/access and the expression these ideas find in policy and allocation of resources reflect traditional power relationships in Irish society. Thus this review has to be contextualised and understood in terms of the failure of the wider society to move the broader discussion around equality and inclusion to the centre of the political agenda.

Underlying philosophical themes

The policy trends identified in the materials reviewed can be connected to a small number of contested ideas, which have informed the understanding of community arts in Ireland. While themes are repeated they are also layered over time with further insights and more refined application.

One such, as identified by the editors of *From Maestro to Manager*, is the ' philosophical polarities on the issue of the arts and their management'. These

> polarities range from the notion that the arts are separate from society and perform their function best in a state of conflict with society ... to the concept of the arts as symbol systems which are essential elements of social communication ... The first premise would have the arts retain their 'mystery' in a state where academic explanation and the 'cherishing

bureaucracy of management' ... have no role to play, while the second reflects the idea that the arts, by expressing universal values, mirror society and are literally part of our social organisation. (Fitzgibbon and Kelly, 1997: 1)[14]

A second theme concerns the notion of a conflict between competing demands for support for professional artists and for 'community' or 'amateur' arts. One side of this perspective was presented by Ciarán Benson more than ten years ago (*Art and the Ordinary – the ACE Report*, 1989). He argued then that 'there is not, nor should there be, any conflict of interest between supports designed to foster and encourage artists and supports which focus upon the development of the artistic and aesthetic lives of non-artists'. This perspective is in opposition to that ascribed to key influencers of arts policy, among them the writer Anthony Cronin: 'His [Cronin's] position relies on "the idea that artists are special people in their sensitivities and innate or acquired powers of expression". He is led by this way of thinking to query the usefulness of most "art education" for adults, to object to art being made into "a mere pastime or social distraction or even therapy" and to condemn the belief that most people have the capacity to experience artistically (productively), rather than aesthetically (receptively) in some degree.'[15]

A third theme concerns notions of cultural democracy. Jenny Harris, in an address to the first conference of CAFE in 1984, talked of the need for a concept of 'cultural democracy' as opposed to the democratisation of culture. The democratisation of culture refers to the creation of greater equality of access to cultural products whose value and importance is defined by cultural élites – in Ireland the Arts Council is the exemplar of this kind of body. The concept of cultural democracy by contrast has to do with culture as a dynamic thing – not as a stagnant, ready-made thing. 'Very simply, what cultural democracy is about is learning to tell your own story on an equal footing with all the other stories. It's discovering ways of giving expression to your own values and heritage and joining with others to do this in some sort of action' (Harris, 1984: 8). Cultural democracy is characterised as a way of administering cultural funds and organising cultural work so as to leave room for all kinds of initiatives, big or small; inside or outside of established institutions; initiatives taken by professional or nonprofessional groups; representing traditional or non-traditional ways of producing and communicating art and culture (Waade, 1997: 329).

The polarity between the democratisation of culture and cultural democracy is reflected in the dual approach to the discussion of access. On the one hand how to make the arts as broadly accessible to as many citizens/consumers as possible, both vertically (social class) and horizontally (geography), and on the other how the making of art can be made available to sections of the community which have been culturally disenfranchised. This latter perspective positions access to and participation in the making of art as a human right, one of which particular groups including the poor, the disabled, ethnic groups such as travellers and women find themselves deprived, in parallel with their exclusion from the wider set of structures and institutions of Irish society. In this way the idea of cultural democracy is integral to the ideas informing new social movements that are challenging the way in which power is disproportionately held by a small number of corporate and political interests.

> Cultural democracy is a deeply radical idea. It is the ultimate extension of the idea of democracy: that each one of us, each community, each cultural minority has rights that deserve respect, and that each must have a voice in the vital decisions that affect the quality of our lives. No one who commands a disproportionate share of power in the world is happy to hear this idea put forward, for it demands that they share this power with those who are locked out by the current order: better to keep us confused and divided. (Goldbard and Adams, 1990)

The concept of culture as used in the above quotation is an all-encompassing idea. Considered in this context the idea of cultural participation is directly related to the more broadly encompassing notion of participative democracy. At its most radical this latter can be described as the collective capacity of systematically marginalised groups to articulate their policy proposals and to gain access to processes and institutions of democratic decision-making.[16]

From new rhetoric to new framework

> It is my strongly held view that it is the fundamental right of all citizens to have full access to and participation in the cultural life of the community. We need to ensure that the barriers that excluded sections of our

community from becoming actively involved in cultural activity are removed. A fundamental quality of community arts must continue to be its concern about empowering communities and encouraging their self expression. (Síle de Valera, Minister for the Arts, in the foreword to the proceedings of the CAFE and Combat Poverty conference, 1998)

From the mid-1990s it is possible to detect a more confident insistence on a politically informed definition of access. The language of a rights-based culture was articulated more forcefully and has found its way into the public utterances of representatives of state policy as can be seen from the above quotation. An important report referred to earlier, *Poverty: Access and Participation in the Arts*, was prepared by a working group which drew on the expertise of community development personnel, cultural institutions, community arts, the Arts Council, Combat Poverty Agency, individual artists and educationalists. It involved a co-operative partnership between two state-funded institutions: the Combat Poverty Agency and the Arts Council. It defined the arts in the language of cultural democracy and of a rights-based culture. The following extracts from the report provide the flavour.

> Our understanding of the arts is as a set of distinctive languages through which individuals and communities represent and come to understand themselves and their worlds. All sections of society have an entitlement to engage in the process of making meaning through the arts. Such expression is not restricted to the expression of a small though culturally dominant, section of society. The arts embrace the expression of the marginalised in their articulation of a contemporary experience. (*Poverty: Access and Participation in the Arts*, 1997: 3)

> There is a need for a greater acceptance of different viewpoints and experiences, including a variety of cultural, class and ethnic views, and a need to challenge the implicit assumptions that determine selection, representation and accessibility in the arts. (*Poverty: Access and Participation in the Arts*, 1997: 7)

A basic principle is that equality of access to the arts is a fundamental democratic right:

> Everyone has the right freely to participate in the cultural life of the community, to enjoy the arts and to share in scientific advancement and its benefits. (*Universal Declaration of Human Rights*: Article 27)

This right refers to access both as a form of expression and access to the arts, culture and heritage of the nation as represented by fine arts institutions and art forms. (*Poverty: Access and Participation in the Arts*, 1997: 23)

A repositioning of the debate around the arts and its role is called for, such as to refocus on 'the value of participation, not as add on marginalia but as central to creativity and to a creative culture. In the near future culture must be more capable of negotiating its position as one of the key determinants of social and communal value within the "real" world and not as an antidote to other powerful determinants in society' (McGonagle, 2002: 18). This refocused debate needs a 'new vocabulary, a new language', and would include 'thinking about civil culture, civil meaning belonging to citizens, and about participatory practices. And part of this is the need to make the discussion about culture and arts part of a political discussion' (McGonagle, 2002: 18). McGonagle does not underestimate the difficulty of the task. 'The values of what I describe as signature culture, in short, artist as genius/producer and the public as consumer, as opposed to participatory culture flow through a powerful armature, have been buttressed by hierarchical memory and conservatism for generations, if not centuries. An imaginative and material conservatism, which is characterised by a dislike of change but curiously also a dislike of the present. Nostalgia is a reflection of that' (McGonagle, 2002: 18).

Thus, those who are at the forefront of advancing the concept of cultural democracy are very conscious that important as issues of resources and of quality and standards are, the need to reframe the debate itself is most urgent. What is believed to be needed is a new way of thinking, challenging perceptions and existing models. Central to this new thinking is the requirement that the process be seen as first and foremost a political one. To transform cultural institutions, structures and processes, such that participation is a central value, it is also necessary to transform our social, economic and political institutions, structures and processes.

Notes

1 The review was conducted through an identification and survey of policy thinking and state action, as revealed in a variety of written materials. These include selected policy documents and annual reports, conference materials, research reports and political statements, which set out the perspectives of Arts Council/government departments and local authorities, arts practitioners, external critics and arts/culture observers.

2 Thomas Bodkin (1949), *The State of the Arts in Ireland*.

3 Examples include the National Gallery, Abbey Theatre, Gate Theatre and Dublin Grand Opera Society.

4 The primary source material for this subsection is Kennedy (1990), *Dreams and Responsibilities*, Criterion Press, Dublin.

5 One direct outcome which went a considerable way towards restoring the perceived relevancy of the Arts Council was the way in which the Council engaged in political debate on the value of public interest over private economic consideration through campaigning against the destruction of Dublin's architectural heritage.

6 There are currently in excess of thirty local arts officers throughout the country.

7 Renamed CREATE in 2003.

8 It is not possible to provide pagination for the quotations taken from the essay 'Art and the Ordinary'.

9 Benson refers to Owen Kelly (1984), Another Standard/The Shelton Trust (1986) and Su Braden (1978).

10 Response of the Arts Council to *Issues and Structures in Education: Discussion Paper*, published by the Curriculum and Examinations Board (undated).

11 Presentation to the National Education Convention (1993) by the Chair of the Arts Council.

12 The 1998 figures are included, as the second Arts Plan ran from 1999–2001.

13 Measuring the impact of policy initiatives, particularly sustained impact, is difficult, not only because of the frequent ambiguity and lack of specificity associated with the statements of goals and objectives but also because of the difficulty inherent in any social-impact analysis of attributing direct cause and effect.

14 The first premise – the arts as separate from society – is presented in D. Donoghue (1982), *The Arts without Mystery*, BBC, London.

15 Quotations taken from this article cannot be referred to by page number.

16 Ideas of Nancy Thede as expressed at the Interdependence between Democracy and Human Rights seminar (November 2002) organised

by the Office of the High Commissioner for Human Rights
(OHCHR), Palais de Nations, Geneva.

Bibliography

A Rationale for the Arts in Irish Education (1987), Government Publications,
Dublin.

Access and Opportunity (1987), White Paper on Cultural Policy, Government
Publications, Dublin.

Acts of the Oireachtas (1922 to present), Dublin.

Arts Council Reports (1951–1989), various, Dublin.

Arts Matters (various from 1986), Arts Council, Dublin.

Benson, C. (1979), *The Place of the Arts in Irish Education*, Arts Council,
Dublin.

Benson, C. (1984) 'Creativity in Education: Personal Development
through Creative Activity' in CAFE (Creative Activity for Everyone),
Seminar Report, Dublin.

Benson, C., ed. (1989), *Art and the Ordinary – The ACE Report*, ACE
Committee, Dublin.

CAFE (Creative Activity for Everyone) (1984), *Seminar Report*, Dublin.

CAFE and the Combat Poverty Agency conference proceedings, Dublin,
1998.

Clancy, P., Drury, M., Kelly, A., Brannick, T. and Pratschke, S. (1994), *The
Public and the Arts*, Arts Council, Dublin.

Cocking, S. (2002) 'Twelve Years of Community Arts: Dublin City Arts
Artsquad' in *Contexts: Arts and Practice in Ireland*, vol. I, CAFE (Creative
Activity for Everyone), pp. 48–52.

Department of Arts, Heritage, Gaeltacht and the Islands (2000), *Towards a
New Framework for the Arts: A Review of Arts Legislation*, Government
Publications, Dublin.

Dublin Arts Report (1992), Dublin Corporation, Dublin.

Duffy, Rita (2001), speaking at 'Community Arts: The Next Five Years'
conference organised by CAFE and CAF, Maynooth.

Durkan, Joe (1994), *The Economics of the Arts*, Arts Council, Dublin.

Fitzgibbon, M. and Kelly, A., eds (1977), *From Maestro to Manager: Critical
Issues in Arts and Culture Management*, Michael Smurfit Graduate School
of Business, University College Dublin, Dublin.

Goldbard, A. and Adams, D. (1990) 'Cultural Policy and Cultural
Democracy' in *Crossroads: Reflections on the Politics of Culture*, DNA
Press, Talmage, CA, pp.107–109.

Harris, Jenny (1984), 'Albany Empire: Creativity and Community
Development' in CAFE (Creative Activity for Everyone), *Seminar
Report*, Dublin.

Higgins, M. D. (1990), 'Review of Art and the Ordinary — The ACE Report', *Economic and Social Review*, vol. XXI, no. 4, July, pp. 431–437.

Kavanagh, Adrian (2002), *Unequal Participation Unequal Influence*, report commissioned by South West Inner City Network, Dublin.

Keane, C. (1991), *Expenditure by Local Authorities on the Arts*, Arts Council, Dublin.

Kennedy, Brian P. (1990), *Dreams and Responsibilities: The State and the Arts in Independent Ireland*, Criterion Press, Dublin.

Local Authorities and the Arts (1998), Arts Council, Dublin.

McGonagle, Declan (1997), in Fitzgibbon, M. and Kelly, A, eds, *From Maestro to Manager: Critical Issues in Arts and Culture Management*, Michael Smurfit Graduate School of Business, University College Dublin, Dublin, pp. 17–30.

McGonagle, Declan (2001), speaking at 'Community Arts: The Next Five Years' conference organised by CAFE and CAF, Maynooth.

McGonagle, Declan (2002), 'The City Arts Centre: I Haven't Gone Away You Know' in *Contexts: Arts and Practice in Ireland*, vol. I, CAFE (Creative Activity for Everyone), Dublin, pp.17–20.

National Education Convention (1993), text presentation by C. Benson, Chairman of the Arts Council, October.

O'Briain, C. (1984), paper given to the First National Conference of CAFE (Creative Activity for Everyone).

O' Hagan, J. and Duffy, C. (1987), *The Performing Arts and the Public Purse: an Economic Analysis*, Arts Council, Dublin.

Poverty: Access and Participation in the Arts (1997), research report by Jeanne Moore, Combat Poverty Agency and the Arts Council, Dublin.

Sinnott, R and Kavanagh, D. (1983), *Audiences, Acquisitions and Amateurs*, Arts Council, Dublin.

Succeeding Better: Report of the Strategic Review of the Arts Plan 1995–1998, Arts Division, The Stationery Office, Dublin.

The Arts Council and Education 1979–1989 (1989), Arts Council, Dublin.

The Arts Plan 1995–1998 (1994), Arts Council, Dublin.

The Arts Plan 1999–2001: Consultative Review (1999), Arts Council, Dublin.

The Arts Plan 2002–2006 (2002), Arts Council, Dublin

Waade, Ann-Marit 'Cultural Project: Management and Cultural Democracy' in Fitzgibbon, M. and Kelly, A., eds (1977), *From Maestro to Manager: Critical Issues in Arts and Culture Management*, Michael Smurfit Graduate School of Business, University College Dublin, Dublin, pp. 319–340.

White Paper on Educational Development (1980), Government Publications, Dublin.

The old triangle
Funding, policy and community arts

SUSAN COUGHLAN

Introduction

Any discussion about the development and direction of community arts over the past twenty-five to thirty years invariably leads to the interlinked issues of funding and the (relative) lack of resources. In the past, these discussions – quite understandably – have often ended in a negative mode of frustration and quiet despair. Now there is a genuine and shared commitment to move beyond this but many of the old issues tend to linger.

The different levels and types of funding applied to community arts, as well as the range of activities incorporated into the term community arts, make the task of documenting the impact of funding on the development of the sector a difficult one. Facts and figures other than those cited in annual reports are hard to come by and little has been written on this subject.

The approach taken here is first to identify and understand the factors affecting funding decisions, such as how funders viewed community arts and what policies dictated funding decisions. Different methods or approaches to funding community arts activity, and the main funders to community arts in the early 1980s, are discussed. This is followed by a more in-depth historical review of the development of the Arts Council's funding and policy relating to community arts, given its role as the primary body invested with supporting arts development in the state. Finally, the impact of funding on community arts, whether from the Arts Council or non-arts sources, is explored and the effects, on both practice and practitioners, are discussed.

Ideology, policy and decisions

Community arts activity in the 1970s and 1980s can best be described as a political and social movement with a desire for cultural democracy at its heart. Initially, the ideologies and methodologies of community arts activists were met with degrees of indifference or misunderstanding from the state, represented principally by the Arts Council.

Over time, community arts methodologies have been whole-heartedly adopted into many other areas of arts practice and have informed (and been informed by) other movements for social change (such as community development), gradually gaining acceptance as an intrinsic part of Irish arts culture. In many ways, community arts practice has developed and diversified because of this inherent capacity to become integral to the articulation and final expression of social and community development agendas.

Were this development balanced with an equal level of success in the acceptance and integration of community arts philosophy and ideology, the general picture would look much healthier than it actually is. Sadly, the ideologies of cultural democracy – whether expressed from a feminist perspective, a socialist one or simply the perspective of one's instinctive belief in the validity and transformative power of arts and cultural participation – continue to be dogged by misunderstandings and false polarisations around which all discussions tend to revolve, regardless of their starting point. The effect is that the dichotomies between 'high art' and 'community art' that existed in the 1970s and 1980s, in truth, still pertain.

This situation directly impacts on funding for a number of critical reasons. The first is that confusion rather than clarity dominated much of the early years of community arts practice. Diverging views about critical issues such as definitions of community arts practice, the role of the artist when working in context, ownership of work produced, quality and standards and the relationship between process and product left funders – particularly those interested in outcomes other than social and community development – feeling insecure about supporting the practice.

Such a lack of clarity and consensus was understandable at first when the variety of approaches and the complexity of practices involved are considered. Community arts practitioners generally lacked the appetite to resolve many of these tensions, and tended to be more concerned with exploring and developing the work than reflecting and critiquing it. This allowed some worthy but generally poor practice to establish itself.

From an arts funder's perspective, the sector, such as it was in the mid-nineties, lacked credible leadership, a coherent shared agenda and, most critically, the capacity to be rigorous and self-critical. This confirmed deep-rooted suspicions and prejudices about the value and efficacy of community arts practice as an area to be engaged with. In addition, the Arts Council did not know how to assess the artistic quality of community arts activity and found it very difficult to define a comfortable role for itself in response to the challenges presented. Instead it chose to apply its resources to clarifying for itself its own role and position in relation to community arts.

In many ways, support for community arts simply lay outside the Arts Council's comfort zone. The Council was severely challenged by the implications of community arts ideology and its likely funding demands should that ideology take root. In response, the Council looked for (and, in the main, still continues to look for) projects that emulate a high arts approach and outcome. Those that are most likely to be successful are those that are similar to any other artist-led proposal or initiative. Consequently, the focus of much of the Arts Council's financial support has been channelled through arts organisations where the commitment to artistic excellence is articulated explicitly.

In the same way that arts funders are suspicious about artistic standards in relation to community arts practice, funders with a development agenda are suspicious of a deep-rooted cultural élitism at the heart of the arts that both the Arts Council and the arts sector have largely failed to address. Such polarisation between the two sectors – community arts practitioners perceived as social radicals lacking in artistic rigour, and the Arts Council and mainstream arts sector perceived as anti-egalitarian and snobbish – is unnecessary and has been highly damaging to the supported development of community arts, making any genuine and progressive dialogue between the established arts sector and community arts principles and practices difficult. Consequently, shared understandings across both sectors of critical concepts (such as what artistic excellence in a community arts project might actually entail or how artistic outcomes might be defined and described) are only beginning to emerge.

Funding types

In the context of the arts, funding is most often thought of as direct funding to organisations and artists for activities and programmes. This kind of funding covers staff, overheads and administration and is often referred to as revenue funding. The Arts Council, FÁS and, increasingly, local authorities fund the arts in this way (though often for different reasons). This form of funding is the most secure, as it is considered an investment and carries an implied commitment from the funder toward the funded. It is generally agreed that, in quantitative terms, FÁS rather than the Arts Council, has been the primary agent of direct revenue funding to community arts in Ireland.

There are a number of problems with revenue funding. First, and most important, there is the truism that there is never enough revenue funding available. For community arts, Arts Council grants seem smaller and harder won as compared with those in other sectors of the arts. In relation to local government funding, the grants have tended to be uniformly low and unrealistic across all arts sectors. Where community arts groups were successful in securing revenue funding they began on a very low base. Revenue funding usually increases incrementally so it follows that growth is extremely slow when there is a low funding base. Often the level of funding was so small as to seem insignificant but, since Arts Council funding also represents a validation of the quality of the work, it has always been important both for the practitioners involved and in levering funds from other sources.

In addition, community arts, a relative newcomer to arts funding in the 1980s, had to struggle to fit into established budget structures and existing funding criteria. This was particularly the case with the Arts Council where the funding system was art-form based and product focused and was structured in a way that was unhelpful to the sustained development of community arts. (It has taken thirty years for these structures to begin to adapt in earnest to the challenges presented by community- and participatory-based arts practice.) Often applications were moved around from one budget to another, with no real 'home' and no executive to advocate on their behalf so inevitably they were at the bottom of an already very competitive pile. Innovative and important community arts organisations or projects emerging from non-arts backgrounds[1] were often caught between a rock and a hard place – development agencies refusing to fund them because the projects were arts-based, and the Arts Council refusing to fund them because their objectives were development-based.

These points about revenue funding are critical influencing factors on the development (or more correctly, the lack of development) of community arts in Ireland. All other factors ultimately stem from them.

Another form of funding is time-limited project funding. The Arts Council's main form of project funding to community arts was through schemes such as the Community Arts Development Fund[2] and the Artist in the Community Scheme[3] (ACE) and through various awards offered to individual artists. Other examples are EU funding initiatives such as Peace II.

Most funding for community arts coming from sources other than FÁS and the Arts Council is project funding. Its main advantages are that it enables experimentation and supports the development of new areas of practice. Consequently, project funding is largely responsible for the growth and development of the diversity within community arts today. The critical drawbacks with project funding are that it is intended for the aims and objectives of a particular project or initiative and not to cover an organisation's core operating costs so its benefits are short term.

Another significant source of support to the development of community arts is indirect funding – funding not directly invested in community arts. This form of funding – much of it from the Arts Council – supports an ever-increasing pool of resources and infrastructure upon which much community arts activity is heavily dependent. Examples are local authority arts officers and services; voluntary sector funding of training opportunities and information sources; and arts funding to venues, production companies and resource organisations involved in supporting and developing community arts practice in different ways.

As both the community and arts sector infrastructure have grown and matured, the range of resources available at a local and regional level has become an increasingly significant source of support for community arts activity around the country. However, the lack of finance to pay staff (particularly development staff such as Outreach Officers and Programme staff) – largely due to the limitations of

'[P]olicy-makers such as members of the Arts Council, and the policy-shapers such as the members of Aosdána, will naturally tend to approach questions of art and society from the viewpoint of the artist. This is because the majority of them are artists. It is also because Arts Council policy has evolved in that direction. But the 1951 Arts Act is especially interesting in the responsibility which it places upon the Arts Council to stimulate public interest in the arts.' Ciarán Benson, *Art and the Ordinary – The ACE Report*, ACE Committee, 1989

project funding mentioned earlier – impedes progress in both drawing on these resources and directing them into areas of community and participative arts practice.

Funding sources

Community arts practice owes much of the speed and rhythm of its evolution, and the diversity of available funding sources, to its close links with community development. Community development was seen by the state to have the potential to address a broad range of social issues. It is no surprise then that community arts is still very dependent on its partnership with community development structures and organisations and that, in Ireland, community arts practice has tended to predominate within community development contexts most particularly in disadvantaged urban communities.

Employment schemes

In 1981 the Youth Employment Scheme (YES)[4] was the first source of significant funding to community arts and is generally regarded as having kick-started the first community arts organisations. The grant levels were significant enough to maintain a core group and base.[5] Peter Sheridan's City Workshop in Dublin's north inner city was the first to be funded, followed by others such as Moving Theatre, Graffiti Theatre and Waterford Arts for All.

From the 1980s to the late 1990s employment schemes were widely recognised to be the most significant source of funding to community-based arts activity. In the late nineties, over 90 per cent of Arts Council-funded community arts organisations, arts centres and community festivals depended upon employment schemes to subsidise their programme.

While employment schemes were excellent resources for kick-starting local art and community arts activities, the schemes' limitations became increasingly problematic in the face of increasing demands for more professionalised arts services and activities. Current policy changes and cutbacks are presenting both community arts and the wider arts sector with serious challenges, as FÁS funding has decreased in line with economic growth and the reduction in unemployment. As a result, much of the additional grant-aid from the state to the Arts Council over the past five or six years has been absorbed by the decreasing arts sector reliance on FÁS funding.

European funding

In the late 1980s and early 1990s EU funding for access programmes, training initiatives and work with disadvantaged groups represented a significant source of funds that arts and community development organisations creatively tapped into for promoting and developing community arts projects.[6] Programme budgets of €200,000 to €300,000 (often significantly more than the annual turnover of the hosting organisation) presented enormous challenges and stimulated an unsustainable level of growth and development.

Current criteria are more focused on economic development and consequently the number of community arts organisations or activities receiving EU funding has decreased. Few arts or cultural organisations have successfully managed to tap into the Leader and Urban programmes and Peace II is currently funding only three community arts projects.

Arts Council

It is enormously difficult to track Arts Council investment and support to community arts for three main reasons. The first is that, in the early 1980s, the Council used the budget heading of 'community arts' as a kind of catch-all for things that didn't fit anywhere else, so what was categorised as 'community arts' activity has changed greatly over time. The second is that 'community arts' and individual art forms ceased to be discrete budget headings in 1998 with the publication of the second Arts Plan. Third, as was suggested earlier, much of the Arts Council's most important support to community arts is in the form of indirect funding.

The Arts Council first funded community arts under the budget heading 'other activities' in 1976. The total budget was €4,000[7] and

The tension between Arts Council funding and Department of Labour funding often led to headlines such as this one from *Magill* magazine, March 1986.

supported amateur and local organisations such as the West Limerick Folk School and the South Tipperary Arts Group.

Up to the early 1980s the Council funded two streams of activities under 'community arts'. The first was professional groups who 'concentrate their activities on, and in, the community'[8] and included TEAM Educational Theatre and Moving Theatre. In both cases the amounts of money were very small. The second was to assist the skills of amateurs to lead to improved standards of excellence and included community festivals, publishers, feiseanna and groups like Waterford Arts for All.

While amateur groups were supported under community arts until 1982, innovative community arts groups such as City Workshop found it almost impossible to secure Arts Council funding at that time, even though their work was widely recognised to be of a high standard. The Arts Council's rationale was that its funding for artists was purely for 'professional' artists whilst City Workshop worked with amateurs.

In funding terms, the first full articulation of the tension between the amateur and the professional artist dates from this time.

By 1984 the Arts Council began to fund CAFE as a lobbying and support organisation for community arts. The Council revised its policies and now began to fund

> Organisations which operate in a direct and loose way with the community, e.g. Ballyfermot Arts Week and the type of organisation which believes that the direct involvement of its audiences in the process of arts activity, is at least, and often more important than the finished object, such as a sculpture, video or novel.[9]

So, the tension between process and product was also articulated during this period.

In 1985 the Arts Council joined with the Calouste Gulbenkian Foundation to establish ACE, a four-year community arts and education project with a budget of £300,000. 'The Arts Council saw it [the ACE project] as a means for understanding the arts and education, but perhaps more particularly its already existing category of community arts.'[10]

The ACE committee's brief was to explore, reflect and recommend on community arts, using grant-assisted exemplary projects. Over a period of four years, the committee discussed the funding, management, evaluation and creativity of these projects.[11] The findings of the ACE project – both theoretical and empirical – published in a report entitled *Art and the Ordinary* – in 1989 significantly informed arts education and community arts policy and practice in Ireland.

ACE advised that

> The Arts Council should continue its policies in, and increase funding to, those aspects of community arts practice which present themselves in conventional organisational contexts and which might be thought of as arts-in-community. Included here would be community festivals; professional performance or resource groups; arts centres with programmes based in community-situated arts.[12]

Many of the recommendations (and some of the thinking) of the ACE report were implemented, such as the Artist in the Community Scheme[13] set up in 1990 and funding directed towards various training initiatives. However, a key recommendation that the Arts Council take a lead role in working with others to co-ordinate funding to community arts was not implemented.[14] The critical question of funding co-ordination got left behind.

From the mid-nineties until recently, the Arts Council's priority has been planning for the arts and adapting its role, structures and policies to meet the challenge of increased growth and demand across all the art forms and practices.

The first Arts Plan (1995–1998) took an area-based approach to arts development and interlinked the fields of community arts, festivals, education, youth arts, regional development and arts centres to the broader themes of access and participation. 'In this way, the Council has placed community arts at the heart of The Arts Plan. This represents an updating of previous major policy statements in the field of community arts.'[15]

However, the Arts Council was not in fact prioritising community arts: it was prioritising access to the arts. The period of the first Arts Plan saw an explosion of growth and development across all arts areas but particularly in the area of audiences and access at local and regional level. Community and youth arts principles and practices were at the heart of much of the increased activity, for example in the areas of public art, local and regional arts and with the increasing number of arts centres and festivals.

The implications of the growth were enormous – how was it to be sustained? An evaluation of the first Arts Plan,[16] commissioned by the Department of Arts, Heritage, Gaeltacht and the Islands, criticised the plan for being too aspirational or unrealistic and the area-based approach for being unworkable. It recommended that the Arts Council undertake extensive consultation with the arts sector in the preparation of the next plan. It also recommended that the Arts Council consolidate what already existed rather than funding new activities and organisations. This led to a re-evaluation of the Council's role and a practical freeze on new revenue funding to arts organisations.

In 1997 the Arts Council commissioned Mapping Community Arts to provide it with up-to-date information on the range and scale of community arts practice in the country and to rehearse some of the key arguments and issues influencing that practice.[17] Those involved in community arts were consulted and the report provided the Arts Council with a better understanding of the activities in the area and the development needs involved. Mapping Community Arts provided both the Arts Council executive and Council with greater comfort about the Council's role in relation to community arts. The report stated the following.

> [T]he Arts Council has a vital role to play, with the arts community, in making policy and adopting strategies to implement that policy towards the development of community arts practice. Areas of influence could include:
>
> • Artistic development and quality bench-marking
> • Policy development for the sector
> • Assuming a role of advocacy and planning in relation to training for artists to ensure skills in art and in community development are balanced
> • Assuming a role of advocacy in relation to other government departments
> • Liaison with other funders (potential and actual)
> • Planning for the future with other stakeholders

In practice, the Arts Council acknowledged that its role in providing for or supporting community arts – twenty years after it had first begun – was still a relatively open question though its emphasis increasingly came to be upon issues of quality and a recognition that issues of 'status' had a bearing on that quality.

> Despite the availability of other funding sources, dependence on Arts Council grant aid is still high ... In practice, there are questions about how best to provide for 'community art' as a dimension of policy for the arts. The Arts Council is committed to ensuring the artistic quality and status of the artistic contribution to community arts practice. We are also concerned that community arts practice informs and is informed by art form practice generally.[18]

Mapping Community Arts recognised that, from an Arts Council perspective, quality community arts practice was occurring:

> Where overall aims and objectives of community arts work are clear, well managed and resourced and where artists of experience and skill have been engaged, participative artistic work of great potential and high quality has emerged over the life of the last arts plan.

The consultation process leading up to the preparation of the second Arts Plan proved to be important for informing clear development agendas within various arts sectors. At the time, there was a lack of coherence within community arts that made consultation difficult and to some extent Mapping Community Arts filled this void.

The report, and the internal processing of it, dovetailed with the arts planning process for the next Arts Plan (1999–2001) where the Arts Council set about transforming its role from being purely a funding agency to being a development agency. On a macro level, the implications of this change are important for the long-term development of the range of community arts practices, as many of the structural barriers to receiving Arts Council support began to be removed. For example, funding budget lines were attached to crosscutting Arts Plan 'objectives' rather than to single art-form budgets.[19]

On a more micro level, the 1999–2001 plan directed funding towards existing clients and categorised them as resource and support organisations for community arts activity, street spectacle and participation-based production companies, local groups that organise professional arts events for remote or socially disadvantaged communities and community arts residences. New initiatives, not previously funded, found it very difficult to obtain Arts Council support.

The recently set-aside Arts Plan (2002–2006) identified sustainability as the key macro direction for Arts Council support. Set against the Council's clear development objectives, the plan opened the way for non-traditional arts activities such as circus, amateur arts, traditional arts and storytelling to be supported. There was also a shift in terminology, with the term community arts largely replaced by terms such as 'participation' or 'participation practice'.

The objective in that plan was 'to broaden and enrich participation in the arts', placing an emphasis on the quality of the participation rather than the quantity. In it, the Council restated its concern about the quality of the arts-participation experience. 'There are many opportunities for participation in the arts, but few are characterised by a high quality of artistic experience for people participating.'[20]

The Arts Council itself continues to be in a period of transition. The new Arts Council members selected to 'set aside' the 2002–2006 Arts Plan and review its mission, aims and objectives in a new planning process. The only documentation available on current Arts Council thinking and policy is an action plan for 2004 available on the web. It continues the emphasis on high artistic standards and refers to the appointment of an arts participation team making it possible for the Arts Council to implement more proactive policies and partnership projects.

Jan Hinde, Participation Officer at the Arts Council, described the Council's current role as one of making specific and strategic interventions rather than shaping and directing community arts development. The current Arts Council policy for addressing participation development needs is to work with realistic levels of resources in a time-limited way with specific partner agencies and organisations, such as the CADMUS community music project with Dublin Corporation, the Arts in Health Project Guidelines with the Eastern Health Board and the preparation of guidelines for good practice for art in schools with the Department of Education and Science.

Overall, the successes of the planning era are that the annual spend on the arts increased from €16 million in 1994 to €53 million in 2004, the Arts Council has more staff than ever before and its structures[21] are increasingly focused on development and change rather than on tradition and maintaining the *status quo*. The failures primarily lie in the Council's consistent refusal to take a co-ordinating or leadership role in the area of community arts or, more crucially, to embrace, as a core value, the idea of cultural democracy itself. In this, the Arts Council is now generally regarded as less significant than many of the more developed arts services within local authorities. In fact, a further essay is required to examine the impact of local authority funding and support to community arts development, as local authorities are increasing their commitment to and investment in locally based arts organisations such as arts venues and festivals where community-based activity is a significant part of the programme.

The challenge to arts funders

The 1951 Arts Act mandated the Arts Council to stimulate public interest in the arts, to promote the knowledge, appreciation and practice of the arts and to improve standards of artistic practice. Over the years, as we have seen here, the Arts Council has chosen to focus strongly on issues of standards and of excellence. This is understandable when we consider the following: the level of investment in the arts by the Irish State was (and remains) the lowest in Europe; Ireland has a very poor level of visual aesthetic in comparison to other European countries and suffers from the consistent failure of the education system to truly value the arts or to provide citizens with a quality arts education experience.

It is also understandable when we consider the way in which the arts have been traditionally undervalued in society. The whole of art history in the western world has revolved around the belief that the best ideas emerge from individual artists working alone. In the arts we have traditionally valued those who advance the aesthetic and structural elements of form and those who use a form in new and innovative ways because these advances open up a world of possibilities for other practitioners and a world of meaning for their audiences.

Within community arts, value and validation are assigned differently. There is always more than one aim in a community arts project and these aims modify each other. This modification challenges the traditional emphasis (within western art) on the individual working alone to produce a work of high aesthetic outcome. It values process as well as product and the group as well as the individual. Meaning resides in the experience rather than merely in the piece of work produced.

When the practice isn't sufficiently valued or validated, the result is that community arts is conceived of as a set of tools and the artist's role as that of a technician or facilitator. The community arts sector needs both funding and validation from the Arts Council. In fact, lack of validation has caused many more established artists to avoid community or contextual work, and practitioners – most particularly in the visual arts – have often eschewed the term 'community artist' for this reason. (This offers some explanation of the shifting terminology from community arts to participatory arts or arts in context mentioned earlier.)

Concurrent changes in the community sector and the arts education sector – as well as society in general – have begun to bring about a change in this situation. Artists are increasingly attracted out of the studio or theatre and into non-traditional contexts, and inter-disciplinary work is a powerful force within arts practice. The general mood is less individualistic and more reflective and open, but validation – particularly from the Arts Council – will be essential to the growth and maintenance of this mood.

The mood within community arts is also reflective. This has become a good time to look back on activity and ask questions with the certain knowledge that a lot has been learned and with the conviction that there is a need for promoters of cultural democracy – in whatever form they appear – to no longer accept a marginalised position. There is a definite sense that practitioners from both the arts and community perspectives have begun to depart from their polarised positions and that a more trusting and confident dialogue can open up between them.

It remains for the Arts Council and other funders to recognise and support these changes and for the community arts sector to engage with both existing and changing funding structures in a way that is ultimately more constructive and mutually beneficial.

Impact of community arts funding

The impact of funding thus far described on community arts has been significant. The lack of coherence that has characterised support for the community arts sector (rather than the activity itself) since the 1980s ultimately has contributed to a situation where the level of development is not commensurate with the commitment, creative energy, potential and funding invested in it. It is not particularly useful to apportion blame for this, as it rests both with the sector itself and with the funders. What may be helpful is an attempt to identify features or characteristics of the funding profile that, over the years, have contributed to this situation.

The short-term and experimental or 'pilot' nature of much of the available funding led to a lack of continuity that, much to the frustration of practitioners, often fundamentally undermined the developmental and innovative aspects of the work itself. This led to a pressure on community arts organisations to be funding-led, seeking project funding for specific initiatives, related but not central to their core mission, to subsidise core operations. This left small organisations distracted from their core purpose, overstretched, unbalanced and dependent on an insecure source of funding. Almost all of the organisations that were successful in attracting significant funds from the EU suffered from this effect and many never recovered once the funding was no longer available. The more positive features need also to be acknowledged, for example the community arts sector is experienced and adept at responding to changing requirements from funders.

The variety of funders involved in community arts activity contributes to the diversity of practice so that, as we have seen, community arts activity spans most art forms and involves many different sectors. This diversity, along with other factors, contributes to a commonly articulated experience of isolation with limited connection and exchange between the different areas of community arts activity and practice and between community arts and other arts sectors. In fact, this sense of isolation persists to this day, so that many community arts organisations and practitioners are unaware of other relevant work occurring in some proximity. The recent growth in local authority investment and support is resulting in a greater sense of connection between artists and arts organisations at a local level, and this is positive, but a coherent national picture for community arts remains elusive and a goal which this publication and other recent initiatives are hoping to address.

The value of art for the state is always related to art's capacity to generate or enable certain kinds of symbolic speech on the part of legislators and politicians acting within the highly circumscribed environment of public policy formation. Public policy debates are one of the central theatres within which the play of participatory democracy is acted out, and policy models or rationales are the scripts that are performed in this theatre. They are the key part of the system by which the state generates consent for the expenditure of public funds.' Grant H. Kester, *Art, Activism and Oppositionality*, Duke University Press, 1998

This experience of isolation described above makes the need for recognition and value, particularly from the Arts Council, ever more critical. As we have seen, this validation and recognition has been slow in coming both from the Arts Council and from the arts sector. This had critical and negative effects – young and emerging artists found it difficult to sustain a practice in community arts and established artists were extremely reluctant to become involved in the area, lest it diminish their hard-won reputation. The lack of critical reflection and discussion on the quality of community arts practice has tended to frustrate and alienate those more-established artists with an interest in community arts.

The quality of community arts work has definitely been affected by the nature and type of funding received. Funding for evaluation was limited – particularly from the arts perspective – so that project learning and outcomes were often poorly documented, understood and generally not well disseminated. There were few shared platforms or opportunities to learn from the work others were doing. Genuine and open discussions about quality have been absent within the sector where the need to be supported has sometimes outweighed the capacity for criticism.

For those practitioners who maintained their involvement over twenty years or more, this has been particularly painful, as much excellent work has suffered from a 'tarred with the same brush' phenomenon, leaving highly innovative work that has pushed the boundaries of art to gain limited critical or collegiate respect or recognition from the wider arts community.

At a time when it may have been possible to talk about a community arts sector, there was no shared or coherent sense amongst practitioners that a sector existed. CAFE,[22] which was best placed to fill this role in some way, was one of the organisations reeling from the experience of managing a number of major EU-funded pilot projects in the late 1990s.

The diversity within the sector was such that assistance to develop sectoral coherence was inevitably needed. This was a role that both the ACE report and Mapping Community Arts recommended that the Arts Council adopt. However, the Arts Council chose not to prioritise this. Without this kind of support, the fragmented sector struggled to provide itself with opportunities for reflection, identification of sectoral needs or the discussion of shared agendas. In the vacuum a number of challenging conditions or confusions took hold.

The first was in relation to language and critical discourse. Such a wide variety of funding sources required (and still requires) community arts practitioners to speak (and write) in a variety of languages – the languages of community development, of peace and reconciliation or of training and accreditation, for example. Understandably enough, non-arts funders are not interested in artistic outcomes so the work is mostly described in terms of social or economic outcomes – reduction in unemployment, numbers of people trained, off drugs, back at school, and so on. Consequently, the language used to describe community arts did not develop in line with the practice but instead became diluted and often confused. Practitioners often found, and continue to find, that they lack the language to articulate the 'arts part' of the community arts experience. This has had serious implications both for developing a critical discourse about the artistic work and its quality and for describing and representing the distinctive qualities of that work to arts funders and the wider arts sector.

The second related confusion involved definitions and shared understandings. There was a general lack of agreement as to a definition of or a set of shared characteristics for community arts. Neither was there a shared understanding of the desired role of a community artist or what constituted good practice. The impact of this is keenly felt when attempting to introduce students of community arts to a framework that they can apply to both develop and locate their individual practice. We find we are still working it out and there are few resources to assist and inform this process.

To summarise these effects, I think it is fair to say that inadequacies in approaches to funding have contributed negatively in two critical and inter-related ways. The failure – particularly by the Arts Council – to transfer proven models of excellence to mainstream provision has ultimately resulted in an inefficient use of scarce resources. It has contributed to a syndrome of continual 'reinvention of the wheel' that has characterised and undermined community arts practice for almost thirty years. What is left is a set of experiences, an ideology but few tangible sustaining outcomes. This makes it easy to forget or not to acknowledge in the first place the significant contribution community arts practice has made both to innovative and cutting-edge arts practice and to the broader themes of cultural democracy and participation in civil society. For example, arts education institutions are only now beginning to develop community arts courses or to include it as a subject on existing courses. It remains to be seen if this contribution is better acknowledged and valued over time or whether, like all challenging movements, the best ideas become absorbed into the dominant culture until a new movement comes along and challenges the *status quo*.

Notes

[1] The Bealtaine festival for older people run by Age and Opportunity and Common Ground, the Arts Development Agency based in the Canal Communities Partnership, are two examples.

[2] Set up in 1998 specifically to support critical reflection and evaluation amongst community arts practitioners, the Community Arts Development fund was absorbed into a general restructured programme of supports for individual artists.

[3] Launched in 1990 with a budget of £6,000, the Artist in Community scheme is currently operated on behalf of the Arts Council by CREATE and has a budget of approximately €50,000.

[4] YES was operated through the Youth Affairs section of the Department of Education.

[5] Tony Ó Dálaigh, involved in operating the YES scheme at the outset, stated at a recent discussion on the history of community arts that the scheme's expenditure on the arts in one year was more than the total annual budget of £3.64 million available to the Arts Council for arts funding.

[6] Examples include CAFE's arts workers course The Learning Wheel; Arts Awareness training for unemployed men; The Roots Project; City Art Centre's arts and disability project.

[7] £3,398.

[8] *Arts Council Annual Report*, 1980, p. 47. The Council's total grant was £3 million.

[9] *Arts Council Annual Report*, 1984, p. 33.

[10] Ciarán Benson (ed.) *Art and the Ordinary — The ACE Report*, 1989, p. 9.

[11] Macnas, CAFE and the Fatima Development Group were funded under the community arts strand of ACE.

[12] Ciarán Benson (ed.) *Art and the Ordinary — The ACE Report*, 1989,

Recommendation 4.4.1, p. 101.

[13] This scheme is still in operation and is now operated by CREATE on behalf of the Arts Council.

[14] ACE recommended setting up an interagency standing committee, facilitated by the Arts Council/Gulbenkian partnership, to explore a collective approach to two major policy priorities – training and the co-ordination of funding. The committee met for two years but dealt only with training.

[15] *Arts Council Annual Report*, 1994, p. 79.

[16] *Succeeding Better: Report of the Strategic Review of the Arts Plan 1995–1998*, prepared by Indecon International Economic Consultants in association with PricewaterhouseCoopers, commissioned by the Department of Arts, Heritage, Gaeltacht and the Islands and published by the Stationery Office, Dublin.

[17] Researched and written by Fiona Ellis and Keith Allen, the report was never published but was distributed in draft form to those consulted.

[18] *The Arts Plan 1999–2001*, p. 50.

[19] For example, to support more public participation in the arts, to increase children's and young people's engagement with the arts and to encourage art organisations and promoters to develop audiences.

[20] *The Arts Plan 2002–2006*, p. 14.

[21] There are now four separate departments: Arts Policy; Arts Programme (responsible for dealing with funding); Arts Development; and Management.

[22] CAFE's name was changed to CREATE in 2003.

Funding environment
in Northern Ireland

HEATHER FLOYD AND CHRIS BALL

Introduction

This essay is a brief overview of the funding and policy environments in relation to community arts in Northern Ireland. Significant funding initiatives are referred to as external political and policy developments but it is the Arts Council of Northern Ireland (ACNI), by necessity, that dominates this essay because its views and funding decisions around community arts are, and continue to be, the most important for the sector in Northern Ireland.

When community arts emerged as a real force in the early 1990s, it is fair to say that the ACNI was somewhat resistant to the concept. So much so, in fact, that the infant Community Arts Forum (CAF) felt compelled to call for the resignation of the entire Arts Council board. One decade on and the change in attitudes could not be more pronounced, with community arts constituting a linchpin of Arts Council policy. However, it could be argued that this growing acceptance of community arts by ACNI represents a further step in the development of the Arts Council of Northern Ireland, not the community art sector.

Arts Council of Northern Ireland: a short history

The first incarnation of ACNI emerged in 1962, replacing the Council for the Encouragement of Music and the Arts (CEMA), which had been in operation since 1943. Initially, funding for the organisation was provided by the Pilgrim Trust and matched by the Ministry of Education for Northern Ireland, a reflection, perhaps, of the position the arts then held in the public-spending pecking order.

The Arts Council of 1962 bore a striking resemblance to its modern day counterpart. As is the case today, its affairs were managed by a Council consisting of fifteen members with a principal executive officer, the chief executive, supported by a professional staff. Back then, of course, the notion of community arts was virtually, if not entirely, unheard of in Northern Ireland. It was not until 1978 that community arts, or at least the notion of arts for all, received statutory recognition and funding as a discrete and distinct area of the arts. The Northern Ireland Education Minister in the then Labour government, Lord Melchett, identified two main aims for the scheme:

1) to encourage existing activity, exhibitions of the visual arts, concerts, plays and so on to expand into the more deprived and isolated areas of Northern Ireland, where they would not be normally available, and to do so in a way that encourages people who would not normally go to see or listen to start doing so

2) to encourage the artistic efforts of people living in deprived areas, particularly when the artistic activity, whatever it is, is especially relevant or linked to the lives and experience of local people.

(Quoted in Northern Ireland Voluntary Trust Community Arts Awards Scheme 1985–1988: A Review by Mark Robinson)

ACNI remained relatively unchanged until the mid-1990s when it underwent a period of quite dramatic upheaval. In 1991, Clive Priestly was employed to undertake a review of arts funding in Northern Ireland and the role, composition and operation of ACNI. In the subsequent report, entitled *Structures and Arrangements for Funding the Arts in Northern Ireland*, Priestly recommended, amongst other points, that more seats on the Arts Council board be reserved for arts practitioners, local councillors and people from the business community. The report also called on the Arts Council to draw up an arts strategy, in addition to taking a more proactive approach to the development of the arts.

The old Arts Council was replaced in 1994 by a company limited by guarantee – the Arts Council of Northern Ireland 1994 Limited. This served as an interim body that in turn gave way to the Arts Council of Northern Ireland, established by the Arts Council (Northern Ireland) Order 1995, on 1 September 1995.

Under the Order, ACNI was charged with four specific statutory functions. These were:

1) to develop and improve the knowledge, appreciation and practice of the arts
2) to increase public access to, and participation in, the arts
3) to advise the Department of Culture, Arts and Leisure and other government departments, district councils and other bodies on matters relating to the arts; and,
4) such other functions as are conferred on the Council by any other statutory provision

In addition to these strategic obligations, ACNI was also given the added responsibility, under the National Lottery etc. Act 1993, to allocate Lottery proceeds to the arts in Northern Ireland, substantially upping the amount of resources available for the ACNI to distribute.

Also in 1995, the publication *To the Millennium* detailed the Arts Council's strategy for the years 1995–2000. It laid out a 'mission to develop the arts in Northern Ireland so that as many people as possible can enjoy as many forms of arts as possible to as high a standard as possible'. To attain this laudable goal the report outlined three main aims, namely: to encourage access to, appreciation of and participation in a broad spectrum of the arts; to promote creative and performing arts of quality and, finally, to increase resources for the arts and ensure their effective and efficient use.

'We cannot rely on a small élite, no matter how highly educated or highly paid. Instead we need the creativity, enterprise and scholarship of all our people.' David Blunkett, Secretary of State for Education and Employment, UK

The restructuring of the Arts Council continued throughout the 1990s with the arrival of the Northern Ireland Assembly in 1998, and the inception of the Department of Culture, Arts and Leisure (DCAL), which assumed control of ACNI from the Department of Education, Northern Ireland. This new department imposed central government policies such as Targeting Social Need (TSN – which was later to become New TSN) on the Council.

As the names suggest, TSN and New TSN were designed to 'tackle social need and social exclusion by targeting efforts and available resources on people, groups and areas in Northern Ireland which are objectively defined as being in greatest social need' (Northern Ireland Office, 1999). This meant that ACNI, as was the case with all public bodies, had to consider its social responsibilities in everything it did – a boost, in theory, to community arts.

While ACNI was grappling with New TSN, DCAL was publishing a series of reports, including the Programme for Government,

Unlocking Creativity and DCAL's own five-year strategy, which collectively had a great bearing on community arts, giving it a pivotal role within the arts sector, as opposed to a marginal position within the wider arts arena. DCAL also commissioned a review of the community arts sector, which, unfortunately, has yet to see the light of day.

As community arts was gaining acceptance from central government, community arts groups were also successfully securing moneys from a variety of other sources. The Belfast Action Teams (BAT) were set up in Belfast in the early 1990s to regenerate socially disadvantaged areas of Belfast. These transformed into the Making Belfast Work initiative (MBW) in July 1988; this later became the Belfast Regeneration Office (BRO). MBW was designed to strengthen and target the efforts being made by the community, private and public sectors in addressing the spectrum of problems facing Belfast's most disadvantaged areas. The then chief executive, Tony McCusker, recognised the untapped potential of community arts in promoting urban regeneration and peace building. His support for the sector led to the creation of a substantial community arts pot of money (£250,000 per annum for three years). The fund proved tremendously useful, allowing many community arts organisations to find their feet, but, unfortunately, its benefits were only felt by groups operating within the Belfast area. The fund was administered by Belfast City Council. MBW and the community arts sector hoped that the fund would be mainstreamed after the initial three-year period. Unfortunately, the fund dried up and was not replaced by mainstream funding.

It was not only MBW which recognised the ability of community arts to tackle the various problems facing Northern Ireland, particularly those arising from the Troubles. Community arts groups were able to access a raft of funding initiatives promoting socio-economic and community development, capacity building, cross-community relations and economic development. This came from organisations such as the Community Relations Council, the Community Foundation (formerly Northern Ireland Voluntary Trust) and the International Fund for Ireland.

However, it was the European Union's Special Support Programme for Peace and Reconciliation for Northern Ireland and the Border

Counties of Ireland (Peace I) that offered the potentially richest pickings for community arts organisations throughout the mid- to late-1990s and, crucially, created an infrastructure for the sector. The seven sub-themes of the programme placed a strong emphasis on community and social development, skills and education, job creation, urban and rural regeneration and peace-building work which would help to embed the peace process. Many community arts projects were funded under Peace I. These fitted in very well with the ethos and goals of community arts allowing groups to secure substantial amounts of monies for projects, staff and core costs. However, the European windfall was short lived and as Peace I gave way to Peace II (which in turn will, we hope, give way to Peace III) the available resources dwindled, projects closed and jobs folded.

Some of the slack left behind by Peace I was picked up by the Arts Council's new lottery programmes, in particular Access and Audience Development. To a certain extent, these have become the next big infrastructure support for the sector, assisting many community arts groups with salary, running and project costs.

The new millennium saw the arrival of *Opening Up the Arts*, a new report commissioned by the Arts Council. Published in 2000, *Opening Up the Arts* evaluated the achievements of the Council over the five-year period from 1995. This evolved into the beginnings of a thorough, future-orientated assessment of the needs of the arts sector in Northern Ireland and the role of the Arts Council in meeting those needs. Following further public and sectoral consultation, in 2001 the Arts Council published its new five-year strategy document, *The Arts Plan 2001–2006*. The priorities outlined in *The Arts Plan* are:

1) increase opportunities for creative opportunities in the arts
2) develop new audiences for the arts and build on existing ones
3) extend opportunities for artists to develop their work and practice
4) strengthen the capacity of arts organisations to deliver quality experiences of the arts

To meet these priorities ACNI identified seven strategic objectives. These were to:

1) increase opportunities for artists working to the highest standards and in innovative ways

2) strengthen the arts infrastructure

3) engage with community arts to increase opportunities for creative participation, to develop new audiences and to expand the range of contexts in which artists work

4) engage with voluntary arts to increase opportunities for creative participation, to develop new audiences and expand the range of contexts in which artists work

5) increase the quality of access for disabled people

6) enhance children and young people's access to creative expression through the arts, in contexts of their own choosing, and increase opportunities for participation as they grow and develop

7) increase audiences for the arts

This was the first time that community arts had actually been enshrined as one of ACNI's strategic objectives and this key aim laid down a number of key tasks that ACNI had to deliver on. These were to:

1) stabilise key community arts organisations

2) increase the quality of experience of participants

3) promote models of good practice to practitioners

4) quantify the benefits to individuals and communities

5) promote synergies across art-form practices

6) provide opportunities for artists to work at community level and in communities of interest

7) anchor the work of community arts organisations in the context of integrated cultural development plans across all local authorities

8) contribute to good community relations

Community arts' inclusion as one of the ACNI's strategic objectives is, perhaps, an indication that it has finally gained acceptance amongst the powers that be. However, although community arts may now be ingrained in ACNI policy, there can be no guarantee that the sector's future is entirely secure. Community arts is now entering a phase of great uncertainty, with the loss of European Peace moneys, declining lottery revenues and ever-increasing pressures on central government funds. The opportunities presented by community arts are slowly being recognised – we can only hope that the necessary resources will be available for this potential to be realised.

Conclusion

The 1990s saw a number of agencies investing in community arts: ACNI; peace moneys; education and back-to-work schemes. One by one, these significant pots of funding have slipped away since the year 2000, eroding the developmental gains of the previous decade and leaving a seriously under-resourced sector. Both Belfast and Derry City Councils have in recent years reduced funding to the arts sectors in these two cities. If the sector is to survive, somebody will have to pick up on this gap. The sector needs a funding strategy to guide it through the next crucial five- to ten-year period, with government departments being pressured to take responsibility for the sector. The truth is that the old understandings of art and culture still dominate funding decision-making and community arts still struggle for recognition and support.

'Can you paint my soul?'
Ethics and community arts

JO EGAN

Ethics: formulated knowledge or principles for behaviour within a group or society according to which actions are judged.

Heinemann English Dictionary,
Heinemann Educational Books, 1979

In 2001 visual artist Rita Duffy initiated a project called 'Drawing the Blinds'. She approached each resident of Divis Flats, in Belfast, and asked them if she could paint something unique to each of them on a blind. As part of the Belfast Festival at Queen's, all the lights were turned on in the flats and the images were on view for the city. Some residents wanted images of themselves, one or two wanted images of things they loved or had lost and one man asked for his false teeth to be painted. One woman asked, 'Can you paint my soul?'

This is the measure of the seriousness of the work. This is the original voice that communities and individuals want when striving for authenticity in their work. Without an essence of self and community present within the content of the work there is a sense of disappointment and missed opportunity.

It is with this end in sight that I propose we judge the ethics of our work.

If we recognise that seeking this essence is of such a degree of importance, it immediately becomes apparent that certain foundation stones are crucial.

1. A strong basic concept

We need a clear starting point: this is our idea, now what is the best possible way in which we can produce our work? This clear artistic concept has to be clearly understood by prospective participants, artists and funders. Some of the processes we need to follow to make the concept a reality may not be immediately apparent to begin with. There will be grey areas. But if the concept aims and objectives are clearly defined; they will guide us through. For example, when the idea of *The Wedding Community Play* was initially discussed, the organisers decided to tell the story of a mixed marriage in Belfast. To facilitate the intensity of the story, they decided to place the story in an interface district. To further heighten the delivery of the story, they decided to place the initial scenes in actual houses in an interface district, on the morning of the fictitious wedding. These houses were small kitchen houses, so bringing the audience from room to room to see the different scenes appeared, at first sight, to be a logistical nightmare. When the idea was presented to the collective community theatre groups they loved the idea but did worry about this potential chaos of the audience moving from room to room. As the houses had not yet been identified, it was impossible to explain the logistics in detail – but because they clearly understood the rest of the concept, the groups were prepared to take a chance with the bits they could not understand clearly.

2. Pairing the right artists with the project needs

When planning a project, it is crucial that project needs can be facilitated by the artist. When seeking to employ an artist you don't just want a *good* artist but the *best* artist for the particular project.

Community Dance UK recently published a report mapping community dance in the UK. As part of this report, they documented the range of skills a community dance facilitator needs to have. These included project planning, skills teacher, facilitation skills, co-ordinator, choreographer, evaluator, administrator, fundraiser and performer. In many cases, one individual artist had to fulfil all of these roles.

Now place that list of skills in front of a group that has decided to do a dance project and thinks they just need a talented dancer.

3. Clarity about levels of engagement and roles

Each process has a different commitment to levels of engagement with participants. For instance, Rita Duffy was quite clear that she would be actually doing the painting on the 'Drawing the Blinds' project and that it was the subject matter of the painting that she was consulting about. A different kind of project may expect participants to contribute to mural design and learn skills to enable them to paint the mural themselves.

This is OK if there is a level of honesty and clarity at the start. As a project progresses, participants can feel a sense of betrayal if this isn't made clear. We also need to specify the points where the consultation between artists and participants occur. Where, in a project, can you honestly commit to equality, to valuing the information you are being given? There should also be clarity about roles. If you don't know where the buck stops, the chances are that important tasks will not happen, therefore adding stress to the creative process. The alternative is that somebody will assume responsibility and will feel incredibly undervalued and exhausted. Artists can feel they are underpaid and undervalued if the goalposts keep on being moved.

'The Mourning Ring' by Ballybeen Community Theatre, 1995

4. Time

Because seeking and capturing essence is such a tall order it immediately becomes apparent that the necessary time is needed. Artists are often approached with a timescale in place that is totally unrealistic and could never deliver any kind of quality work. Most artists will be familiar with the unrealistic delivery request: 'Can you come and do a one-day drama workshop. And can you get them to do a thirty-minute presentation at the end of the day for family and friends?'

The appropriate reply should be obvious, but at some time most artists have gone down the road of trying to deliver quality work within an unrealistic timescale.

5. A commitment to keep asking questions

About ten years ago I was working on a project where the participants, mainly women, decided that they would like to devise a play exploring the theme of emotional blackmail. Initially, they were drawn to the use of silence as a weapon but then one woman said, 'I don't know if this is relevant but I would like to say I feel trapped by my son. I hate him. I don't just mean this is a temporary thing. I don't like him. I don't even like that I gave birth to him. By being his mother I don't have a right to say this. My hands are tied by emotions I am expected to have and boundaries I am not entitled to cross.' As she spoke some women were nodding their heads. Others were shocked.

For me, it was one of the most memorable statements I have ever heard during research for a play. It unlocked a vast reservoir that allowed us to explore social myths and expectations related to being a mother. This work was incredibly valuable in the creation of characters and storylines.

Having the courage to face up to these answers and not compromise a project with a 'this will do' or 'I haven't got the answers so I think I know myself what they want to say' can be difficult. The minute artists or a production team feel they must create to make up for a shortfall in participant input is probably the death knell of any good project. It is even more crucial to have the commitment to keep asking questions, even when it's, 'I'm lost, where do we go from here?' Asking the questions that unlock is the fuel that stokes the furnace both during the process and in framing the finished product.

If the previous points have highlighted some of the cornerstones of good process, the following points will hopefully shed light on some of the issues that can devour creative energy and make engagement in community arts a nightmare.

a. Red Adair syndrome

A favourite misconception is the idea that focusing on the problems within a community and trying to fix them with an artistic process and product will somehow solve social problems or miraculously heal community division.

If you try to build on what's negative, it puts you in the position of being a doctor or guru. Great for your ego but no use at all to a process that seeks to leave sustainable skills. Harnessing creativity is about building on the positive aspects of what's there. It's about drawing on undiscovered skills. It's like a search for gold that, once unearthed, leads to the most explosive release of creativity and excitement. It's a huge part of the fun and joy of the work. It is the start of the process of leaving sustainable skills and also informs participants about quality of engagement that they may want to access in their future lives.

I was once asked to work with a group of young women from a community where teenage pregnancies were very common. 'Maybe you could do a play with the girls on this issue?' I was asked. None of the participants had yet become pregnant so they could only comment as onlookers. 'Anyway, that's boring,' said one of the girls. So we ended up creating a really funny piece about their dreams and expectations. Not one of them mentioned getting pregnant as an ambition. Getting participants to think creatively is the key. Dwelling on 'the boring stuff' is boring and, more importantly, can often lead you up a blind alley that you are not equipped to deal with. It is impossible to establish any kind of equal dialogue if you are the facilitator from the healthy world and participants reside in some kind of no man's land from which they need rescuing.

b. Emotional avoidance

Bad is not having the sense to acknowledge safe space, trust, risk, chaos and emotions as being crucial to the process of creativity. They may be

'My first teacher said that's what a work of art does – provides a stimulating point of departure. When I asked him in class what it was, that was his answer and it's as good a one as I ever heard. All you do, working as an artist, is to keep asking the questions – and the world needs this or we are sliding.' Jack Nicholson (actor), interviewed in *Uncut* magazine, February 2003

embarrassing to admit, some issues may be too touchy-feely, too new age.

Get over it or get that job in the sausage factory.

c. Repeating the same old mistakes

Bad is making the same old mistakes over and over again.

The list of familiar stumbling blocks is boringly repetitive. They include poor project management and allowing our new artists entering the sector to trip over familiar stumbling blocks. This leads to another recurring problem – the continual loss of artists to the sector due to burnout and poor standards of pay. Deep knowledge is assimilated during a project process. It is housed within the artist's memory so the loss of an artist can be the loss of the practical learning.

Another common creative drain is the tendency to become tied up in bureaucracy. This ultimately inhibits the amount of work produced. It is essential that we take time to assess where we have been and where we want to go. The word 'ethics' indicates formulated or recorded knowledge. What we have learned over the last couple of decades has not been collated into usable information yet. If we don't gather the crucial information for ourselves and communicate this to relevant agencies, we only have ourselves to blame for being undervalued and not taken seriously.

d. Disowning our own practice

Bad is not owning up to what we do.

Many artists and organisations feel that it is detrimental to own up to the term community arts. It's all arts, they say. Yes, of course it is, but it is very specific work with its own frame of reference. If we cannot name what we do that is different, how on earth will we ever move forward? If we see it as demeaning to use the term 'community arts', we undervalue the skills, speciality and the incredible creative power of the work.

While most of these points are project related, they also inform the need for the creation of sector support for infrastructures.

For many organisations, the challenge facing them has changed from birthing problems to facilitating a growing sector's needs. So the issue becomes one of re-learning how to serve the sector effectively. The same ethics that govern the creation of a piece of community art are also applicable to the infrastructures that support these projects.

We need to be clear about what and whom we are serving and keep striving to ask the questions and listening to the answers that will help us to provide a dynamic delivery of services.

We need to define our ethics – ethics that liberate rather than restrict and inhibit the work being done within the community arts sector.

References

Cleveland William, *Philanthropy, the Arts and Programs for Youth*, Center for the Study of Art and Community.

Cleveland William, *Touching the Stone: The Trials and Triumphs of a Community Mural*.

Foundation for Community Dance, *Mapping Community Dance*.

I would also like to acknowledge the help I received from Gerri Moriarty during the editing of this essay.

Community arts and the quality issue

GERRI MORIARTY

Chambers Twentieth Century Dictionary offers two very different definitions of the word 'quality'. One is 'of a high grade of excellence'. The other is 'persons of the upper class collectively'. In the early days of community arts, at the beginning of the seventies, it felt as if it was this second meaning that was constantly being evoked, as members of the arts establishment strove to stifle the growth and development of the work with indiscriminate and derogatory references to lack of quality. Quality was a word that could, it seemed, only be associated with 'high' arts venues such as opera houses or art galleries; to a small coterie of bourgeois arts bureaucrats, it was simply inconceivable that work of any kind of quality could be taking place in council estates or in village halls. They were not interested in upholding the principle of participation in creating and enjoying arts as a universal human cultural right but in pursuing narrow policies that favoured the moneyed and well educated. The word was not used to identify and promote good practice in the field but to disguise ill-informed prejudice from behind a desk. It was not used dynamically to open up constructive developmental debate but as an ill-disguised weapon of attack. Such an abuse of the word 'quality' is not, unfortunately, entirely historic. In my view, it diverts attention away from the first and much more important definition of quality – 'of a high grade of excellence' – and discourages an ongoing dialogue as to what this might signify or how this might be achieved within the context of community arts work.

The search for quality in community arts, I would suggest, begins not at the moment of consumption by an external audience, but during the journey of creation and exploration in workshop by participants. The initial stages of this have three distinct elements. First, the participant is engaged in a process that concerns learning and technique, coming to terms with the discipline and demands of an art form – framing a photograph, remembering a movement sequence, mastering a craft skill. Second, the participant is engaged in an individual authorial process, giving voice, developing confidence, finding expression for his/her own ideas, identity, feelings, observations. Third, he/she is engaged in group processes, such as discussing, reflecting or negotiating with others, developing a collective creative approach. This implies that evidence of excellence is to be found first in the degree of learning and second in the degree of authorship (individual authorship and co-authorship) that is taking place within the workshop.

Focusing on the importance of the quality of the workshop experience draws attention to the variety of skills expected of the community artist or artists. He/she must have a confident knowledge of the art form, with the flexibility and adaptability to meet the needs of participants with different levels of ability. Participants will be learning throughout the process but are likely to respond badly to formal teaching styles and this requires imagination and enthusiasm from the workshop leader. The community artist needs to be able to lead, develop and suggest a shape for creative work but also be able to leave ego aside and make room for others to contribute. There will be points when his/her professional experience is vital in ensuring that time is not spent in futile culs-de-sac, in developing bad techniques or in creating work which will speak to no one, and there will be points when the voice of the professional needs to be silent. The unexpected is bound to happen and requires attention – whether dramatic, such as the street violence that interrupts rehearsals, or more mundane, such as the friends who fall out and carry their feud into the workshop situation. There has to be a constant interrogation of or reflection on the workshop process that includes the learning and creative experience of individual participants, dynamics within the group and progress with the creative work.

Providing a high level of excellence in workshop experience is not easy for the artist, particularly given the marginalised social contexts in which community arts usually takes place. Workshop venues can be cramped, cold, uninviting. Attendance by participants can be sporadic, given such factors as illness, lack of transport, personal difficulties and political disputes. Resources and time available can be very limited. The dominant culture in an institution within which a workshop is taking place, for example a prison, can be at odds with the culture needed for creative engagement. Community artists can also compound such problems by accepting impossible tasks. As a drama practitioner in Belfast, I have worked in the kind of youth club where workers insisted on a public performance after a handful of taster workshops, abandoned artists to work without support with large numbers of young people of different ages, in a noisy sports hall, with older young people running in and out of the space. At the same time, I have also worked alongside an experienced youth worker, with a well-established small group of young people, in a quiet, self-contained space. It would not be difficult to guess which environment offered a higher quality of experience for the young people concerned.

Insisting that the spotlight plays as much on the quality of the workshop process as on the quality of the final production presents developmental challenges to community artists. Budgets on community arts projects can be so tight that artists are often asked to work on their own, sometimes with large groups, managing a whole range of delicate individual and group creative activity with no support, no one with whom to discuss options, or no one to offer a different perspective. Community artists, often moving quickly from one project to another, have little space to reflect on or develop their workshop practice – a vital aspect of their own professional development. For newcomers to the field, opportunities of working with an experienced mentor in an apprenticeship role can be invaluable but hard to finance. In my own workshop practice, I have increasingly tried to work alongside another artist, sometimes from my own discipline, sometimes from another discipline, to give me the benefit of that additional critical eye, alternative approach and opportunity for training.

It also suggests that participants (and other observers of the process, such as teachers, youth workers, carers) have a key role to play in reflecting on and assessing the journey they are taking through the workshop – to build their own definition of a quality experience. It is as much about their subjective response to that experience as it is about an objective analysis of what has taken place, and their judgements should be sought and respected.

This reflection can be built into the workshop and draw on the strengths of the art form itself; for example, I once asked a group of young dancers in Ethiopia to create three still images of their journey through a community dance training. The first image showed bodies turned inwards, in hopeless slumps, cramped, eyes cast down. The final image showed proud extended limbs, eyes open and alert, a physical and mental stretch. The transformation of mind, body and spirit was startlingly clear. Reflection can also be additional to the workshop process – for example, using video, audio or written diaries.

Although some community arts work remains consciously and appropriately at the workshop level – for example, because of the vulnerability of participants – most projects will, at some time or other, move out of workshop into public exhibition, performance or publication. The concept of aspiring to 'a high grade of excellence' now takes on another dimension. Workshop material must be edited, shaped, rehearsed, framed to communicate with a wider audience, for whom the longer creative journey will be, to some extent, invisible.

At this point, the responsibility of the community artist to manage this transition with integrity becomes intense. For example, at the core of a community play should be a unique voice – content or forms of expression which could only be brought to the surface by this group of people, living, observing, struggling in this specific socio-cultural context. That is what authentic authorship means. In a community arts context, it can be necessary to try out different options for performance, to experiment, to take time to decide – no different from the route taken by individual artists, but this time carried out within a group context. At the same time, not every idea conceived in the workshop is interesting, not all will translate into a dramatic medium, not all will speak equally strongly to an audience. In the search for a conventional definition of quality, it can be easy for the artist to wield knowledge and power dictatorially, ignoring the previous search in workshops for dialogue and understanding. At the same time, rehearsals inevitably call for a focused discipline and direction that is very different from the atmosphere in exploratory workshops. It is a testing time for all concerned. For example, I have sometimes found achieving this level of negotiation and balance difficult when working with a writer and a group to develop a community play; a writer is more accustomed to taking an individual route and can find it difficult to develop an approach which is more transparent and shared.

There is also a responsibility to ensure that the skills that the participant has been developing in the art form continue to be stretched through performance/presentation but not to a point where they are encouraged to fail dismally in a public arena. This means working to create a form, a container, which allows growing strengths to shine through and weaknesses to be minimised. An important element of this can be the use of additional technical expertise – for example, production management, sound recording, lighting design – to create a clear and coherent frame for presenter and audience alike. I would suggest that, at this stage of the endeavour, a juggling act is going on between the conventional demands of the context in which the final piece is going to be presented (whether this is a school hall, a prison gymnasium, a city centre arts venue, a piece of waste ground) and the particular needs of the work and of participants. Quality lies in not neglecting any of these priorities.

And now it is possible to ask what happens at the point of performance or exhibition – how does the audience or spectator perceive quality in a piece of community arts work? At its best, in common with other arts practices, it changes their understanding of the world, asks them to look with different eyes, to hear another part of the story. It challenges assumptions, confounds stereotypes, helps people to look at the extraordinary in the ordinary and the ordinary in the extraordinary. Community arts work also speaks of the specific, the local, that which is often ignored or disregarded in more privileged discourse. This shift in viewpoint can be radical – for example, community theatre in Belfast was prepared to speak of the weariness of conflict in working-class communities in Belfast long before there was a peace process and to explore Protestant identity and culture at a time when there was an overpowering silence in the media and in the arts on such issues.

Excellent community arts work, however, also calls attention to the power of the ensemble, of human beings committed to working together to achieve something that is more engaging, more inspiring than any one person could achieve alone. It asks us to engage with the potential of the arts to release positive energy and discipline, no matter how apparently chaotic or negative the circumstances. It is this that, I believe, tends to induce the tingle factor, the shiver up the back of the spine. In our capitalist society, we are so overwhelmed by messages about the supremacy of the individual, it is immensely exciting to be faced with evidence to the contrary.

Experience suggests to me that excellent community arts work also invites the audience to engage directly, to be drawn into the creative experience, rather than to sit on the sidelines as passive consumers. My metaphor for this is *The Wedding Community Play* in Belfast, where audiences sat in the kitchens and bedrooms of terraced houses in east Belfast and the Short Strand to watch performances. It was extremely difficult not to acknowledge one's own part in the issues raised by the drama being played out inches from your face. Although this is an extreme example, there is often a feeling that the viewer/audience member is being asked to contribute to the final moments of creation of the community arts work, that their response has been eagerly awaited and has an impact on what will happen next. This is not always the case with more conventional arts practices, which can distance rather than include.

Workshop, devising, production, dissemination – there is yet another area of community arts practice that calls for 'a high grade of excellence'. Underpinning this creative journey from initial workshop to final presentation is the hidden hand of arts management. Funders, in particular, are unlikely to give a stamp of quality if budgets are not controlled, documentation is not clear and precise, objectives are not achieved, time-tables are not met. But the truth is that the consequences of poor management are inevitably experienced by all involved – participants, artists and audience – and all have a vested interest in its success.

Delivering quality consistently in a community arts context is therefore multi-faceted, extremely demanding and requires a constant critical practice. It is important to acknowledge that the highest standards are not always achieved. As I said before, I have been completely defeated as a practitioner by the environment in which I was expected to work – and yes, I should have known better than to take on the assignment in the first place. I have watched artists who are extremely accomplished in their own art form yet quite unable to lead workshops with young people. I can think of projects where the workshop process has seemed to be going well but the final performance has failed to communicate to its audience, and other projects where the final performance has been acclaimed when the workshop process has been seriously flawed. I have seen work with excellent content that is let down by its technical standards and work that seems derivative, unoriginal or more reflective of the perceptions and views of the artist than of the participants.

There are very real difficulties in identifying and rectifying poor quality in community arts practice, which also need to be acknowledged. In the early nineties, I recorded the following description of a workshop from someone applying (unsuccessfully) for a community arts job. 'Four of us jump in a van and we go down to the community centre. We do some wee models beforehand, and then we give the clay to the kiddies and let them get on with it. But they got hold of some black paint last time and it was all over the floor. It's awful difficult to keep them in control. No, I haven't got any photos of what we did, because the kids wrecked them all.' A horrific example of bad practice, perhaps. But if, for example, you are a youth worker in a club with very limited resources, you may be unwilling to question uninspiring project delivery in case you damage a relationship with an organisation which is able to provide you with some additional help; indeed, it may not even be clear to you how you might talk about your concerns with that organisation. External evaluators can be so sympathetic to the difficult conditions within which work is taking place or so enthused by its positive aspects that they find it hard to voice negatives. Alternatively, their honest informative work can lie unread and unimplemented in office filing cabinets for years. The desire for advocacy of the work to funding agencies and decision-makers or the fear of handing over ammunition to the anti-community-arts lobby can lead to self-evaluation reports by arts organisations and artists that minimise their problems and difficulties. Given that community arts now has a history, it is possible for funders to be trapped in historic funding decisions that unfairly favour the established organisation over newer, less familiar approaches, failing to take account of consideration of comparative artistic and participative outcomes. But it is sometimes also the case that community artists have to work hard to persuade their funders or partners of the importance of delivering the resources to offer a high quality arts experience when those agencies' primary concerns may be improvements in education, health awareness or engagement.

Quality also needs to be witnessed and acknowledged. I have seen workshops that have stretched participants to the fullest extent, encouraging them to dig deep to create final work that is valuable, unique and extremely well presented. I have observed arts organisations develop their programmes over time, making collaborations and connections across sectors and settings, growing more ambitious in their aspirations, regarding the achievement of quality as a dynamic goal, requiring constant reflection and critical analysis. As documentation of community arts has improved, I have been able to watch excellent practice on video and in photographs/written testimony. It is good news that serious and sympathetic institutions are working to record and archive the sector, as the Linenhall Library is doing for community theatre as part of its detailed work on theatre in Northern Ireland. Coverage in the media has increased. In the pages of this document, the debate continues.

There is a final aspect of quality in community arts to which I would like to draw attention: the degree of excellence it demonstrates in its sectoral position in critiquing established norms, in drawing attention to the silenced voice, not of the individual, nor of small groups, but of whole sections of populations. Just as once it queried why access to the arts in the western model was the preserve of a small élite, just as it worked alongside disabled arts organisations to lobby for their cultural objectives, so now it draws attention, for example, to the creative needs of older people and to cultural work in the context of international development. Community arts needs to maintain a radical, political function, which requires collaboration between those engaged in the field and activists in other sectors. Excellence demands attention to published material, seminars, conferences, exchanges, as well as to workshop and production. This wider remit should not be overlooked in the search for excellence within individual projects or programmes.

I was asked in this essay to consider the term 'quality' as it applied to community arts. I am not entirely sure that it is possible to shake off the feeling that it is a word which suggests some kind of external kite mark which will be conferred or withheld by some powerful and remote bureaucratic agency. More important, and infinitely more subtle, are aspirational internal goals, defined in detail at the beginning

'Ideally quality should be self-evident; within the company it usually is. We expect of each other that things are well made and they usually are. You have to believe that everyone wants to do their best. If something is badly produced it usually means a shortage of time, a lack of resources (a lack of belief in what you are doing – either because you are doing the wrong thing or someone's ripping you off) or a lack of experience and practice. I believe if you set up the right situation there's no problem. People are open with each other, they can take honest criticism from each other and quality is self-controlling.' John Fox, 'Engineers of the Imagination', *The Welfare State Handbook*, Methuen, 1983

of a journey and reflected upon and refined at key points during that journey by the arts organisation, its partner organisations, the artists, participants and close observers. Achieving excellence, after all, is not an end point, but a new beginning.

SECTION 3

PRACTICE

BeatStyle performers in Larne Carnival Parade (Co. Antrim) organised by the Beat Initiative.
Photo: David Boyd

The practice of community arts began with a few activists. Today, some thirty years later, it is hard to quantify where exactly community arts begin and end, with thousands of projects and participants engaging in creative activity. While this success is to be applauded, support and recognition for community arts continues to be a problem and practitioners on the ground often find themselves isolated and under-resourced. Equally, the rich and empowering nature of the work that is community arts continues to attract more and more people to become involved in the creative process. In this section, some of the practitioners of community arts speak about their work and their experiences.

Community arts as socially engaged art

Rhona Henderson

In this essay I want to try to situate community arts within the broader discourses and institutions of contemporary art practice. My aim here is not to provide a history of community arts but instead to outline a theory and methodology of community arts – as socially engaged art – which corresponds to my practice as an artist working in a community context. In this light I will be referring to the writing of Grant Kester, Associate Professor of Art History at the University of California, who defines socially engaged art, or in his own terms Littoral art, as a participatory or collaborative model of art practice based on a process of equitable discursive exchange between artists and audiences. I have chosen to focus on Kester here because to date his critical framework for the analysis and evaluation of Littoral art projects has been of most practical use to me in helping me to understand and improve upon my practice as an artist working in a community context. I also want to highlight the importance of understanding collaborative relations as embodied inter-subjective relations, which I am suggesting can return the critical edge to participatory and collaborative practice amidst concerns that it has been blunted recently.

It is difficult if not impossible to find a consensus of opinion when it comes to definitions of socially engaged art. A useful reference is *Interrupt: Artists in Socially Engaged Practice*, a series of five symposia hosted by the Arts Council of England (ACE) in 2003.[1] One of the issues raised by those participating in the symposia was this very same lack of consensus, and concern was expressed that ACE was attempting to force a definition to meet with policy and funding imperatives. In response Grant Kester appealed to critics, theorists and practitioners to 'move beyond these sort of synoptic events that try to comprehend the entire field and begin working more deeply in and on specific areas and methodologies'.[2] Nevertheless I want to attempt my own definition of socially engaged art here for those who are unfamiliar with the term. Since my definition is provisional it is, of course, open to contestation.

'What strikes me is the fact that in our society, art has become something which is related only to objects and not to individuals or to life. That art is something which is specialized or which is done by experts who are artists. But couldn't everyone's life become a work of art?' Michel Foucault

While it may indeed be true that all art is socially engaged, it is also true that in the 1990s a range of art practices came to be specifically defined as such, including 'new genre public art', 'site-specific art', 'issue-based art', 'activist art' and 'community arts'; a genealogy of which would include constructivism, productivism, minimalism, conceptualism and institutional critique. I would define socially engaged art as a form of ideology critique which takes as its object the social function of art and artists and in doing so presents a challenge to dominant artistic hegemonies by rejecting the autonomy of the institution of art in favour of a revitalisation of the avant-garde attempt to integrate art and everyday life. Physically located outside the space of the gallery or museum, socially engaged art engages with non-art audiences, discourses and institutions in the social field with the aim of effecting social change through an art allied with politics. Privileging collective over individual modes of artistic production and reception by encouraging audience participation through collaboration, socially engaged art insists on the essentially collective nature of art practice and of creative activity in general, while the artistic production process is itself privileged over any finished product; hence the familiar refrain of 'process over product!' In spite of these credentials, socially engaged art has become increasingly reliant upon art institutions acting as commissioning and funding intermediaries and theories and methodologies of socially engaged art have been incorporated into galleries and museums by way of access and outreach programmes.

In similar fashion community arts engages with and in non-art communities that are socially, economically and/or geographically marginalised, and the match between an artist and a community is also increasingly mediated by a sponsoring art institution. The level of interaction between an artist and a community can range from nominal participation on the part of the community to full-blown collaboration. Community arts also has links with, on the one hand, community development, and on the other, community activism. Of course an idealised notion of community as a coherent unity based on an exclusion of difference has come under fire recently, and yet, while I have difficulties with the term community arts, I have decided to retain its use here in the context of this reader – for the time being at least.

Before I look at Kester's model of socially engaged art in more detail, I want to outline briefly my own career trajectory as it relates to community arts, to identify some of the factors that have contributed to my decision to work in this way. For ten years I have worked as a visual artist on a variety of community arts projects in Dublin, as well as in the formal and informal education sectors. Shortly after graduating from the National College of Art and Design in 1992 with a degree in fine art, I set up an art studio in Dublin city centre with other graduates and began supplementing my income teaching art in adult and extramural education. In 1994, like many artists of my generation in Ireland in the 1990s, I stumbled onto a community employment scheme and began work as a community artist in a Dublin maternity hospital where I helped to deliver, not babies, but an arts programme as part of the hospital's centenary celebrations: teaching art to groups from the local community. This job brought security in the form of a small but regular income, plus I enjoyed the opportunities for social interaction brought about by group work as a change from the occasional isolation of working in a studio. As a student at the National College of Art and Design in the late 1980s and early 1990s, curriculum, teaching and assessment tended to be geared towards art practice as individual practice. This emphasis is still prevalent in art schools today. It came as a complete surprise then when I discovered just how much I enjoyed teaching and especially group work. Then, in 1995, I was invited to join the Department of Education and Community at the Irish Museum of Modern Art (IMMA) where I began work as an artist educator on a project-by-project basis. I have been with the department ever since. One of the first projects I collaborated on was the major community arts project and exhibition 'Once Is Too Much', which I will be returning to below. Joining the department gave me the opportunity to experience working collaboratively for the first time, not just with groups, but also with other artists and curators. Over the years, I have met and worked with a wide range of groups and communities and experienced first-hand the differences in project outcomes resulting from different levels of interaction and rates of turnover. The casual status of my employment at IMMA has also enabled me to work on a variety of community arts projects outside the museum and experience in addition the effect on project outcomes of various commissioning and funding structures.

After completing an M.Phil. in 1999, I began lecturing in Cultural Studies and Critical Theory to third-level students of art and design. More recently I have taken a break from lecturing and art practice for research purposes while continuing to work at IMMA. I am currently involved in researching and developing a number of initiatives in Ireland and the UK designed to highlight and promote effective international practice in the field of socially engaged art and create opportunities for critical (academic and non-academic) debate and 'the voicing of dissent'. In spite of my current research activities I still regard myself first and foremost as an artist. What working in a community context has inspired in me is an ongoing interest in collaborative art practice, which I hope that my current research will help me to understand more fully.

The exhibition 'Once Is Too Much', which addressed the issue of domestic violence, was the result of the highest profile community arts project I have collaborated on to date. The project was part of a programme of community development undertaken by the St Michael's Estate Family Resource Centre (FRC) in conjunction with Women's Aid and was facilitated by the Department of Education and Community at IMMA as part of the museum's access and outreach programme. Funding for the project came from public and private sources.

When 'Once Is Too Much' opened at IMMA in 1997, it was the culmination of a two-year-long collaboration between a group of women from St Michael's Estate and four artists (Joe Lee, Ailbhe Murphy, Rochelle Rubinstein Kaplan and me). The match between artists and community was mediated by the Department of Education and Community. The FRC and the Department of Education and Community had been working together on various art projects since 1991 and by the time this project started had already established a good working relationship. The project itself was initiated by the FRC, which had been working in conjunction with Women's Aid, also since 1991, to develop a community approach to domestic violence that would address the inadequacy and ineffectiveness of existing approaches. The women from St Michael's Estate who collaborated on 'Once Is Too Much' had participated in the programme and had received education and training relevant to the issue. From the outset the exhibition was intended as a consciousness-raising exercise that attempted to account for the social determinants of domestic violence, to communicate something of the power dynamics of violent and abusive relationships to deepen understanding of the psychology of abuse and to honour the lives of Irish women who had died and are still dying today as a result of domestic violence. Some of the women who collaborated on 'Once Is Too Much' had already participated in another successful community arts project – 'Unspoken Truths' – with artist Ailbhe Murphy in 1992. In preparation for the exhibition the group attended talks and exhibitions at IMMA and participated in workshops with artists visiting the museum, picking up along the way a good basic knowledge and understanding of contemporary visual art practice. This, combined with a strong sense of their collective identity (the women were neighbours who had known each other for many years) and purpose, made it easier for the artists to collaborate with the group on an equal footing. The artworks in the exhibition were created through an extended process of equitable discursive exchange, consultation and negotiation between artists and group. The group also played a major role in the planning, organisation and installation of the exhibition at IMMA and at all subsequent venues. Since the exhibition first opened at IMMA it has toured to regional galleries throughout Ireland and has attracted many thousands of visitors. At each location the gallery space has served as a venue for local groups to participate in talks and workshops on domestic violence and access information, advice and support. The exhibition is still touring in 2004, seven years after its official launch.

One of the most intriguing things for me about the project was the complex process of consultation and negotiation that took place between a local community organisation and a national cultural institution. This process was not always easy and inevitably minor conflicts did arise. However it is through these kinds of conflictual processes that struggles over power are waged and new knowledges produced. This is why I have chosen in the preceding account to focus not on the artworks exhibited but on the project's organisational structures and procedures. This is not to devalue the considerable achievement of the women who made the artworks, or indeed the artworks themselves, but because it is precisely the organisation of socially engaged art projects that to me constitutes the real difference between socially engaged and other models of art practice.

Contemporary reviews of the exhibition in the popular press, on the other hand, tended to do just the opposite and focus instead on the artworks exhibited. This elision, by ignoring the project's organisational structures and procedures and the mode and relations of the artistic production process, effectively erased the community from the picture leaving the 'professional' artists to be erroneously construed as the singular producers of the artworks.

In this it is possible to establish a correspondence with the demands of the art market which privileges artworks produced by individual artists, both of which it is better equipped to package and sell as fetishised commodities. Collective modes of artistic production present a challenge to the economy of the art market, especially when process is privileged over product and even more so when there is no product at all and the work of art is just that: the mode and relations of the artistic production process itself. This tactic has been used strategically by individual artists and by activist art collectives who have employed alternative modes of artistic production and distribution to resist incorporation into the art world or culture industry – two once relatively autonomous spheres (of high and mass culture) between which, as Theodor Adorno rightly predicted, it has become increasingly difficult to distinguish. But this strategy has not always been successful and today the rhetoric of process has become a staple of corporate ideology and artists as 'aesthetic service providers' have become the prototype for the trans-national corporate worker under the hegemony of global capital.

Viewed in this light 'Once Is Too Much' could justifiably be held up as just one more example of the institutionalisation of a critical art practice. While I have concerns about the institutionalisation of socially engaged art, not least because of the determining influence of curatorial and institutional power, on this occasion I would argue that 'Once Is Too Much' managed to go beyond any simple fulfilment of access requirements on the part of a gallery or museum. That the project was not simply a case of the incorporation of the theory and methodology of socially engaged art into an art institution was undoubtedly due to the critical intervention of all those involved. Which is not to say that my concerns are unfounded. However it is probably also fair to say that 'The art world has not been subject to much empirical analysis or theorised sociologically, to such an extent that categorical judgements on institutionalisation can only remain speculative.'[3]

As I write, a critical analysis and evaluation of 'Once Is Too Much' by all those involved in the project has not been undertaken. Until this task has been accomplished it would be inappropriate and indeed irresponsible to speculate on the successes and failures of the project and for this reason I am not going to draw any such conclusions here. In the meantime, however, I hope that my account of the project's organisational structures and procedures serves to illustrate the complexity of such projects and highlight the importance of struggles to maintain democratic process which, while not always successful, act as a welcome antidote to the corrupt structures and procedures of many of our public institutions.

In the period immediately following my collaboration on 'Once Is Too Much', what persuaded me to continue to seek out opportunities for collaborative work, as well as the opportunities for social interaction, was the 'buzz' I'd experience during and after a collaborative session with a group. Gradually I came to associate this buzz with the inter-subjective relations that are a vital but inadequately theorised aspect of collaboration. Collaboration requires face-to-face interaction between embodied subjects in shared physical space, and because collaborative relations are embodied they are not just about mind: they are about bodily sensations and emotions too. My experience of collaborative work has been one filled with joy and laughter and, importantly, with love and care, which has made the collaborative experience a pleasurable one for everyone involved. In 'Eros, Eroticism and the Pedagogical Process', African American academic bell hooks relates her own experience of embodied inter-subjective relations. Noting how her academic colleagues tended to teach 'as though only the mind is present, and not the body',[4] she describes how she re-introduced the body into her own teaching practice and is consequently able to offer love and care to her students. In my experience a pleasurable collaborative experience has the additional benefit of encouraging bonding between collaborative partners and the forging of strong emotional bonds engenders the trust that is essential for effective collaboration. As activist art collective Critical Art Ensemble explain: 'Members [of Critical Art Ensemble] must be able to interact in a direct face-to-face manner, so everyone is sure that they have been heard as a person (and not as an anonymous or marginalised voice). Second, the members must trust one another; that is, sustained collective action requires social intimacy and a belief that the other members have each individual member's interests at heart. A recognition and understanding of the non-rational components of collective action is crucial – without it, the practice cannot sustain itself.'[5]

My intention here is not to idealise collaboration; it can be difficult and frustrating at times and, because of the emotional investments made in other members of the group, devastating when it goes wrong. Conflict is as inherent to collaboration as it is to community and struggles to maintain democratic process in 'decision making, divisions of labour, and power sharing' can be relentless. Group work does not suit everyone. What I do want to do, however, is to highlight an aspect of collaboration – collaborative relations as embodied inter-subjective relations developed slowly over time – which I would suggest merits closer attention. Collaborative relations are about pleasure and pain, love and hate or aggression, and they are also about individual and collective needs, desires and fantasies. For this reason I prefer to work with groups of adults rather than children and on long-term rather than on short-term projects, which allow the time needed for relationships to mature. Unfortunately, existing commissioning and funding structures tend not to support long-term projects, with sponsoring institutions tending instead to 'parachute' artists into communities to work on short-term projects. This is not to imply that short-term projects have no value but that to date I have found long-term projects more stimulating.

Needless to say, the relationships I have forged through collaborative work have had a considerable impact on my personal, professional and political development. It wasn't just the buzz that got me hooked though! I was beginning to appreciate the potential challenge to traditional aesthetic paradigms and artistic identities presented by this model of art practice. Moreover, as a teenager in Scotland during the 1980s I had been involved in activist politics and was beginning to seek out ways in which I could introduce politics into my art practice.

As a direct result of my earliest collaborative experiences I began re-

Detail from 'Once Is Too Much' exhibition, 1997

reading cultural studies material I had first encountered as a student. I was drawn to cultural studies through a need to understand community arts not just as an art practice but also as a cultural practice, and to try to unravel the complexities of the relationship between art, culture and society; my interest grew from there on in. In simple terms, cultural studies takes as its object of study the culture of everyday life, from high culture or 'the arts' to mass or popular culture. Cultural studies then sets itself the task of theorising the relationship between culture and power and the struggles over power which arise between dominant and subordinate social groups. If we accept that the unequal distribution of power in society is based on differences of class, race, gender, and so on, then in this light community arts might be understood as a form of counter-hegemonic resistance on the part of subordinated social groups to the hegemony of dominant social groups. Cultural studies intellectuals are also concerned with the relationship between theory and practice and with how their theories can be put to practical use in struggles over power that aim to effect social change.

From the beginning, and increasingly so in recent years, cultural studies has also concerned itself with theories and methodologies of education. There is of course a pedagogic dimension to socially engaged art too. Artists who practise socially engaged art as well as artists and educators working in the formal and informal education sectors often cite the 'critical' or 'engaged' pedagogy of educationalists such as Paolo Freire, bell hooks and Henry Giroux as important influences on their practice. The educational philosophy of Brazilian Paolo Freire will also be familiar to those working in the fields of community development and community activism. Against traditional teaching and learning methodologies, or the 'banking' model of education, Freire's critical pedagogy sets the 'problem-posing' model of education, which is based upon a two-way dialogue between teacher and students, rather than the uni-directional monologue of the teacher. In this way the unequal power relationship between teacher and students is balanced out and 'the teacher-of-the-students and the students-of-the-teacher cease to exist and a new term emerges: teacher-student with students-teachers. The teacher is no longer merely the one-who-teaches, but one who is himself [sic] taught in dialogue with the students, who in turn while being taught also teach. They become jointly responsible for a process

'We need a type of theatre which not only releases the feelings, insights and impulses possible within the particular historical field of human relations in which the action takes place, but employs and encourages those thoughts and feelings which help transform the field itself.' Bertolt Brecht

in which all grow.'[5] Through dialogue, teachers help students to 'problematise' social reality, with the aim of creating critical consciousness and effecting social change. However, objections have been raised to the effect that critical consciousness is not enough in and of itself to effect change.

The theory and methodology of critical pedagogy has influenced not only my collaborative work but also my work as an artist educator at IMMA. I share with other artist educators a belief in the basic principle of access. Teaching and learning models used by artist educators are non-didactic and participatory, with artists assuming the role of facilitator and co-learner. At IMMA many forms of engagement with audiences take place, ranging from talks about artists and exhibitions, one-off workshops teaching practical art skills, to participatory and collaborative projects which require deeper and more sustained levels of interaction between artists and audiences over extended periods of time. Most unusually, projects can last for many years. Sometimes artist educators are employed as gallery or museum staff; at other times artists may be invited or commissioned by a gallery or museum to work on a project with a particular group or community; or a gallery or museum might mediate in the match between artists and groups at their own request. The forms of engagement audiences have with galleries and museums are far richer and more varied than most people imagine them to be. As an artist educator I see my role as facilitating individuals and groups, often those previously denied access to the arts, to think critically about contemporary art, its discourses and its institutions and to make audiences more aware of the power relations embodied by the museum. Access for me is about much more than audience development.

Most museums and galleries now operate access programmes in some form or another. The principle of access, however, is a controversial one. Critics of access argue that when museums and galleries adopt the principle of access it leads inevitably to a 'dumbing down' of art. While this argument should be taken seriously, there is another argument that maintains that access to and participation in the arts is a right not a privilege and should be equally available to all members of society regardless of their social or economic status. The question is, why is this right denied to certain social groups? French sociologist Pierre Bourdieu has written extensively about the role of culture in the reproduction of social structure. In his study of gallery and museum audiences he analyses class determinants of attitudes towards and the ability to use galleries and museums, backed up by extensive empirical research. Bourdieu argues that all societies are structured hierarchically and are characterised by a struggle between social groups and/or classes and class fractions to maximise their interests to ensure their reproduction. In the field of culture this struggle is governed by a logic of difference or 'distinction'. Museums and galleries often appear as élitist to subordinate classes traditionally denied access to formal art education, and art is often viewed as too difficult and in any way irrelevant to people's everyday lives. Good taste or the ability to appreciate art is generally considered to be an innate quality. However Bourdieu argues that there is nothing natural or pre-given about the competencies required to understand and appreciate art, which are instead learned through the family in the home environment or through formal art education. 'Whereas the ideology of charisma regards taste in legitimate culture as a gift of nature, scientific observation shows that cultural needs are the product of upbringing and education: surveys establish that all cultural practices (museum visits, concert-going, reading etc.), and preferences in literature, painting or music, are closely linked to educational level (measured by qualification or length of schooling) and secondarily to social origin.'[7] The means to acquire these competencies are more freely available to the dominant class; therefore taste, thought to be an innate quality and associated with the dominant class, acts as a marker of 'distinction' between dominant and subordinate classes and serves to legitimise the power of the former. That the subordinate classes are denied the opportunity to learn the competencies required to understand and appreciate art is an act of 'symbolic violence' on the part of the dominant class. Access programmes can and do provide this opportunity. Indeed one benchmark against which access programmes can be measured is the effective transmission of these competencies by gallery and museum staff.

Just as importantly, in a move from the consumption to the production of culture, access programmes can also grant subordinate social groups access to the means of artistic production that they have previously been denied. That artwork from the exhibition 'Once Is Too Much' that has been purchased by IMMA and is now part of the museum's collection could be, and indeed has been, interpreted as a direct and potent challenge by a group of working-class women to the powerful élites who control the production, distribution and consumption of art in the 'cultural economy' or art market.

I want to now look at Grant Kester's model of socially engaged art in more detail. In the 1990s a large and important body of critical and theoretical writing on socially engaged art began to emerge in North America. These essays and books, by artists and theorists such as Martha Rosler, Suzanne Lacy, Lucy Lippard, Suzy Gablick, Carol Becker, and so on, described a set of practices, examples of which tended to be drawn from the specific political, historical and geographical context of North America and as such any claims made on their behalf should not be generalised unproblematically. Nevetheless, Grant Kester's definition of Littoral art, which draws its examples from both North America and the UK, has made a significant contribution to the development of my own practice. In what follows I want to highlight some of the issues raised by Kester that have had particular relevance to me as an artist working in a community context. It should be made clear from the start that the critical framework Kester outlines focuses on just one aspect of the range of practices that fall under the descriptive term of socially engaged art.

In a paper delivered at the conference 'Critical Sites: Issues in Critical Art Practice and Pedagogy' in 1997,[8] Grant Kester outlined a critical framework for the analysis and evaluation of socially engaged, or in Kester's terms Littoral, art projects. To this end Kester proposes a new aesthetic paradigm – 'dialogical aesthetics' – which he presents as a challenge to the scopism of traditional aesthetic paradigms. Littoral art is defined as an open-ended, two-way discursive exchange between an artist and an audience; a model of artistic production and reception that challenges conventional notions of artistic authorship by demolishing the traditional separation of artist and audience, both of whom now participate collaboratively in the production of meaning. The value of Littoral art projects, according to Kester, lies in 'the condition and character' of discursive exchange itself and, because the production of (visible) artworks is not the aim of Littoral art, everyone who participates in the (invisible) process of discursive exchange becomes an artist, and artistic practice and creative activity in general cease to be the specialised domain of professional artists.

It's not difficult to make the leap from Littoral art to community arts, which can just as easily be defined as an open-ended, two-way discursive exchange between an artist and an audience, where the audience is the community collaborating with an artist on a particular project. This process of discursive exchange, Kester claims, 'is most easily facilitated in those cases in which the artist collaborates with a politically coherent community, that is, with a community or collectivity that has, through its own internal processes, achieved some degree of coherence, and a sense of its own political interests, and is able to enter into a discursive collaboration on more equal footing.'[9] The politically coherent community is an a priori community as opposed to a community that comes together temporarily for the sole purpose of collaborating on a particular project. The latter is a looser coalition of individuals over whom the artist is more likely to assert their authority. However, Miwon Kwon has argued that the politically coherent community may in fact be more, not less, susceptible to the authority of the artist, while a community that comes together temporarily for the sole purpose of collaborating on a particular project can 'productively reinvent or critique'[10] an idealised notion of community as a coherent unity based on an exclusion of difference. Indeed some artists like Critical Art Ensemble have chosen to abandon the notion of community altogether in favour of what they refer to as 'friendship networks'.

Staying with the issue of authority, Kester warns that artists do not have the authority to represent or 'exhibit' the community without recourse to due procedure of consultation and negotiation – the very conditions essential to democratic process. It is not that artists cannot or should not represent the community (it is equally a mistake to believe that the community or the subordinated other is the only 'repository of truth') but that the authority to do so must be sanctioned by the community itself. Though identification is an essential part of social interaction and interpersonal relations, artists claiming the authority to represent the community can be guilty of a reductive over-identification with the community, owing to a lack of a facility for critical self-reflection. Even more damning, though, is Kester's allegation that some artists claiming the authority to represent the community do so to advance their own careers. However, Miwon Kwon qualifies Kester's allegations by drawing our attention to the extent to which the authority to represent the community is sanctioned by an external source – a sponsoring institution, for example, which 'often reduces, sometimes stereotypes, the identities of the artist and the community group'.[11] The 'indignity of [artists and institutions] speaking for others'[12] means that in some community arts projects 'it is precisely the community whose voice is never heard'.[13]

As I mentioned earlier there is also a pedagogic dimension to socially engaged art. When an artist and a community collaborate they participate in a process of discursive exchange, which provides the opportunity for artist and community to learn from each other and to have their preconceived notions about themselves and each other challenged. Like critical pedagogy, Littoral art aims to create critical consciousness through dialogue and effect social change, but just like critical pedagogy, critical consciousness is not enough in and of itself to effect social change. To effect change, Kester urges, artists must cross disciplinary boundaries and affiliate with groups, organisations and institutions already working to effect change. This interdisciplinarity, Kester claims, in contrast to traditional models of art practice that operate solely within the discipline of art, is what gives Littoral art its critical edge, as it enables artists 'to develop a systematic critique that can be actualised through specific political or social struggles'.[14] The crossing of disciplinary boundaries, however, is not always easy. As Greg Sholette, a member of art collective REPOhistory, reports: '[REPO-history] has collaborated with historians, urban geographers, legal activists, unions and architects nevertheless an extended dialogue between these various [disciplines] and the artists has not taken root.'[15]

Finally, I want to highlight Kester's mandate that Littoral art must also take account of 'the broader discursive context within which a given Littoral project operates – for example, relevant public policies and debates, corporate ideologies … and numerous other sites which structure the political and cultural meaning that a specific work is capable of producing, and which are susceptible to being transformed by the work in turn'.[16] To do this, an ability to draw on a broad interdisciplinary knowledge base is required which, let's face it, artists just don't possess. A solution to this problem might of course be found in the interdisciplinary crossovers of Littoral art. In light of this demand, however, certain questions immediately spring to mind regarding European policy on social inclusion currently being implemented in Ireland and the UK that have a direct bearing on socially engaged art.

First of all, what is socially engaged art trying to change, at whose request and in whose interest? Moreover, in spite of its claims, can socially engaged art practice actually effect social change? This question is of crucial importance in a society in which it is has become increasingly difficult to imagine alternatives to the dominant hegemony of neo-liberal democracy, global capital and the 'totally administered world'. As I mentioned earlier in relation to cultural studies, socially engaged art might be understood as a form of counter-hegemonic resistance to the hegemony of dominant social groups. Recently, however, socially engaged art has become implicated in the continuing debate over the management and administration of culture and the arts by state bureaucracies, as outlined in the recent PEER publication *Art for All? Their Policies and Our Culture,* which collected together arguments for and against state funding of culture and the arts from across the political spectrum.

Like public art before it, participatory and collaborative art practice has been co-opted into state programmes of urban regeneration, and so on, under the banner of social inclusion, which has led some critics to argue that in this context socially engaged art becomes an instrument of policy while artists become mere 'social workers' or 'therapists'. Are these charges of instrumentalisation justifiable and if so is it the case that in this context participation and collaboration becomes an empty gesture, losing its critical edge and failing to live up to its subversive potential? What evaluative criteria come into play when it comes to decisions regarding the allocation of public funding in this context? Is a particular project valued for its artistic merit or solely on its effectiveness as an instrument of policy? Is there discrimination in the allocation of public funding? Is to be critical to lose out on public-funding opportunities? When a funding application fails can discrimination be proved? What roles can and do progressive curators, managers and administrators play as commissioning and funding intermediaries? To what extent has public funding and policy capitulated to private interests? Are there alternative sources of funding? Are there ways in which artists and cultural workers can and indeed must work together with state bureaucracies to effect changes in policy and redress the balance of power? What does social inclusion really mean anyway?

Returning to the question of why certain social groups are denied access to the arts — often elided from discussions of community arts by a rhetoric of 'empowerment' — community arts must be about more than just 'creative activity for all'. If community arts is going to continue to engage with and in marginalised communities, then critics, theorists and practitioners of community arts must also work to expose the structural causes of the oppression which produces social, economic and geographic marginalisation in the first place and face up to the possibility that community arts might itself play a role in the reproduction of an oppressive social structure (not least through social inclusion policy); to understand access to the arts, in other words, as part of a broader set of concerns about social, political and economic domination and subordination. As long ago as 1970, Paolo Freire explained how community development involves the breaking down of a nation-state or a region into local communities: 'As the oppressor minority subordinates and dominates the majority, it must divide it and keep it divided in order to remain in power. The minority cannot permit itself the luxury of tolerating the unification of the people, which would undoubtedly signify a serious threat to their own hegemony … One of the characteristics of oppressive cultural action which is almost never perceived by the dedicated but naïve professionals who are involved is the emphasis on a focalised view of problems rather than on seeing them as dimensions of a totality.'[17] And yet over thirty years later local communities are still competing against each other for the limited public funding available for programmes of community development. Even more importantly we need to understand community arts not just in a local, regional or national context but also in a global context. For example, the co-option of community arts into state programmes of urban regeneration needs to be understood as a local consequence of globalisation.

Do artists and communities need to be thinking less about social

'Because of the capacity of community arts activities to depict and represent recognisable community situations, events and characters, they have an important function in promoting community groups' sense of identity and belonging.' Creating Connections, Combat Poverty Agency, 1995

inclusion and more about social justice; turning away from community development and towards community activism or even further towards organised political and social movements? What is the relationship between small local or regional pockets of resistance and larger, organised political and social movements? Whatever the case may be, community artists must finally ask themselves – am I working for or against the *status quo*?

There are, of course, other models of socially engaged practice but for me, to date, Kester's model of Littoral art has been of most practical use in helping me to understand and improve upon my practice as an artist working in a community context – not least for highlighting the importance of dialogue for effective collaboration. The value of Littoral projects according to Kester's dialogical aesthetics, lies in 'the condition and character' of discursive exchange itself and in 'the specific effects [produced by these exchanges] in a given context',[18] and while Kester himself admits that due to inequalities in discursive power there is no such thing as 'an ideal discursive process', he does suggest ways in which artists can manufacture the best conditions possible for equitable discursive exchange, consultation and negotiation and for democratic process to take place. However, I would argue that Kester fails to elaborate on the precise mechanism by which 'systematic critique … can be actualised through specific political or social struggles' and evidence needs to be provided of examples of actual projects where, in Kester's opinion, this goal has been achieved. Finally though, Kester's insistence that 'systematic critique is precisely where the transgressive powers of Littoral art, and of dialogical aesthetics, are most needed today'[19] has been vital for me as it confirms my own conviction that socially engaged art and community arts must necessarily be critical art practices.

But does socially engaged art always have to try to effect change directly? Indeed, can socially engaged art actually effect social change? In its most extreme form socially engaged art can be difficult to differentiate from other forms of activism. Some, like Kester, have made it their job to distinguish between socially engaged art, other models of art practice and other forms of activism, whereas others, like London-based art collective Platform, don't care if their work is classified as art or as activism: if change is effected then who cares? But what about socially engaged artists whose practice is participatory and collaborative but who don't view their work as overtly political?

Curator and critic Nicolas Bourriaud has recently developed the concept of 'relational aesthetics' to describe a range of practices that focus on discursive exchange and social interaction as a response to the fragmentation and atomisation of contemporary social life. If, as I mentioned earlier, socially engaged art entails a revitalisation of the avant-garde attempt to integrate art and everyday life, then what kind of everyday life is art attempting to integrate with? Everyday life as invaded by the commodity form of the spectacle? Attempts to integrate art and everyday life must acknowledge the fundamental role played by everyday life in the exercise of power and work to change everyday life itself. Amidst concerns that the critical edge of participation and collaboration has been blunted recently, I want to take my cue from Kester's appeal to 'begin working more deeply in and on specific areas and methodologies' and finish with a suggestion for another way of looking at participatory and collaborative art practice.

Much important work has already been done to analyse the collective nature of collaboration within activist art collectives by, for example, Greg Sholette and Critical Art Ensemble. Indeed Critical Art Ensemble claims that 'artists' research into alternative forms of social organisation is just as important as the traditional research into materials, processes, and products'.[20] Of course, research of any kind into alternative forms of social organisation is nothing new but I would argue that it has become a matter of some urgency today. For this reason I would prefer not to talk about community arts at all but instead about collective artistic or cultural praxis. However, art is not culture *per se* and there are also important lessons to be learned from other kinds of informal and frequently collective creative activity operating at grassroots level.[21]

In conclusion, I want to suggest that the real value of socially engaged art could in fact lie in 'the condition and character' of collaborative relations as embodied inter-subjective relations. Coincidentally, while researching this essay I came across a recent posting by Kester on the Interrupt web site in which he revealed that, in his current research, 'I want to ask', he explains, 'how collaborative work, extended through time, can generate new insights into difference and new modes of solidarity.' For Kester, this line of research will involve an analysis of the 'physical, somatic and non-verbal components of collaboration'.[22] My own suggestion is that if theorists and practitioners 'begin to work more deeply in and on' collaborative relations as embodied inter-subjective relations and pay closer attention to the role of the body and to the articulation of need, desire and fantasy within collaboration, then it might just be possible to return the critical edge to participation and collaboration as a model of art practice which has not yet in and of itself exhausted its subversive potential. And yet this would also be a Utopian project in that, while it might not set out to effect change directly, it opens up the possibility of an idea; of alternative forms of social organisation and of transformed social relations; indeed of urgently needed alternatives to contemporary social reality, the seeds of which are already present in everyday life itself.

Notes

[1] See Emily Pringle, *We Did Stir Things Up: The Role of Artists in Sites for Learning*, ACE, 2002.

[2] Grant Kester, Interrupt web site. Currently available to Interrupt core group members only.

[3] Jonathan Vickery, 'Art without Administration: Radical Art and Critique after the Neo-Avant-Garde' in *Third Text*, vol. 16, Issue 4, 2002, p. 407.

[4] bell hooks, 'Eros, Eroticism and the Pedagogical Process' in *Teaching to Transgress*, Routledge, 1994, p. 191.

[5] Critical Art Ensemble, 'Collective Cultural Action' in *Variant*, Summer 2002, p. 25.

[6] Paolo Freire, *Pedagogy of the Oppressed*, Penguin, 1996, p. 61.

[7] Pierre Bourdieu, *Distinction: A Social Critique of the Judgement of Taste*, Routledge, 1989, p. 1.

[8] The conference took place at the Institute of Art, Design and Technology, Dun Laoghaire, and was co-organised by Littoral and Critical Access. The paper was subsequently published as Grant Kester, 'Dialogical Aesthetics: A Critical Framework for Littoral Art' in *Variant* supplement Socially Engaged Art Forum, Winter 1999/2000.

[9] Kester, ibid., p. 7.

[10] Miwon Kwon, *One Place after Another: Site-Specific Art and Locational Identity*, MIT Press, 2002, p. 147.

[11] Ibid., p. 141.

[12] 'Intellectuals and Power: A Conversation between Michel Foucault and

Giles Deleuze' in *Language, Counter-Memory, Practice*, p. 209.

[13] Grant Kester, 'Aesthetic Evangelists: Conversion and Empowerment in Contemporary Community Arts' in *AFTERIMAGE*, January 1995, p. 6.

[14] Kester, 'Dialogical Aesthetics', p. 4.

[15] Greg Sholette, *News from Nowhere: Activist Art and After, A Report from New York City*, 1998

[16] Kester, 'Dialogical Aesthetics', p. 4.

[17] Freire, p. 122.

[18] Kester, 'Dialogical Aesthetics', p. 8.

[19] Kester, 'Dialogical Aesthetics', p. 4.

[20] Critical Art Ensemble, p. 25; see also Sholette, *Dark Matter, Activist Art and the Counter Public Sphere: MAVN Conference, and the Battles Lost*, 2003, and *Counting on Your Collective Silence: Notes on Activist Art as Collaborative Practice*, 1999.

[21] Sholette, *Some Call it Art: From Imaginary Autonomy to Autonomous Collectivity*, 2000.

[22] Kester, Interrupt web site.

The fine art of floating horses

AILBHE MURPHY

After many years of frustrated effort, a psychologist friend of mine finally modified his hopes for organisational transformation, placing them wryly within the scope of the miraculous as he concluded, 'You can bring a horse to water … if you can get it to float on its back you're really onto something.'

Applying the more familiar version of this old maxim to the field of community arts suggests a set of transformational relations between the community, the artist and art practice. In this modest drama, the community is led by the guiding hands of the artist towards the restorative waters of art. If the community should refuse the invitation, the role of the artist is cast primarily as one of persuasion. The artist successfully employs his or her skills of encouragement and eventually the transformation of the uncertain community is complete … a sense of satisfaction and self-congratulation pervades before the artist moves on to greener pastures.

I personally favour the more ambitious spectacle of the floating horse. I believe it offers a compelling rather than miraculous analogy for community arts practice. But I would reverse the symbolic relations so that it is the art practice that is being brought to the community and, whilst it is once again the artist that 'brings the horse to water', the anticipated results are, at the very least, surprising. The relationship between the artist, their practice and community has shifted and changed and yielded something more than the sum of its parts. Something surprising, something new has happened to the art, by way of its connection to the artist and to the community and the field of practice is never quite the same again.

Community arts practice resides within these complex and shifting relations between artists, art practice and community. While practice is progressed through the diverse working relationships initiated by artists and by communities, it is shaped, in my view, by the nature of the invitations they extend to each other. In this essay I would like to reflect on my own experience in this complex relational field and to consider the challenges and rewards of a potent but equally problematic area of arts practice.

My interest in community arts began as a student in the National College of Art and Design (NCAD) in Dublin. At that time in the college the relevance of art practice that attempted to connect to the wider social sphere of art in community contexts seldom, if ever, arose.[1] In my final year, following my interests in architecture, changing urban landscapes and the effects of such change on the social, political and cultural life of communities, I began to establish connections with community groups in the north inner city. These groups were representing a constituency who, at that time, found themselves at the epicentre of an accelerated transformation of their social and physical landscape. The arrival of the Financial Services Centre was to herald the total redevelopment of the Dublin Docklands area.[2]

Over a twelve-month period, this exploration led to a series of large mixed media photo-works and a slide-sound installation that reproduced the recorded testimonies of people living in the area. The work was presented in the context of my NCAD degree show. Although I was reasonably happy with the formal resolution of the work, which read comfortably enough in the context of the college's fine-art degree show, something had been lost in the translation from the engagement with community to the exhibited outcome. I was left with many questions and challenges concerning the validity of what had been essentially an observer position in relation to the community. Not surprisingly, I had questions about this process and its effectiveness in making a genuine contribution to the wider debates circulating around the real-life issues of the day. I now wondered if it would be possible to work with those communities to articulate the dynamics of change as experienced directly by them. I hoped it would be possible to build on the dialogue already initiated towards creating new collaborations that could make the art practice a more collective process and therefore more visible in a way that was not so evident in my degree show. If I could work more directly with this community, what might they have to say about their experience and how would they choose to articulate that experience?

These questions led to my re-engagement with one of the

community development organisations in the north inner city, the Lourdes Youth and Community Services (LYCS) based in Rutland Street, to work for a six-month period with an older women's group. A short time later, in the context of one of the earliest outreach projects of the newly opened Irish Museum of Modern Art (IMMA), I began to work with a second community development organisation, the Family Resource Centre in St Michael's Estate, Inchicore. At an open meeting for artists in May 1991, Declan McGonagle, the then director of the Irish Museum of Modern Art, extended an invitation to artists to consider how they might be involved in shaping the direction of this new cultural institution. He indicated the possibilities for artists to engage with the museum's programme and invited us to consider potential engagements in relation to the museum's culture of access and participation. I began to develop the idea of a collaborative project that would engage women from the north and south sides of the city, their community development organisations and the Education and Community Department of IMMA. The impetus for the project was in no small way inspired by the quality and openness of the museum's invitation, combined with my recent experiences of working with both community development organisations and with the Education and Community Department of the museum.

Although it is beyond the scope of this essay to revisit in detail the project narrative of what was to become 'Unspoken Truths', which has been well documented elsewhere,[3] in the context of addressing the kinds of relationships artists can have to community it is important to draw attention to both the diversity of experience and the nature of the collaborative relationships within that project, which extended over a five-year period.

'Perhaps in "Unspoken Truths" time has been the critical resource. There has been time crucially for the unlearning before the learning could begin. The unlearning of muteness of reticence as regards the kinds of intimacy you could have with a group and the kinds of ways of working, kinds of materials that could be employed. Above all though, the time seemed to allow for some reclamation of the lost or abandoned artistic self and its re-grafting onto the mother self, the daughter self, the private self, the wife self, the working self and the domestic self' (Drury, 1996: 79).

Certainly 'Unspoken Truths' was made up of many novel intersections: an artist just out of college, a new national contemporary-arts institution, two community development organisations with a long history of arts and crafts activities in their respective centres but new to engaging with professional artists in the context of a major cultural institution and thirty-two women embarking for the first time on a cross-community arts project. However, 'Unspoken Truths' also brought together a range of expertise and experience within contemporary arts practice, arts education and community-based arts practice, and harnessed a wealth of community development expertise and local leadership, particularly in the provision of social, educational and personal development resources for women. This range of expertise was represented on the 'Unspoken Truths' co-ordinating team and, though fourteen artworks became the public manifestation of the project, 'Unspoken Truths' had at its heart an ongoing process of dialogue through which it took shape.[4] There was much to be negotiated. Although we each recognised the potential of the collaboration, our coming together was by no means a *fait accompli*. It was very important to establish and respect the premise and the terms of our respective engagements with the project. The collaboration required a project framework that was as flexible conceptually as it was robust organisationally.

From my perspective, a central question on entering into the project was the extent to which I could develop a collaborative process in which the navigation of such a complex set of relationships and their different discourses could be as much at the core of my work practice as was the facilitation of the development of any artworks that would emerge. The community development organisations were establishing a new relationship with a new cultural institution. They had to be sure that they could enter on their own terms so that the range of experience they were bringing to the project could seriously inform and shape the direction of the collaboration and not simply be appropriated for institutional gains. For the newly opened Irish Museum of Modern Art and its education and community department the stakes were high. In the face of considerable expectations from the national and international contemporary arts community, it had made a cross-community arts project a central aspect of its initial and therefore defining work programme. The working relationship with the museum afforded access to the extensive experience of its education and community department and once the collective decision to have an exhibition was taken six months into the project, all the resources of the museum were made available to facilitate that process. Our working together was not simply a happy accident of well-disposed individuals engaging in a discourse of benevolent patience towards each other and in turn enjoying the benign patronage of a cultural institution. We tested each other and learned a lot from each other. Certainly 'Unspoken Truths' was where my education in community-based arts really began.

With any collaboration, the question of who gets to speak about the work and whose experience is represented is crucial. In the exhibition and, later, in the *Unspoken Truths* publication it was the voices of the thirty-two women that were to the fore. The transition of private experience into the public realm, first in the context of a group and subsequently interpreted and mediated through the artwork, required absolute and ongoing attention to the various roles and responsibilities within the project. My role as an artist was to facilitate the exploration and realisation of a range of ideas through the visual arts, within the sensitive navigational complexities that made up the relational field of 'Unspoken Truths'. This was my 'process'. The community development organisations might place a different emphasis drawn from community development principles but they too expected the quality of the journey to be reflected in the quality of the finished work and in the story and analysis of the project. Each of these major points of transition within 'Unspoken Truths' was accompanied by a rigorous, collective decision-making process through which the most appropriate representation and subsequent mediation for each stage of the project was decided. We took our collective responsibility to safeguard the journey from the intimacy of a women's group to larger, ever more public contexts, from exhibition to public workshops and eventually to publication, very seriously.

Following the exhibition phase at IMMA I worked on the *Unspoken Truths* publication, compiling the texts and the testaments that together made up its story. We had a responsibility to communicate the level of work invested in achieving the necessary framework for the project. In

'Our deepest fear is not that we are inadequate. Our deepest fear is that we are powerful beyond measure. It is our light not our darkness that most frightens us. We ask ourselves who am I to be brilliant, gorgeous, talented and fabulous. Actually who are you not to be? ... As we let our own light shine, we unconsciously give other people permission to do the same. As we are liberated from our own fear our presence automatically liberates others.' Nelson Mandela

the absence of any coherent body of knowledge to serve as a reference for placing 'Unspoken Truths' in a historical relation to the kinds of community arts initiatives that had preceded it, and without any unifying discourse which could incorporate and respect the diversity of experience activated, the project story was assembled from a number of points of view, with the women's testimonies leading all others, as was appropriate.

I welcome the opportunity to reflect on 'Unspoken Truths' that writing this essay has afforded. With the benefit of some distance, the impulse is less to revisit the rich life experience and project narrative that resides in each of the fourteen artworks. Instead, I feel more compelled to draw attention to the very hard work that led us to identify the points of connection, to test each other's views, to trust each other's experience and to work closely with each other for over five years.

The work of compiling and co-editing the *Unspoken Truths* publication (1996) was naturally a process of reflection that extended into my time on the newly established artists' work programme at IMMA. In this context I considered how to progress my practice within or alongside an arts institution where we had both sought to challenge the meaning of such a relationship, through the process of 'Unspoken Truths'. My time on the artists' work programme evolved as a series of informal meetings with key community workers based in the Inchicore area and with other artists on the programme. I also made connections with artists working collaboratively in an international context when I attended the second Littoral conference held in Sydney in 1994.[5] It was through this network that I became aware of the extent of work being developed internationally in the field of socially engaged art practice. The artists' work programme became an exploration of the kind of relationships artists can have to community in the broadest sense.

That exploration led into my involvement with the next major art project developed by the Family Resource Centre.[6] 'Once Is Too Much' centred around the single issue of violence against women and was initiated and led by the Family Resource Centre as part of a wider community development strategy. At the time, the Family Resource Centre was working very closely with the national agency Women's Aid[7] towards shaping for the first time a model of community practice in

Ireland that would address the question of community response and action to domestic violence at both a local and national level. 'Once Is Too Much' differed in many ways from 'Unspoken Truths', perhaps most significantly in its mode of initiation. Whereas 'Unspoken Truths' combined one principal facilitating artist with other artists invited in to complement the project at key moments, the Family Resource Centre identified and invited four artists to work with them to realise 'Once Is Too Much'.[8] My engagement with this project was at the very beginning of the process and, again, more intensively in its later stages. The other three artists were more closely involved with the development of the project throughout.

The Family Resource Centre had very clear ideas in relation to the overall direction of the project and more specifically about the form and content of many of the artworks. At times there was much debate within the project about whether the role of the artist ought to be as a facilitator of ideas or as a technician lending support for the final resolution of a work already in progress. My role as an artist working on the installation *And They Tell Me* seemed to oscillate between those two positions. I had been asked to facilitate the making of a piece of work that had already been well imagined in both form and content by the group. We had a short timeframe in which to complete the work: the date for the exhibition opening was looming. We worked intensely but failed to resolve the form of the piece as originally imagined to our satisfaction and so we changed direction. In the eleventh hour we spent time in the exhibition space and stood where this work was to be placed. We considered the overall content of the exhibition. It was at that point that we realised that 'Once Is Too Much' needed to acknowledge and remember those who had died as a result of male violence during the course of the making of the project: *And They Tell Me* took shape there and then. The central idea for *And They Tell Me* was realised through the culmination of much work and discussion. Long-established working relationships allowed us to challenge each other and to relinquish unsuccessful strategies. We were able to work intensely together until that moment when the final content and form had fallen into place.

The finished work in 'Once Is Too Much' represented a significant progression from 'Unspoken Truths' both formally and conceptually. As the exhibition travelled nationally, the organisational framework extended to include involvement by state agencies to facilitate its presence at various art venues. In this way the exhibition went beyond a static representation of a brutalising experience and acted as a catalyst for other individuals and community organisations dealing with the issue. 'Once Is Too Much' was embedded in a wider set of aims and objectives within a community development agenda, to which the art did not take second place. On the contrary it was absolutely central to its expression.

By this time I had been engaged in some form of collaborative art practice for over ten years. In the face of ongoing scepticism expressed by others in relation to my levels of satisfaction as an artist in the absence of 'my own work', I became increasingly preoccupied with how an artist who collaborates with a community might articulate that experience and I sought time to reflect on my practice to date. Certain questions had emerged from my work in community contexts and, along with those questions, a degree of frustration with the rather self-perpetuating discourse that seemed to hold currency among artists like myself, working in the field of community-based art practice in Ireland. This discourse tended to be somewhat effusive when it came to describing the richness of the working relationships in past or current projects, communicating in earnest the personal immediacy of the collective experience. An emphasis on the innovative nature of project structures was typically combined with pleas for the rather nebulous appreciation of 'process over product'. At times one could not help suspecting a general, misguided elevation of the novelty of the institutional and organisational intersections at the expense of artistic innovation and quality. All these accounts were pertinent but my point is that they were overly anecdotal. They did not constitute a discourse with the accumulative power to conceptualise one project experience with or against another, nor offer a broader register that could place a local experience in relation to the field of collaborative arts practice nationally or internationally. Every collaborative experience seemed to be sealed within the logic of its own practice, as though it had unfolded in its own isolated moment in time, de-coupled from any cumulative history.

I had formulated a series of questions which began by asking whether being an artist in a community context required announcing oneself as engaging in a vocational model of art practice (as someone who has relinquished one's own practice in favour of others) with all the overly earnest energy that such testimony demands. At the same time if one chooses to make work about or with any particular set of issues affecting community, as I had attempted to do in my college work, is this process of re-presenting the community essentially colonial? In short, I felt I was caught between two equally unpalatable models of practice.

I also began to consider what limits might be set on artists and the legitimate practice of contemporary art by the expectations and understandings of the communities they engage with. In my case I had been fortunate to work with very experienced community development organisations. My presence in communities was brokered by them and sealed with the community arts promise of inclusiveness. In the context of public art practice where artists extend themselves and/or their work into the public domain, they encounter 'community' primarily as audience or as participants, less often as collaborators. Consequently the demands and challenges of communities on artists can sometimes make the community seem more like gatekeepers than facilitators for contemporary art practice and all that it might have to offer. The tensions of expectation inevitably encountered between artists and community is a dynamic I will return to later on. For artists who have successfully navigated the territory of collaboration from the point of initiation to a project's natural conclusion, what judgements await their endeavour? Can contemporary art criticism, coming from a tradition of reflection within a self-referential art historical framework, address the breadth and diversity of the elements that come into play in the collaborative arts process? Equally, in community development contexts are the models of evaluation that place emphasis on the educational and developmental process appropriate to all of the elements within collaborative arts practice? It is in the aftermath of community arts engagements, when the readings and subsequent counter-readings of these initiatives emerge, that the absence of models of practice and evaluation that can resolve the historical separation of individualistic artistic production and collaborative art practice are most keenly felt.

I engaged in a series of conversations with practitioners, arts organisations and others either directly involved or with an interest in the field of collaborative arts practice.[9] I travelled to the United States to visit other practitioners and attended the public analysis of projects which had taken place in the public domain. I gained a sense of the range and scale of artists' interventions, which were accompanied by a more evolved and robust critical armature which could interrogate the work and place it within a wider contemporary arts context.[10]

I also began to gain a much broader perspective on the different ways in which artists can engage with community. Although artists' engagements with any given community will differ, they all tend to share a common point of entry, which almost invariably is in the form of an invitation. This invitation may come from the community to the artist, or from the artist to the community, or from the curator to the artist or to both the artist and community. Whatever the sequence, in my view it is the quality of this invitation that has a huge bearing on the integrity of the work and on the experience that follows. If the initial negotiations of the terms of engagement and the roles and expectations are reasonably clear and well understood, this will be reflected in the integrity of subsequent relationships and, ultimately, in the quality of the work. The critic Grant Kester addresses the question of equity between the community and the artist, guarding against the patronage of the former by the latter.

'The artist occupies a socially constructed position of privileged subjectivity, reinforced by both institutional sponsorship and deeply embedded cultural connotations. It is the achievement of Littoral practitioners to work to mitigate the effects of these associations as much as possible, and to open up and equalize the process of dialogical exchange. This process is most easily facilitated in those cases which the artist collaborates with a politically coherent community, that is with a community or collectivity that has, through its own internal processes, achieved a degree of coherence and a sense of its own political interests and is able to enter into a discursive collaboration on more equal footing. This is perhaps the most effective way in which to avoid the problems posed by the "salvage" paradigm in which the artist takes on the task of "improving" the implicitly flawed subject' (Kester, 1998).

The initial, negotiated understandings between artist and community largely determine the equality and balance of the contract. Also crucial in determining the quality of the engagement is the artist's

'A painting is never finished, it simply stops in interesting places.' Paul Gardner

sense of responsibility, their ability to respond to the various relationships that have become activated when working in the complex social and political landscape of community. A strong organisational framework at community level can make a significant positive difference to the mediation of the work of the artist and, in addition, can ensure ongoing attention to the 'afterlife' of a project, when the artist inevitably moves on and the artistic intervention is incorporated by the community it addresses and represents.

In recent years the parameters of public art practice in Ireland have widened beyond the spectacle of the permanent monument to include new territories and new audiences. For arts in community contexts, the public domain also presents a compelling arena for new work to emerge. This shift in direction away from more traditional venues and methods of art production towards negotiating the complexities of public space represents an opportunity to open up new territory for creative alliances between practising artists, experienced community development leaders and their constituencies. Much public art in Ireland is currently funded as a direct result of profound changes in the urban landscape.[11] The community development sector is often at the coalface, negotiating and supporting the endeavours of their communities to have a voice and to be heard in the complex dynamics of these changes. This sector has felt that the struggle to represent community experience and to reclaim lost voices and lost experience has been a defining feature of their history and work practice. Indeed, much community arts has been explicitly preoccupied with reclaiming that which has been lost. The arena for public art practice is now made up of multiple views and interests from within community development, from within arts practice and from regional and local government, which together form the complex institutional framework in which artists increasingly must work. Progressing work in the public domain, either in the context of the Per Cent for Art platform or in community contexts, calls for delicate negotiations involving many stakeholders, including local authorities, local communities and a range of funding sources. Somehow within this intersection of artistic, social and technocratic discourses it is crucial to protect the space for the unpredictable and to generate work that tests assumptions and expectations.

Whether artists position themselves as 'artists in the community' or as 'working in the public domain' they inevitably open up their practice to multiple critiques and points of reference. These can include questions of authorship, community development perspectives, the discourse of civil and human rights activism, community expectations and the institutional objectives of local authorities, to name but a few. In the absence of a model for articulating arts practice in this permanently contested space, any one element of concern or experience within this relational field is at risk of disappearing. The articulation of experiences and critical reflections on community arts practice has tended to surface in a fragmented and occasional fashion, sometimes finding its way into the broader arts constituency to make a contribution to an understanding of the field of collaborative art practice. The sporadic nature of such contributions is in part due to an emphasis on process and modes of production within community arts at the expense of any rigorous articulation of the spectrum of ideas or range of perspectives that might contribute to the broader field of cultural production.

In my experience, when these contributions do emerge there are two standard approaches to the critique of collaborative art projects, each with a distinctly different point of articulation. Modes of evaluation from the community development tradition are typically set in train at the outset or as a project builds momentum. In contrast, forms of evaluation derived from art criticism typically pass judgement on a project based on the moment of its public manifestation. The former utilises the language, values and sensibilities of community development principles and serves the discursive requirements of community very well; less so the artist and their own arts constituency. The latter practice casts its critical gaze on the resulting art object(s), bringing the entire history of art production to bear on the collective endeavours of a modest group of individuals. It is at this point that we can expect to hear a certain righteous indignation on the part of the artist and his or her community of collaborators at the shortcomings of contemporary art criticism and its methods of validation. A rigorous art critique, which is both attentive to the social and political context and respectful of the moment of articulation of a set of working relationships, is rare. We need a model for critique that is present at the outset, when the context and framework for any major project is first established. We need to ensure that the premise of a project's evolution and any collective conceptual journey in a community context can be tested within a critical framework that is equally cognisant of the histories and experiences of community development and contemporary arts practice both in national and international contexts.

Perhaps it is now time for artists working in community contexts to imagine and develop models of engagement that privilege the articulation of contemporary community experience as a cultural process over the collective making of art objects and the subsequent critical judgements that inform that domain of reference. If artists and their collaborators are to articulate the dynamics of their work together beyond the description of a certain marvel at being able to participate in art-making in the first place, in short, beyond the anecdotal, then the field of collaborative art practice must set out to destabilise, challenge and finally dissolve the very terms within which it has been constructed and contained: the community, the artist, the art work and the audience.

'The challenge, then, is to figure out a way beyond and through the impossibility of community. This is not to invoke a transcendent plateau from which one will find a new synthetic resolution free of contradictions. Quite the contrary, it is meant to suggest the impossibility of total consolidation, wholeness and unity – in an individual, a collective social body like the "community" or an institution or discipline – and, perhaps more importantly to suggest that such an impossibility is a welcome premise upon which a collective artistic praxis, as opposed to "community-based art", might be theorized' (Kwon, 2002: 154).

Either that, or we may find that the proper space for the articulation of the collaborative experience keeps eluding us, somewhere between the disciplinary constraints of art history and the elation of participation. At the risk of overusing equestrian metaphors, we may be condemned, like the poet Keats and his faithful companion Chapman in *The Best of Myles,* to 'Dogging a fled horse.'[12]

Notes

[1] Since 2002 The National College of Art and Design offers a Higher Diploma in Community Arts through the education faculty. Third-year

fine-art students also have the option of a short-term placement with community groups located within the vicinity of the college.

[2] In 1990 the working-class community of Sheriff Street, one of the longest established in Dublin, was facing complete redevelopment as part of the transformation of the Dublin Docklands. The North City Centre Community Action Project, among other community organisations, was to the fore in the negotiations on behalf of the residents of Sheriff Street. Through the NCCCAP, I worked closely with the North Inner City Folklore Project, which gathered stories from the residents of Sheriff Street, building a valuable archive of the Docklands communities.

[3] The *Unspoken Truths* publication (Irish Museum of Modern Art, 1996) documents in detail the sequence and narrative of 'Unspoken Truths'. It begins with the fourteen artworks and the stories behind the work. It describes the project framework in depth. It outlines the community development and art education principles that informed the project. The publication also includes a number of commentaries from the community development and cultural sectors.

[4] There were four members of the 'Unspoken Truths' co-ordinating team: Rita Fagan, director of the Family Resource Centre; Maureen Downey, co-ordinator of the Adult Programme in the Lourdes Youth and Community Services; Helen O'Donoghue, senior curator, Education and Community Programmes, Irish Museum of Modern Art; and myself. The co-ordinating team was charged with the responsibility of advancing the project and we worked very closely together over a five-year period, meeting every week initially, more often as the work intensified. The direction of the project took shape through ongoing and extensive discussions at our regular meetings and in close collaboration with the thirty-two women involved.

[5] The Littoral international conference and research programme is co-ordinated by an independent network of artists, critics, curators and academics with an interest in contributing to new thinking on contemporary arts practice and critical theory. The participants have a particular interest in promoting socially engaged art practice and long-term collaborative projects in which artists work with communities on issues about rural development, health, new media, agricultural change and other social, educational and environmental issues.

The first Littoral conference, 'New Zones for Critical Art Practice', was held in Manchester in 1994. The second, 'Chimera' was held in Sydney in 1995 with presentations by a range of practitioners including Wochenklauser, an artists' collective based in Austria, and the keynote address given by Professor Bruce Barber from the Nova Scotia

School of Art and Design. The third Littoral conference, 'Critical Sites: Issues in Critical Art Practice and Pedagogy' was held at the Institute of Art, Design and Technology, Dun Laoghaire, Dublin in 1998.

[6] Following 'Unspoken Truths' the Family Resource Centre went on to work with a number of different artists in the context of the Education and Community Department of IMMA. These projects were more short term. For example, the Family Resource Centre men's group worked with American artist John Ahern when he was on the Artist Work Programme and with the Irish artist and filmmaker Joe Lee, who was working closely with the Education and Community Department of IMMA. A number of the women also worked with Canadian artist Rochelle Rubenstein Kaplan when she was on the Artist Work Programme, to make work about the issue of violence against women.

[7] Women's Aid is a voluntary organisation that provides a range of services to women experiencing male violence and abuse. Women's Aid has worked closely with a number of community development organisations in developing training and education programmes, in particular the Family Resource Centre. The Women's Aid Community Development Support Agency was set up in 1998 and is funded by the Department of Social, Community and Family Affairs.

[8] The four artists were Joe Lee (from Dublin), Rhona Henderson (from Dublin), Rochelle Rubenstein Kaplan (from Canada) and myself (from Dublin).

[9] This reflection took the form of 'The Conversations Project', which was a research project engaging with a number of practitioners, curators, critics and community development workers with an interest or direct involvement in the field of collaborative art practice. The premise of this research was to critically reflect on my own experience of community-based arts and to examine that experience within the broader context of collaborative art practice, nationally and internationally. The research took the form of a series of conversations with key individuals and afforded me the opportunity to participate in a number of fora in the context of other collaborative initiatives over a two-year period. 'The Conversations Project' was funded through the Arts Council's Community Artist's Development Fund

[10] Specifically I visited inSITE 2000, a biennial public art programme which takes place throughout the San Diego/Tijuana region. Thirty artists were commissioned to make work in response to the region, with many of the works addressing the particular context of the USA/Mexico border. As part of the programme, inSITE 2000 organised a series of conversation weekends. Conversation IV (Feb

2002) was titled 'Image Power: Cultural Interventions as Public
Memory in Post-Modern Spaces' and it brought together cultural
anthropologists, sociologists, artists and critics to discuss the work of
artist Krzyzstof Wodiczko with the participation of the women's
organisation Factor X in Tijuana. This 'conversation' followed two
nights of Wodiczko's projections on the Centro Cultural in Tijuana. I
subsequently returned to Tijuana a year later to meet with Factor X to
discuss their experience as collaborators in the project. As part of this
trip myself and Rita Fagan, the Director of the Family Resource
Centre, were invited by Mary Jane Jacob to present an overview of our
work together at the School of Art Institute in Chicago. These fora
presented me with valuable opportunities to reflect on international
collaborative and public arts practice.

[11] The Per Cent for Art Scheme was first introduced in Ireland in 1988 by
the Department of Environment and Local Government. It allows for
1 per cent (up to a current maximum of €63,486) on any public-
housing construction budget, either new build or repairs or
maintenance, to be spent on commissioning art. Funds may be pooled
to allow for major commissions and diversity in the nature of public
art commissioned under the scheme is encouraged. The Arts Council
of Ireland is currently drawing up a set of National Guidelines for the
use and future development of the Per Cent for Art Scheme.

[12] Flann O'Brien (1975), *The Best of Myles na Gopaleen*, Picador, London, p.
182.

References

Drury, Martin (1996), 'The Muse and the Mute' in *Unspoken Truths*, Irish
Museum of Modern Art, Dublin.

Kester, Grant (1998), 'Dialogical Aesthetics: A Critical Framework for
Littoral Art', presented at the conference 'Critical Sites: Issues in
Critical Art Practice and Pedagogy' at the Institute of Art, Design and
Technology, Dun Laoghaire, Dublin.

Kwon, Miwon (2002), *One Place after Another: Site-Specific Art and Locational
Identity*, MIT Press, Cambridge Massachusetts.

Murphy, Ailbhe (1994), *Artists' Work Programme Catalogue*, Irish Museum of
Modern Art, Dublin.

Murphy, Ailbhe, et al., eds. (1996) *Unspoken Truths*, Irish Museum of
Modern Art, Dublin.

O'Brien, Flann (1975), *The Best of Myles na Gopaleen*, Picador, London.

Access, authorship, participation and ownership

(much-disputed definition of community arts, but still the only one that works!)

WILL CHAMBERLAIN

Five years ago community arts in Northern Ireland was in the ascendancy – a militant, eloquent and vocal sector growing in size and growing in confidence. We were convinced that the inequalities regarding funding and esteem would soon begin to be rectified. With the election of an assembly of MLAs representing local communities, surely great things would follow. Demonstration through the streets of Belfast to the doors of the new Department for Culture Arts and Leisure (DCAL) was swiftly followed by the first real increase in funding for community arts in a decade. *The Wedding Community Play* focused the eyes of the arts world on our work and the public was increasingly aware of the powerful impact engagement with community arts could have. The appointment of three respected community arts practitioners onto the new Arts Council board surely put the seal on it. Things were going to be different from now on. Many grumblings were heard from the traditionally well-funded sectors of the arts world. The barbarians were not just at the gates, but somebody had started inviting them in for tea and biccies. Surely it was just a matter of time before the much-heralded Targeting of Social Need became a real factor in deciding where arts resources would be directed. In a short time we would see artists and organisations who put people at the heart of their work flourish with long-term investment. Who knows, perhaps we would finally see the renaissance for the arts that we all knew was possible if enough people committed themselves to pursuing the community arts mantra of access, authorship, participation and ownership.

Five years later, there are few in the sector who would claim that the promise has been fulfilled. Parity of esteem and equitable funding still feel a long way off. Of course, the arts will always wrestle over the issue of scarce resources when there is no limit to the potential levels of expenditure, but the apparent inequitable distributions of resources continues to disadvantage community arts to the degree that the debate over resources continues to dominate the sector.

In my own practice, it is the single issue that dominates year after year and the absence of sufficient funding from government means that my time is taken up with chasing the necessary resources to present a full programme of community circus that is accessible across Northern Ireland – in a context of funding for the arts where an independent theatre company receives more money to safeguard administrative support for one production a year than my organisation (Belfast Community Circus School) receives for presenting one major production each year, a central youth circus training programme for forty weeks a year, a circus training programme for adults for forty-five weeks of the year, an outreach programme working with twenty-five groups of young people from many of the most margnialised communities in our society over the year, providing professional development for artists and community circus teachers and so on. I'm sure you get the picture. It's not a level playing field and our ability to maximise the potential for community arts is severely impeded. For this reason, the thrust of this essay will focus on the resource debate rather than the amazing results that are being seen from community arts work.

Here in Northern Ireland, we have a situation where the arts are, in any case, viewed as luxury goods. Any reference to public funding for the arts in the media always talks of it as a 'windfall' or 'cash bonanza', summoning up images of indolent artists rolling around in lorry-loads of lolly. Historically, the arts have been seen by governments as something ethereal, which doesn't really have an impact on real life – something which is not readily understandable by your average person in the street. As a result the arts were left to a cultural élite to dominate. We have seen many groups that were supported by the first round of EU Peace funding fade from existence – victims of, amongst other things, extraordinary incompetence at government level over the almost criminally inept and bureaucratic phasing in of the second round of EU Peace money. The impact of this 'transition' was wilfully ignored by DCAL, despite evidence produced by their own research department that showed the devastating impact on activity levels and employment in the sector. Of course, there are organisations (including the Belfast Community Circus School) that have grown and thrived over this period of time and support has been received from various government agencies. However, the sustainability of these organisations has been achieved through the sourcing and securing of funds from a range of trusts, foundations and entrepreneurial activity rather than through the fabled 'mainstreaming'. There are, we are told, more resources available for community arts now than ever before, but the fact is that most funding is in the form of the smallest of grants schemes. It would seem that community arts is being encouraged so long as it doesn't get above itself and start nurturing any grand ambitions.

So, here we are, following another assembly election, and the sense of anticipation has long since dissipated to be replaced by the old companions of community arts: frustration and disappointment tinged with anger. But now, there is a new feeling and one that is felt by many of those who were at the forefront of the struggle for recognition – the feeling of exhaustion. Trying to get a voice heard is never easy, but when it's talking about the disenfranchised and marginalised members of our society – 'Puhleeease! We've got better things to do with our time. We're trying to run a business (I mean country) here.' So five years after the doors were thrown open, it would now appear that these doors simply led to an elaborate waiting-room where the receptionist keeps popping her head round the door to apologise for the delay and to say that it won't be long now. What has been going on with community arts in Northern Ireland over the past five years?

On the plus side, it would seem to me that standards within the sector have generally continued to improve as we all spend more time dedicating ourselves to our work. Communities are now much better informed than they were, with a greater awareness of the kind of projects they could create, the range and standards of provision available and what kind of outcomes they can expect. The larger provision organisations have grown stronger and appear more sustainable simply by virtue of their longevity and the resourcefulness shown in finding the funds necessary to ensure survival thus far. The range and complexity of projects being undertaken has grown in many instances as has the depth of partnerships with local communities – indeed more centres are

Cross-community project, Crumlin Road, north Belfast, 1997.
Photo: Belfast Exposed

employing community arts to build capacity in a community, with some even employing full-time community artists to help realise the creative and expressive potential that lies within every individual. For much of the past five years the community arts agenda in Northern Ireland has largely been driven from Belfast with the Community Arts Forum (CAF) setting the tone for many years with the dissemination of a community arts ethos and practice amongst smaller and emerging groups and initiatives: organisations such as WheelWorks, combining art forms and working with young people in a manner that enabled new forms of self expression about the issues which concern them; Northern Visions and the expansion into community media to give ordinary voices an audience beyond their own community; and, of course, Belfast Community Circus School, which has employed the process of community arts across the entire circus spectrum to ensure that commercial and professional ventures provide community opportunities. Most of the community arts organisations which operate on a regional/national basis have their roots in Belfast, perhaps because of the concentration of population, but I feel that, more than that, there is a combination of radicalism and mutual support that drives individuals and organisations forward.

The downside over the past number of years is that we have seen many smaller provision and facilitation organisations in the sector fall away as funds have been withdrawn or not replaced (for many community arts initiatives, EU Peace money breathed life into them and provided the kiss of death as the transition to Peace II was handled by government with all the finesse of an elephant tap-dancing); many communities have found resources harder to secure for anything which deviates from IT learning and basic numeracy/literacy skills. Analysis of funding levels from the Arts Council of Northern Ireland shows that the level of funding support is still far from equal with other sectors (hence the need for access to private trusts and foundations for survival). Despite sustained increases in levels of provision from many organisations, that growth has not been rewarded with a proportionate increase in funding. In most instances, the growth is being delivered through an increase in workloads for the same number of employees, leading to burnout. It should be pointed out that the demand for community arts continues to grow apace whilst other forms of artistic practice continue to find it difficult to maintain audience levels. The Arts Council of Northern Ireland itself has changed, with the new Council having only one community arts practitioner on the board and a much greater representation from the 'mainstream' supporters.

On the face of things, community arts should be thriving. One of the key factors that is supposed to be present in all public expenditure is Targeting Social Need (TSN). Much heralded when New Labour came to power, it should have seen a massive investment in community arts in Northern Ireland, given that much of the activity was located in areas of highest social need. Another aspiration that would appear to favour community arts is the determination of DCAL, along with the departments for Education, Employment and Trade and Investment, to 'unlock creativity', something which the sector has been doing succ-essfully for so many years through the process of engagement with large swathes of the population historically distanced from 'mainstream arts'. So why, in the face of such a promising climate for community arts, has so little progress been made?

It has never been clear to me how TSN works. OK, so all govern-ment expenditure is supposed to be weighted to take into account that certain areas experience serious deprivation in terms of income, employment, health and education. Policy is supposed to reflect this concern and to ensure that overall expenditure is skewed to assist in eradicating the inequality in social need. A good theory, but what are the mechanics? Is there a statistical analysis that can be applied to check whether this is happening? Is all expenditure supposed to address this equally? Is there any mechanism for measuring the impact of expenditure on reducing the level of social need? The answer to the last three questions would seem to be no, no and no, from the evidence of experience. There appears to be neither quantitative, nor qualitative evidence available in relation to TSN and the arts. So what is going on here? Is TSN being interpreted as *any* expenditure, which takes place in these areas, counts as targeting the need? I suspect this to be the case. I suspect that a one-off performance in an area of high social need means that boxes can be ticked, obligations can be seen as being met and everyone can carry on as before. I suspect that too many organisations within the arts world see this as a box-ticking exercise and as a result we have a proliferation of education and outreach workers with every large organisation (and in some sectors even quite small organisations have all the trappings).

It is hard to blame organisations for adopting this approach when they feel it necessary to continue to access the level of public funding they seek, but it is time to start being honest about this one. The type of interventions offered within these models is not core to the work of the organisations. They do not exist to improve social conditions or to provide access to personal expression and creativity. Many performing arts organisations are about recreation and interpretation, not about primary creativity for individuals. The community arts sector, on the other hand, occupies the other end of the spectrum. It is about encouraging individuals to explore what they have to say and to find a vehicle for that voice. In doing so, community arts deliberately seeks to give individuals and communities access to methods of improving their situation and addressing the issues which contribute to social need. Given that this is self-evidently true, it is time that government/DCAL got honest about TSN and acknowledged that there are some organisations within the arts sphere that are capable of delivering as a core commitment and there are others that would rather be focusing on investing in their own performance. This is not to say that resources should solely be given to community arts to address social need, but there needs to be recognition that different sectors have very different things to offer in this respect and that community arts organisations should receive additional funding to support their work. With regards to the 'groundbreaking initiative' whereby four departments come together to unlock the creativity of the people (particularly young people) we need to look at what is really happening here. There is no intrinsic value being attached by government here to creativity itself. No, the exercise is driven by economics. This is all about wealth creation, not artistic creation. Let's face it, governments are never going to encourage the people to think for themselves, certainly not those people most marginalised in our society. What if they began to think that the government was badly letting them down? So an initiative that could have looked as if it could provide assistance for community arts to encourage creativity and imaginative thinking amongst the most neglected sections of society is in fact more interested in the other end of the spectrum, those who can create wealth.

There are other initiatives where opportunities for harnessing the experience and enthusiasm of the community arts sector have been spurned in favour of more conservative models of arts practice with the result that the most disadvantaged in our society will not experience the benefits of public expenditure. So, why does this happen? What is the pattern here? It appears to me that there are two main reasons for this happening time and again. First, the way in which government operates is so hierarchical that any notion that the people affected by initiatives should somehow be involved in drawing them up in any meaningful way poses a threat. After all, if the people can do it better than government, doesn't that make it rather difficult for those in government to justify their own jobs? I suspect it is also quite reassuring to exercise power – after all, by imposing a situation on others, you are confirming to them and to yourself that you know better than they do. The challenge here is to persuade, demonstrate, convince government that they actually end up with a much better model – one devised by the people for the people – if there is an openness of approach and disclosure than if they try to do it all by themselves. This holds particularly true of the arts where the level of expertise is often extremely limited. If government could be persuaded of the virtues of this model then there is little doubt that they would also begin to recognise the advantages that lie behind community arts as an approach and a process.

The other, and perhaps more important, reason is that the arts continue to be seen as a commodity rather than an experience. This leads to the value placed on them being defined in terms of direct revenue and employment they can generate rather than any holistic assessment of their impact. The language being used to justify the expenditure on the arts is increasingly simplified in terms of cultural tourism, economic impact, and so on. It is almost unheard of for politicians to extol the virtues of the arts in terms of the impact on individuals or enhancing the quality of life. I suspect that this is frustrating for people right across the arts world, but it is more worrying for those in the community arts sector simply because the investment goes into a process and the success is judged on the impact of that process rather than on the ability to entice good box-office figures. So important decisions are being made about huge investments in the arts (including major new projects) based on economic assessments and business plans that focus on revenue-generating capacity and leave no space whatsoever for community arts, which, economically speaking, would just show up as a deficit on the budget sheet.

Now, of course there is nothing wrong with huge investments in the arts, but money can only be spent once and we have the most limited arts budget in the UK and Ireland. This means that if you spend it all on the business model, community arts will cease to be supported altogether. I am sure that few in the arts world are delighted with this form of decision-making, but it is only community arts that will be excluded through this method. I would argue that it is imperative that government begins, as a matter of urgency, to ascribe economic value to the work done by the community arts sector. The argument here is that there is no data to back up any valuation, but it is hardly the fault of a chronically underfunded sector that it hasn't been able to translate the social and community benefits seen from community arts work into financial equivalents. I would argue that a provisional method of calculation be agreed between the sector and government to give the sector the parity of bargaining when it comes to bidding for funding. This method can then be employed until it is replaced by properly funded and researched data.

Of course, it would be wrong of me to suggest that the business model was being deliberately employed to serve the purpose of those who believe that community arts should be pushed aside and that certain 'mainstream arts' are the only ones worthy of funding through the arts. It's clear that the business model is imposed throughout government these days, but it is also clear that there is still a huge imbalance in the arts world with regards to resource allocation and access. Part of the imbalance, as I've said, comes from the business-model approach, but there is a huge element which derives from a very strong bias held by many of the 'great and the good', which is that community arts doesn't really count when it comes to allocation of resources for the arts. There is a hugely powerful body of opinion within the funding world that believes certain forms are better than others and that we have our very own set of untouchables. It sometimes appears that the more élite the artistic practice, the less need to demonstrate its value and the more money it is given. So we, in the community arts sector, are left to dive through innumerable hoops to claim our share of the remaining crumbs. In a world of limited resources we have to ask ourselves whether we can continue to justify spending 25 per cent of annual ACNI expenditure on one organisation with an elderly audience drawn almost exclusively from the middle and upper classes at a subsidy of around £40 for each ticket sold. Surely, in the twenty-first century, the smart approach is to ensure that such exclusivity becomes a thing of the past. There are a number of ways to do this – increase audiences dramatically and broaden their demographic; reduce public subsidy dramatically; increase expenditure in other areas of the arts. Let's face it, if we were talking health or education here we would not be suggesting such an inequitable spend on items of social class or percentages. However, the arts remains a bastion of prejudice, which is somehow seen as justifiable by otherwise sane and reasonable people. It's as if we are expected to accept that art is a privilege and not a right.

Furthermore, there appears to be widespread media complicity that fails to question public money being spent on minority pursuits because the purveyors of the news are the self-same élite who enjoy the highly subsidised arts. Don't misunderstand me: I am not arguing that arts that aren't accessible to all should not be funded at all; but I do believe that the assumptions that inform arts funding need to be done away with and a new basis for resource allocation needs to emerge. At present, we appear to be in a situation where certain art forms and approaches to creating art need to do no more than exist to prove their worthiness, whereas community arts is constantly having to prove itself in a myriad ways – from number-crunching through to proving outcomes and impacts – before we can be considered for a minor slice of the pie. It's not an easy issue, but it is time that it was debated and addressed in light of the world we live in, not the world our grandparents were born into. It's a scary thing to do, but it might be one way of making the arts more relevant and understandable to many people in our society. It's worth bearing in mind also that all sides have strong arguments to advance and that the arts could emerge at the other end of the process with stronger support all round and a greater commitment from people to invest and investigate for themselves.

It also strikes me that, while we are questioning the way the arts function, we could have a little look at the way the arts model in

Northern Ireland seems to be so closely based on the English perspective. At this moment in our history, we have an opportunity to define our own values and methods of delivery. Instead, every major initiative comes across to Northern Ireland a few years after it's been done in England and then implemented without recognition that we are not England. Northern Ireland can realign itself with other models within the world if we wish and I would argue that any realignment takes into account the unique strengths of the community arts sector in Northern Ireland instead of being led by civil servants immersed in a culture where initiative, creativity and risk taking are seen as dangerous qualities to exhibit. If people were faced with a choice between the élitist and often joyless approach to the arts seen in Northern Ireland or the all-embracing face of culture and the near-universal rejoicing in and celebration of the arts in, say, France, it is hard to see many people opting to continue down the path we are on. Certainly, if my experience of encounters with European colleagues is anything to go by, community arts would benefit enormously from the subvention practised on the Continent. The two things I hear from these colleagues in relation to the work of the Community Circus are praise for the quality and volume of work carried out and astonishment that this work is not directly and fully supported by the local and regional government.

It seems to me that, after all these years, we are still facing a situation where ignorance about community arts abounds amongst those holding the purse strings, whilst awareness on local level has grown and this has led to increased demand without increased levels of support. Of course we have made progress over the past five years, but it remains the case that the sector is still waiting to be understood and embraced. If this is to be achieved, we will have to muster our collective forces once again and shout loud and clear about what we bring to the table and why we should be supported. We will have to articulate that, but we also have to find people who are prepared to listen. I believe, as I always have done, that if it were understood what community arts does and the contribution it can make to this society, then we would be able to play a hugely valuable role in defining a distinct and diverse cultural future for this part of our world.

So, one last time, with feeling now …

Notes on a practice

BRIAN MAGUIRE

What follows is a personal story. I was a student at the NCA (National College of Art) from 1969 to 1974. It was a period when collective action by students and some staff forced the ending of a system of management of the college by the Department of Education, together with involvement by members of the officer board of the RHA (Royal Hibernian Academy). This arrangement was replaced by a board established under an act of the Oireachtas. Engagement with a political dispute over a period of five years brings about an active relationship with many issues, including those of power, solidarity and class; communication, media and group dynamics; confidence, bullying and manipulation. These issues, rather than the history of art or aesthetics, formed the intellectual basis for the education we received. The college at this time was based in the stables of Leinster House, Kildare Street. Its proximity to the houses of the Oireachtas was a strong contributing factor to its politicisation. Experiencing ethics as practical problems needing solutions suits painters whose expression is practice as against pure theory. Franz Fannon, Paolo Freire and Bobby Seal were writers whose works gave a context. The other big influence of the time was the civil rights movement in Northern Ireland and the subsequent state repression. At this time the Irish artist Brian O'Doherty changed his name to Patrick Ireland in protest at the murders of civil rights marchers in Derry by units of the British Army.

There is a contradiction between methods of agitation and the activity of painting, the necessary studio condition of isolation seemed at odds with everything that I was experiencing. Painting seemed to me to be a history of the ruling class both at ease and at war and also a kind of pleasant bank vault. Berger's not so simple book *Ways of Seeing* deals with this while it conversely shows that, at other times, painting can communicate timeless human conditions. An important event that had lasting influence was a lecture given by Joseph Beúys in the Hugh Lane Municipal Gallery of Modern Art, Dublin, in the early 1970s. This lecture was part of a major exhibition by Beúys, including drawings, mixed media pieces and performances. While I found the specifics of the lecture difficult, there was no missing the linkage of politics, art, government and personal fate. This has remained with me as a sounding board.

After leaving college I stopped painting, partly due to being disillusioned with what I saw of the gallery system, both public and private. It all seemed to confirm the painted object as an exchange item. The whole business was presented as if it was an *Irish Times* page three! But this is all reflective and one doesn't lead a life in reflection. Eventually, waiting at four in the morning, one begins to draw some man in a room for no reason at all. Painting was for me a private means of confirming reality.

In the early 1980s I began to work in a studio in Dublin. I supported this work by exhibiting in a gallery. This arrangement of trying to live from one's work was a more responsible approach than not working. The German communist Brecht had written of the duty of the artist to make his/her own living. At this time my primary interest in painting was in the making of a work. The subjects of the exhibitions ranged from fathers and their children to the war in the north, addiction and childhood. The work from those early years was shown in the Douglas Hyde Gallery in 1988 with a critical essay by Donald Kuspit. His contention was that this form of painting could be understood within a psychoanalytical context. This connected with my own understanding of existentialism. Another view saw it as a history of the Worker's Party. From the point of view of this essay, the painting was still coming from within a studio. The audience was outside; their role was passive and came at the conclusion of the making.

I had a show in Wexford Arts Centre during the opera festival around this time. The Wexford Arts Centre asked that I do a number of workshops with a group of young people who were judged not socially compliant enough to be in school. There were many groups like this one, in high-population areas, funded by FÁS at that time. I was similarly invited to work with groups of young people in the inner cities of Dublin and Cork. I recall the expressed intention by these groups' management was to assist the establishment of a process of socialisation for the young people. Recently, teachers used this word to describe the education of asylum seekers. I felt it was like, when all else fails, bring on the art. Of course, when treated with respect and an attempted understanding, the need for socialisation vanishes. On the other hand the need for education is always there.

My memory of Wexford is of attending the opera (the exhibition fee was a ticket), a tiny, two-hundred-seat theatre presenting an obscure German opera, with a Finn, the day after meeting a pregnant fifteen-year-old orphan in the FÁS group. The connection between both is tenuous until one considers the investment and judgement criteria the state makes in both cases. From my viewpoint, a different experience of art was being presented to and understood by the teenagers and the opera-goers. While I enjoy, to this day, the aftertaste of that opera, my sense of reality comes from the young orphan.

In 1986, I was asked by the Arts Council to do a pilot workshop in Portlaoise Prison. The prison at this time held political prisoners sentenced by the special criminal court. This prison's population has since grown to include non-political prisoners. Over the next decade I did workshops of around four weeks' duration in most prisons in the state, in some cases returning to do projects a second or third time. In Portlaoise Prison, the NCAD (National College of Art and Design) established a course in which I have been teaching since 1988. I was aware of comments like the one from the Master of one of Dublin's Maternity Hospitals where he maintained that the family's address would indicate a baby's likelihood of ending up as an adult in prison. If prison was the university of the republicans, for the rest of its population it seemed to have a predetermined place in their lives. The men came from the same urban estates throughout Ireland, with similar educational backgrounds. It's the same in other countries except that in the USA the colour of one's skin as well as one's address is the indicator for jail. Ostensibly jails are society's response to an individual's specific criminal actions. The prisons are, in themselves, the largest criminal action we have in society. The prisons, with the honourable exceptions of Holland and the Scandinavian countries, are the most important ingredient in a process of criminalising people. The prisons are a growth industry in the past decade, but for all the money spent, very little is used to address the underlying causes of crime. The people who deliver educational programs in prison are working in a context that is committed to undermining their work. In our regime, the man leaving

'When people hear about "crimes against humanity", they immediately think of a war torn country in whatever part of the world it is happening in at that moment. When I think of crimes against humanity, I think of the Women, the Children and the Men that can be violated and brutalised in their own homes or on the streets of any city in the world, whether it would be for the colour of their skin or their religious beliefs. The victims of crime, abuse or war atrocities have to live with the legacy of the perpetrator's actions and find some way to carry on with their lives. Some survive to tell the story and that's the hope we as victims and survivors hold on to, that our story will be told, thus enabling us to try and make some kind of life for ourselves and our families.' Artist Tony Crosbie from his exhibition catalogue Crimes Against Humanity, City Arts Centre, 1999

is marked as unemployable with no new or different skills to negotiate his passage in society other than those he had when he began his term.

The work in the prison is very honourable where it helps facilitate a physical and mental space for self-expression. This establishes a counterpoint to the process of prison. This was the intention of the NCAD course. To educate is to draw out. Art is particularly important where sensory deprivation occurs. There was a welcome for the classes in art in jails here and abroad. A non-academic vocational approach is real and involved the artist doing the same work as the men. This led to a series of observations – for example, the involvement of the men, both as subjects and doers, marked the process as different. In recent years, video is available as well as the more traditional media. In whatever media, the process is one of self-actualisation.

Working in the prison affected my work. I made a group of large canvases that showed the conditions in the prison. This was a simple matter of painting the architecture of the jails. This architecture is unique in that it contains both its practical purpose and its reason, its emotional content. Having done these paintings I wanted to go beyond the physical place and say something about the system and the people kept there. I wanted to acknowledge the men serving their time and comment on the bureaucratic process that runs these places. This involved a group of men from Limerick's A wing, Spike Island and E1, E3 and E4 in Portlaoise Prison who agreed to sit for a portrait in the knowledge that the paintings would be filmed with a voice-over of the current rules for the operation of prisons, as adopted in 1947. This work, *Predgedical Portraits*, was the first time I negotiated a work with others. I continued to make some paintings that connected to the jails. I use these paintings to introduce myself to new groups of prisoners with slide shows. In 2002, in Antwerp, I gave a lecture on consecutive days in the local art college and in the local prison. There was a polite ten-minute discourse in the art school and a two-hour animated discussion in the prison. This experience underlined for me the fact that I had an audience for these works.

In tandem with this work I was asked to make a project by the Orchard Gallery in 1993 in Gransha Hospital, the mental-health institution in Derry. I used the format of portraiture, as the question of being a mental patient always revolved, for me, around the issue of individual human rights. This was formed when, as a student, I was party to a café discussion by slightly older medical students around whether mental patients should be allowed to have sex with each other. I was horrified at the arrogance of the medical students who seemed to think they had god-like authority over the private life of the ill. Portraiture was attractive to me because it underlines the individual authority of the sitter. It is primarily an act of respect for the sitter. This is understood by all classes and ages, world-wide.

In the prisons, the concept of normalisation was being adopted at this time by the EU. This meant whatever is normal on the outside is replicated, where possible, on the inside. With a nod to this policy I set up a studio easel in the day-room of Gransha and waited. About one-third of the patients presented themselves for their portrait. An interview with one person, Anne, accompanied the showing of the works in the Orchard Gallery across the river in Derry. This interview gives a clear perspective on what it was like to be a mental patient in Derry in 1993. By just quietly moving this project along I had arrived at a way of working which involved the other in the making.

The value of the work in Gransha was confirmed in the responses of those whose experience was similar to the residents of the day-room. The use of portraiture is a means to both personalise the process and use the status-baring nature of the portrait to give a shift to the perception of the social position of the sitter. In a way, a prejudice located in the mind of the viewer both changes and charges the work. This was the basis for the public showings of the Gransha Project and later the Casa De Cultura project in Brazil, which emerged from these early experiences and became part of my ongoing practice. The Brazilian projects in 1998 and 2000, Casa de Cultura and Favela Vila Prudente and Dario Popular, were gestures of solidarity. The first two involved local people in the *favela* Vile Prudente in Sao Paulo. The latter project was derived from the local newspaper. They both involved a series of negotiation. As in earlier projects, portraiture was a central means. Ownership of the artworks stayed with the sitters. To allow the work to travel a second drawing was made. The *favela* came to the Biennial by means of these works and their loan to the Biennial. Visits and workshops in Sao Paulo's Carandiru Detention Centre (today a subject of a brilliant film *Carandiru*) brought the circle to a close, where eyewitness accounts and survivors' memories of that 1992 massacre were the basis for the work *Memorial*.

Diario Popular Drawings (12.3.98) by Brian Maguire. Mixed media on paper 50 x 70 cm. *Kerlin Gallery, Dublin*

The next projects were again in jails: Long Kesh, outside Belfast, in 1999 and in the Bayview Prison in Chelsea, New York, 2000–2002. In Long Kesh the idea was to celebrate the return of the prisoners to their community. Posters and billboards were done in east Belfast and at the top of the Shankill Road. And an exhibition was held on prisoners' day in The Felons' Club, west Belfast. This work uncovered the real hypocrisy and distaste the authorities had for the prisoners on all sides. I still work with the people from east Belfast on community projects. Ormeau Baths Gallery commissioned the work and exhibited the results. The Bayview Project was one where eighteen women held in Bayview Corrections Centre, Twentieth Street East, Manhattan, worked for under two years making a series of works which were descriptions of important events in their lives. The drawings and portraits I made during that time were shown in the White Box in Chelsea. A sixty-foot billboard, at the traffic entry to Twentieth Street on Tenth Avenue, advertised the show for two months. The White Box, working with the project's curator Fergus McCaffery, had asked that I bring knowledge of the prison to the art world and knowledge of art to the prisoners. The show had the political effect of reversing a ban on prisoners' exhibitions imposed by Governor Patacki's office in March 2001. The director of the White Box, Juan Pontes, was supported in this achievment by the New York Branch of the American Council of Civil Liberty's lawyer, Cris Dunn. Exhibiting the women's work and my own was a shift in my practice. In the most recent work (2003/4), a public art project in Geel in Belgium, the participants and I work on the same images, which become lithographs printed by Jacque Champhlurie in Paris.

I think there is some crossover in terms of public presentation between the studio work of paintings and drawings and the collaborations. Both contain elements of performance, content and intention. Both stem from the attempt to integrate art into life and vice versa, the art-life project. Both are based firmly on the aesthetic surface of painting and drawing. This seems a contradiction in the positioning of, for example, painting and collaborative performance. Earlier I mentioned Joseph Beúys' drawings and his performative blackboard lecture in the Hugh Lane Gallery and these contradictory approaches were seamless. Contradictions are there only to be resolved.

The political viewpoint that drives my work has developed over many years from active engagement in all levels of politics. These concerns have informed my work rather than the dominant changes in art theory and practice. The dominant change in the politics of the late 1980s and 1990s has been the change from the model of class war to one of class dialogue, with its consequences from on one level the peace process and on another level the enlargement of the EU. This is played out in many communities at local level. This is very apparent in Sao Paulo where theatre is used to explore the contradictions between poor and rich and in the work of Raul Araujo and his group Mudanca do Cena, which teased out the contradictions between the prisoners, men and women and the prison guards in the penal system, presenting the performances not in the prison Chapel but in the auditorium of the Parliament of Latin America in Sao Paulo.

While working on projects with Gae Lairn in east Belfast from 1999 to today, we were both engaged in a very modest and individual way to reposition a republican and loyalist antagonism by seeking out points of

'Adults and children sometimes have boards in their bedrooms or living-rooms on which they pin pieces of paper: letters, snapshots, reproductions of paintings, newspaper cuttings, original drawings, postcards. On each board all the images belong to the same language and all are more or less equal within it, because they have been chosen in a highly personal way to match and express the experiences of the room's inhabitant. Logically, these boards should replace museums.' John Berger, *Ways of Seeing*, Pelican, 1972

agreement and mutual support. The work I have done in the mental hospitals in Northern Ireland and in Belgium has a similar template in that the process leads to the breaking down of the barriers between the patient and the citizen in the local area. In these works there is a two-part strategy, one which is internal to the group, and this is self contained and sufficient; the second strategy is when a work derived from the first stage goes into the public domain. This representation requires the agreement of all involved. The first strategy is one where the work is made collaboratively by the audience for the work – in most cases the end product is only a part of the process.

Of course there are problems – for example, where people were hurt and this hurt can be re-aroused, as happened when an image of Michael Stone was shown as part of a work in progress in the Ormeau Baths Gallery in 1999. This question of the victim has been addressed by those working against the death penalty in the US and recently by those Americans actively opposing the war in Iraq. Steve Earle spoke recently about using the model of respect for the victims, while resisting the operation of the death penalty as the template for supporting the soldiers, while resisting the US government's involvement in the affairs of Iraq.

The structure of these notes has been to attempt a description of the development of my practice and to offer a brief overview. That it has been written in the middle of a European-election campaign doesn't help a situation that is already fraught with subjectivity. There are some simple points I'd like to underline. Art always begins at the personal and intimate; it has got a process, and usually this is empathetic and collaborative; it is concerned with generating and expressing solidarity in its widest meaning. Its aesthetic is usually its honesty; its context is often hostile. Its intention is argumentative. Its means is beauty. It is usually ineffective.

COMMUNITY ARTS FORUM 2
CORK, 13 OCTOBER 2003

See introductory note to Historical Forum on p.5

Parade of Innocence, Dublin, 1989.
Photo: Derek Speirs/Report

Contemporary forum

Participants

Val Ballance, Emma Bowell, Heather Floyd, Declan Gorman, Lynne McCarthy, Niall O'Baoill, Tony Sheehan, Conor Shields, Wes Wilkie.

Chairperson

Doireann Ní Bhriain (assisted by Susan Coughlan).

Participants' biographies

Val Ballance founded the Iniscealtra Festival with Nicola Henley in 1996. In 2000 Val founded Áras Éanna, an arts centre on the small Irish-speaking island of Inisheer in the group of islands known as Árann off the west coast of Ireland, developing it as a contemporary arts centre with artists-in-residence, concerts, theatre and dance.

Emma Bowell is a film-maker working primarily in community-based films and documentaries. With a background in theatre and film, she set up Frameworks Films in 1999 with fellow film-maker and community arts practitioner Eddie Noonan. In her work for Frameworks, Emma facilitates film-making workshops in schools and community settings and works in a variety of roles on collaborative film productions within the community. She is actively involved in the development of both community arts and community media in Cork.

Heather Floyd has worked in the Community Arts Forum (CAF) for the past five years, first as training officer and subsequently as director. She came to CAF from a community education background, having worked in Shankill Women's Centre for eight years developing educational and cultural programmes.

Declan Gorman is artistic director and resident writer with Upstate Theatre Project, Drogheda, a professional touring and community theatre company. He was formerly an actor and producer with Co-Motion Theatre Company, Dublin (1985–90); development officer at City Arts Centre (1990–95); and co-ordinator of the Arts Council Theatre Review 1995–96. He is a recipient of a Stewart Parker playwriting award for his first play, *Hades* (1999), and he occasionally lectures and writes in various journals on arts policy matters. He is currently a member of the board of City Arts Centre.

Lynne McCarthy graduated from Trinity with a BA Hons degree in Drama and Theatre Studies in 1998. She began work as a community artist for Macnas (1999–2001), in the capacity of performance director for projects including Clifden Community Arts Week, the Bealtaine Festival, Newbridge, Kildare, and as assistant director on the Galway Arts Festival Parades 'Cargo de Nuit' (1999) and 'The Listening Wind' (2000). Lynne has worked with one-third of Irish secondary schools through the Coca-Cola Form and Fusion Design Awards, which she directed in 2001. Since 1999 Lynne has developed a professional relationship with Cork Community Artlink, collaborating with them on site-specific, participatory arts projects, the most recent of which was 'The Difference Engine'.

Niall O'Baoill is a founder and director of Wet Paint – a seminal youth arts organisation established in 1984. He has since been active in policy, education/training and programming initiatives related to participatory culture. He is currently the arts and culture co-ordinator in Fatima Mansions – a distinct community-led regeneration process in the south-west inner city of Dublin – and is chairperson of City Arts and The Civil Arts Inquiry.

Tony Sheehan is director of Community Based Projects for Cork 2005, the company established to manage Cork's designation as Europe's Capital of Culture. Previously he was director of the Fire Station Artists Studios in Dublin. He is also involved in community development organisations and continues to work with the Inner City Renewal Group in Dublin, which he chairs.

Conor Shields is a proud Belfast man and an experienced musical performer and songwriter, who has contributed to a variety of bands and recordings over the last twenty years. He has conducted workshops for community groups and in prisons and has worked with various theatre companies (Vesuvius, Tinderbox, Rapid House). Conor has also made documentaries, worked in television news and is now the programme director of New Belfast Community Arts Initiative, a city-wide pro-gramme working in over eighty communities in the Belfast area, employing more than ninety artists per year.

Wes Wilkie comes from Liverpool, UK. After five years as an arts development officer with Liverpool City Council, he became the director of The Centre for Arts Development Training, Liverpool, in 1995. He has been the executive director of CREATE since 1999.

Doireann Ní Bhriain: Do you all share the notion that community arts is what you're involved in at the moment and that it's important and if so why?

Heather Floyd: The CAF [Community Arts Forum – Northern Ireland] definition of community arts is an original artwork that contains significant elements of access, participation, authorship and ownership.

Doireann Ní Bhriain: Is that definition very important?

Heather Floyd: Very important, yes.

Doireann Ní Bhriain: Was it easy to reach that definition?

Heather Floyd: No. I wasn't working in CAF at the time but I think that it took quite a lot of debate and dialogue to come up with that definition. But it's been there for eleven years now and most of CAF's members, which is about 280, would sign up to that definition. It's a definition of a process.

Doireann Ní Bhriain: Would you share that, Wes, from CREATE's side of things?

Wes Wilkie: We don't define in that we don't judge. The view that we take is that the service is there for any arts practitioner, any arts organisation. We're not going to put the label on the organisation or on the individual that they are a community arts organisation, or a community arts project, or a community artist. We try to keep it as open as possible. It's important for us not to put labels where we cannot put labels and let everyone find their own level. If they choose to define themselves as a community arts practitioner, that's fine by us. If they also choose to define themselves as arts practitioners in a particular context, that's also fine by us.

Doireann Ní Bhriain: Why do you call yourself a community artist, Lynne?

Lynne McCarthy: I suppose just in relation to people I've worked with and how they define me as much as in relation to how I define myself. I see it as a cultural response to a social condition.

Emma Bowell: In Cork city we have an umbrella organisation for the arts called the Cork Arts Development Committee and within that we have different art forms: a film sector, a theatre sector and we have a community arts sector. We spent some time recently debating this as part of our response to Cork 2005 [Capital of Culture] and what we felt very strongly was that there are really two strands within what's now labelled as community arts. One would be artist in the community and the other would be developmental community arts. I think there needs to be recognition that there is arts in the community in terms of maybe an artist working within a community or bringing access to a particular art form to people, whereas community arts as a long-term developmental process is a much more complex process and needs to be funded separately and needs to be addressed and debated and analysed in a separate way to arts in the community. I just think that it's worrying for community arts practice that there is no access to funding for that type of work, because at the end of the day it is art that we are working on, and so by putting it 'over there' it creates a division and moves it again away from art and I think it just perpetuates the notion that this type of work is not art.

Doireann Ní Bhriain: Does anybody else share Emma's concerns about that division?

Tony Sheehan: Well, I don't know if I'd share the concern so much, but I do note that there is a greater tension arising now between what community development sees as arts practice, and what practitioners see as community arts practice, and I've seen community development agendas dominate arts practice. And in rarer cases arts practice dominating community development identity. There are huge assumptions made out there by all sectors of society of what constitutes a community for a start, what constitutes cultural as opposed to just arts activity in a community. We in Cork 2005 are trying to devise a kind of statement of confidence, almost a statement of intent about what we do in our different areas and yet there's always this gap that we're not quite sure about, and that's why we can't have a discussion any longer about the definition of community arts. I think it's actually proved to be a pointless discussion because we'll never reach a conclusion.

Doireann Ní Bhriain: At the time when community arts started in the Republic – and in the North as well – it was exciting and dangerous and threatening and radical – all of those things. I wonder whether that's still the case?

Conor Shields: Absolutely. As an arts organisation we're trying to position ourselves where we can actually have the greatest impact. We see that there is a social mission behind community arts that we're trying to sustain. I think that community arts can step up to that challenge because we're trying to offer a dialogue through the arts so that we can actually mediate what's going on between two dangerously distanced communities at times. But you're also putting yourself in potentially difficult situations and having to mediate at very adverse political outputs and outlooks, so I think that that spirit of the sixties and seventies is still definitely alive and well in Belfast.

Declan Gorman: Can I come in on this? I was attracted into my own area of work in community arts through a kind of mildly dangerous politics. At the same time I think one of the burdens that actually hangs on contemporary practitioners is, in fact, that radical history. But if you look at the kind of practice that my own organisation is involved in, working with members of Macra na Feirme in a village outside Drogheda, there are no visible life-threatening threats to be radical against. And in fact I ended up having to write my excuses about this eventually, in our book a couple of years ago, saying that I had to search my soul and say, 'Is it community arts if in fact it's not set against a radical background?' And of course we found that the answer was yes, because there are profound questions that impact on ordinary men and women which have to do with fundamental issues of how we are living now. I think that at its purest community arts is actually a challenge to those things that we are meant to accept as being beyond question: international global consumerism, for instance, or the inevitability of certain approaches to contemporary life – for instance, commuter living.

Tony Sheehan: I've witnessed a huge amount of practice, of intent, of wanting to get on with the job of being a practitioner. I echo what Declan is saying about it being a polar opposite to a corporate view of the world. And yet we find ourselves as a sector within the corporate structure. The Arts Council is a corporate structure. I don't know but I think that unless we have a greater sense of our own values they will be appropriated.

Doireann Ní Bhriain: How do you arrive at that sense of your own values?

Heather Floyd: My feeling about community arts in the North is that we have a very strong sense of our values and our value base. Do you feel that that is missing for you in your work here?

Tony Sheehan: No, that is not what I'm saying. What I'm saying is that, over the thirty or forty years, we have now arrived at the point where things are complex to the point where in actual fact the core set of beliefs or core intent is being in some way diluted, taken away or else it's been fractured. For example 'community arts can only be valid if it's political and if it's to the left politically' or 'it can only be valuable if it is dealing with just one class' or 'it can only be valuable if it either deals with communities of interest or geographical communities'. There are all these things that rage against each other, until someone else determines what funding will suddenly make itself available.

Emma Bowell: I think there is a need for just recognition of different slants. If there is that recognition then there can be targeted funding at different types of projects. It's not that one should be funded over the other, that one is better than the other. I think that everybody is going for the same sort of funding and I just think that that creates problems. Speaking with other community artists in Cork this is a major problem. I just rang them in advance to see if this is still an issue for people and I feel that it is. There's a need to recognise that there are different kinds of community arts so that different funding strategies can be put in place.

Niall O'Baoill: I think it's very difficult to expect recognition in some ways from a field of work that is evolving, that has so many dimensions, so many starting points.

Emma Bowell: Do you mean recognition among ourselves?

Niall O'Baoill: I mean it on every level. I can count the number of times on my hand that I've heard conversations going on at this level in the last twenty years. It's very rare. So if I don't know you and if I don't recognise your work and you've been at it for twenty years, you know that says something about the field that we're in. In some ways I think community arts is best seen as an historical term and as a creative response at a particular time to a largely indifferent political and arts establishment. There were also other factors at play at that time. But now – almost thirty years on – we have to take an amount of personal responsibility about the extent to which we have failed in effectively communicating and supporting the complexity of this unique field of practice. The establishment – as Declan McGonagle would put it – has its armature, through which it exercises the means by which to reaffirm, sustain and perpetuate a somewhat formalised and static sense of culture. We on the other hand do not and it shows. To take up on Tony's point, we are separate and dissonant. People are still struggling with concepts around value and what the work is and what we need to draw together to create a healthy dynamic out of which the essential identity and strength of what is termed 'community arts' practice might fully assert itself. It is very hard to sustain a commitment in this area of work. If you are a dedicated practitioner there is a persistent challenge in retaining your sense of self and in remaining enthusiastic. Finding ways of refreshing your practice is an art in itself. And there is nobody going to give you that, no Arts Council, no Department of Culture, no European funding programme. They all exist for other reasons. Now, it is possible to remain optimistic and opportunistic; you can bend circumstances to suit yourself for a while. The example of the 'pilot project' syndrome has been around for a long time now. But there's the crux of the matter, which is that the broad church of community arts practice hasn't tried to correspond with itself particularly well; it hasn't tried out actions together, and not so much on an intellectual and theoretical level, but even on an interpersonal or practical level. As such we have forfeited what is it distinctive and common between us and with it the potential to lead our own change. That's the way I experience it and so that I feel the frustration for recognition comes, in some ways, with the loneliness of the field.

Emma Bowell: Yeah, I totally agree with that and I think maybe recognition is the wrong word. It's more an understanding, I suppose, among ourselves of what we do and the differences amongst ourselves and mutual respect for that. When I said recognition I meant just more of an awareness, because I would find that even within our community arts in Cork that there are quite a lot of differences and that some people just wouldn't be aware of those differences.

Niall O'Baoill: I think it's because the two terms are there, 'art' and 'community'. I mean everyone feels that to some degree they can lay claim to that. The 'arts' because they're pissed off as others define the term more powerfully and possessively than themselves and 'community' because what are you if you're not a member of some community. So when you put those two terms together it's a very large and contestable space.

Emma Bowell: My main fear is that it's leading in some cases to bad practice and I think it's leading to projects where artists are engaged in community arts projects who are very good at doing what they do, but who have absolutely no skills in group work. This has created bad experiences for communities who maybe then would not get engaged in another project and that's my only fear, it's not about trying to create division. I feel absolutely that there is a need to work together. It's only when it results in bad practice or when it results in local authorities feeling that the only artist that they can bring into a community is a professional artist, maybe somebody working in a studio rather than within a community arts context, that I would worry. So that's really my fear with it, that if we don't talk about it and decide upon it then it leads to very loose practice sometimes.

Declan Gorman: I understand where that fear is coming from but I think it's very unwise — that kind of fear about sporadic bad practice being the governing factor around the difficult process of recognition. I come to this debate having the luxury of having moved on from having to define community arts any more because I've spent a number of years and an earlier career grappling with what does it mean and how do we define it. And in that context I am loathe to create that difference because there are times when I find it enormously rewarding for me, and I know it is rewarding for the people I work among, to create work that will never have an exposition, that is simply a process that somehow makes sense in that particular setting, a collaborative process. And there are other times when I am actually driven by the imperative not only for the work to be delivered to the public but in fact to get the world's media to come down and film it. And across that entire arc there is the practice of community arts and as an artist and a policy advisor I can roam very happily across without having to worry about the distinctions. I don't envy those of you whose organisations are obliged to define the field because I think it's a deathly exercise to try to define it for the bigger and wider world. It's more helpful as an individual if you can afford that luxury to know your own definition and to be comfortable with it.

Doireann Ní Bhriain: You've got to in some way justify yourself to funders. Does that have a bad impact on what people actually do in the end?

Wes Wilkie: We can't programme that way, you know. We have observed a number of organisations, groups, projects over the years that have been trying to play both ends against the middle, so to speak, and the net result is that there is no clarity in the objective when the project is designed. Trying to please the criteria of one fund and then another fund. The projects are often not written up separately and then the document is used as the source to perform for all applications. So when you look at the project you wonder why there's no attempt at proper evaluation either for the people who are doing it or for the funders. The planning is poor, the resources aren't adequate and it goes on and on, but you know it's going to end, you know it's going to be delivered because that's what people do, is to make sure it's delivered, which is not the best possible thing it could be. Say you need a hundred thousand to deliver a project and someone says to you, we're not going to give you a hundred thousand, we're going to give you thirty thousand. That's too much money to walk away from but far less than you need to actually deliver the programme, so what you get is a cobbled end.

Niall O'Baoill: I think the main problem with money in this field is that virtually none of the funds have been clearly predicated on meeting real identifiable needs and development opportunities within the field of community arts practice, and with that come the added features of what Wes talks about. If we look to the future, we will need to be a little more intelligent around how it is we're looking for our money, and how we try and correlate and challenge the existing policies and mechanisms that purport to be concerned with community arts.

Doireann Ní Bhriain: So is it your responsibility as community arts practitioners to drive that forward and to create the agenda rather than waiting and having to respond?

Emma Bowell: Ideally, yes, it is our case, but for a lot of people there simply isn't the time and energy. As practitioners you can be so busy just trying to actually survive. We spend a lot of time talking, debating locally here, trying to improve the recognition of community arts, to promote community arts but, you know, that's not funded at all, so, yes, I think ideally we do need to be doing it, to be pushing the agenda, but we need to be supported to do that as well.

Niall O'Baoill: I think that's missing. I don't mean it to sound like a simple prospect but I think it's unavoidable that we establish the means of reflecting upon provision and practice in community and relating its efficacy to the wider public and policy-making and funding bodies. I think some small improvements have taken place however in terms of artists' formation and their willingness to look outside the box. But in broader terms, if you were to analyse the policy and funding disposition of the bodies that are under legislation responsible for this area of Irish cultural life, local government and the Arts Council, they are both hiding at the moment from the reality and challenges of community arts, hiding and mute.

Doireann Ní Bhriain: Can I ask, Val, as you have worked in a rural context more than most of the people who have spoken, whether any of what's been said resonates with you?

Val Ballance: Well, it doesn't really, because people here are working at a generally high level within an urban environment, whereas I work a double rural thing, the rural and the Gaeltacht at the same time. I was just thinking of the Arts Council, the VEC, Údarás na Gaeltachta, the Department of Education, Cumas, Cóir, FÁS, the Ireland Fund, that's just a few, I could think of another dozen places I would go for money. But they would all have one thing in common, which would be that they wouldn't want to give me any [table members laughing]. But they also would have a formal policy of refusing something to force you to go around to all the funding agencies to get formal refusals so they know that you're not double funding to start off with. But this is a job-creation scheme; you know it's tremendously wasteful of people's time, but I've mentioned that because it supports the idea of what is community arts. To me I'm not particularly a practitioner of this; I use it and become involved in it from time to time. At this stage I think it's more of a campaign than any one thing. What is community arts? You know, I couldn't even be bothered to come up with a definition for it because it's so diverse, but it certainly needs to have some kind of a profile in order to campaign for changes in areas that still need it in Ireland. For instance, in education, which is something that I've been involved in, it's always kind of left out there in the porch. The arts centre that I work in has three major funding agencies, all of whom give for no more than a year, if you're lucky. So you're constantly justifying your existence. You know you'd just go out of business, you'd just give up. So I will say of community arts, there's a big argument here to campaign for change, and this would be my own interest in it now, in creating an infrastructure for artists who'd wish to work. You just talked about artists who are suitable, I've come across artists who are really unsuited to what would be called community arts, they're really dreadful, no communication ability whatsoever, no organisation ability, but there is this idea that, especially where I live now, that artists should work in the community. Most artists aren't suited to working with anyone else. But there are some other artists who are absolutely brilliant and if there was some kind of structure for artists to work within, where there is an established way of working if you wish to, within schools, palliative care, local community centres.

Doireann Ní Bhriain: That leads us to the issue of training and formation of artists.

Declan Gorman: I think Val brought up a very interesting issue. It is so ironic given that there are people who have years and years of excellent practice who find this sense that your value as a contributing artist in the community is directly proportionate to the number of hours' community service that you do. I think that's very, very unhelpful to the arts, and I say that as somebody who does happen to work most happily in participatory circumstances, but I also work very, very happily with artists who I wouldn't think of sending out to work with a group of teenagers. I simply wouldn't think of it. When that allegedly definitive distinction was created in the mid-nineties between developmental community arts and the rest of community arts, it was almost as if to say, well now there is an area of practice which has been endorsed by Combat Poverty [in the report *Poverty: Access and Participation in the Arts*, 1997], which is deserving of funding from where ever because it is very important in the war against poverty, very important in the war against disadvantage, and so on and so forth, but I think, such is the weight of that report, such is the weight of the kind of embracing of that report, that it began to create difficulties for artists who might wish to work outside of those kind of contexts. If you look at very first Arts Plan in the Republic, sorry to be so Republic-centred but it's where most of my knowledge is on this, in the wake of the publication of the first Arts Plan, those of us who were working with arts organisations began to receive a new variation of the application form [from the Arts Council] where you were asked to outline the work you were doing with children, people with disabilities and so on. It was a box-ticking exercise and it was very, very worrying for organisations which were struggling to simply define their own practice, who weren't necessarily working in that way. But there was a great kind of weight on organisations and it was completely the wrong approach and it hasn't really gone away. The correct approach obviously is to identify organisations or individuals who may wish to work that way and to identify communities who may wish to work that way and provide substantial and substantive support of equal weight for different approaches to the making of art.

Niall O'Baoill: I think that goes back to what you were saying earlier about how there has been an absence of critical thinking and serious planning in relation to certain areas of the arts. Remember the first significant cultural policy statement in Ireland – it was called *Access and Opportunity* – actually heralded the idea of participation in the arts. The Arts Council thereafter got around to re-pointing in some ways its policies and funding dispositions to incorporate this statement of intent. They gathered lists of the different types of ideas of disadvantage or cultural alienation and they put them into little boxes and lines into their application forms, and who did they go with the application form to – only their existing client base. So straight away they were asking people who had been formed and working in a particular way, and who were already financially strapped themselves and worried about where the crust will come from, to jump that hurdle, tick that box, pretend you can, either way you won't be caught out. So an extraordinary opportunity was lost. The last time I was down here in Cork, it was in the Firkin Crane Dance Centre. The Arts Council had invited people to talk about partnership in the arts, as they had just produced their first five-year Arts Plan. I had studied it and counted forty-eight instances where the Council had stated boldly that they were going to partner other statutory and community/voluntary sectors in opening up access and participation in the arts. I remember reading them aloud out like a

Van Morrison homily – RTÉ, BBC, VEC, dee dee dee, etc. – and people started to laugh in the audience. Understandably so, because there was no sane belief that you could start from scratch with a stated aim of forty-eight strategic partnerships. If you could go back and examine the breadth of that ambition, and how many actual organisations were profoundly actually engaged with in the course of that Arts Plan, I suspect the evidence would be damning. How measurably improved was access and participation in the arts as a consequence of this supposed blitzkrieg? It remains a fantasy world in which there is no real accountability. It would appear that everything is possible for as long as you can write it or describe it, and there's no constituency actively reviewing or analysing their satisfaction or otherwise with such matters other than the essentially self-satisfied establishment.

Doireann Ní Bhriain: Declan did make the point earlier that this is very Republic-centred, this discussion. Does it have any resonance for those of you from Northern Ireland and the way you work? [To Heather.]

Heather Floyd: A lot of the issues are very, very similar. I think, Niall, you were saying about the Arts Council, your Arts Council, runs away from community arts at the minute. We've found the opposite actually in the North and to a certain extent they [the Arts Council of Northern Ireland] are embracing it. We now have, for six counties, a community arts officer and a social inclusion officer, which has been a big, big shift, and generally within the Arts Council of Northern Ireland a recognition of community arts after years of battle. Apart from that, loads of the same issues, you know, short-term funding, the need for innovative projects all the time, lack of sustainability, lack of strategy, lack of planning. A lot of small towns in the North have now got arts centres, without any thought of how these can be sustained long-term and the money has to come from somewhere. The way sectarianism is embedded in our institutions and public bodies means that if such and such a town has an arts centre, this one has to have one as well. Certainly in some cities, Derry maybe in particular, there's been a huge drain on the city. They've had a big new theatre, the Millennium Forum, which has been nothing but trouble really from day one, even before day one.

Declan Gorman: I'm a little bit familiar with that. I remember when they were building the Forum, actually people on the ground knew before the foundation stone was laid that it would be a disaster for the very reasons that you're articulating, and that would lead you to despair about the way in which intelligent opinion on the ground is very often not listened to.

Doireann Ní Bhriain: It goes back to what Tony was saying earlier about the appropriation.

Tony Sheehan: Well, it's consultation with a PFO letter at the end of it. It's bring you in, give you the cup of tea and the biscuit, feign interest in what you're saying and telling you to fuck off. And then that vacuous type of consultation process whereby decisions will be made that will be politically expedient. The local elections are due all around the country this year. It would be very interesting to do a scientific study of the mayhem that will be caused at local level by politicians all of a sudden wanting to know what's in it for them or their constituents. And I mean that nationally.

Doireann Ní Bhriain: Has that not always been so? Is that not something that you have to grapple with all the time?

Tony Sheehan: But it's interesting, Doireann, that after so many years of independence as a state we are still so far behind in what is obvious to all of us. The reason that things are continually pilot projects is that no organisation has ever been mandated to take on that fifty- or sixty-year mission. About the only people who do it are the ESRI, and that's because they're looking at pensions in fifty or sixty years. We actually don't have in our organisations that level of investment into forward thinking. The European Capital of Culture is a serious intervention in the life of this city. It's going to be a huge traumatic event, there's a €13 million budget suddenly being landed into a city with a population of less than 150,000 and already the way people are reacting is a combination of what they're used to in terms of applying to the committee. You just go and you ask for things, and you get them and go away. A younger generation is really hungry to make a big statement, whether it's at a community level or otherwise, but they feel a sense of cynicism. It is the old guard who smugly expect, because they have patrolled the city up till now, to receive the lion's share of the thing.

Niall O'Baoill: Tony has brought us into the whole area of power, political structures and, to some degree, what pathological difficulties we have as a nation in terms of facing up to ourselves and getting on. It's a considerable conundrum and one that has created great difficulty because there is a depth of feeling and a genuine, natural, indignation among a lot of practitioners in this field of work that is not finding adequate expression.

Tony Sheehan: The danger of that though is that it brings us straight back to the pilot-project phenomena. The learning has been done but has been packed away; the reports have been shelved. There is a whole lot of inertia; there's been a lot of damping down and, unless we stop that cycle of innovation and then putting aside, another generation will be back here in twenty years time having the same discussion.

Conor Shields: I was just thinking that it's the connectivity between these organisations and what we do that really needs to be established as well, especially the connectivity of our funders, of the environment that we're working within, because from one organisation to the next to the next, there isn't a continuum of a baseline, so you're constantly reinventing the wheel every time in order to bring those people up to speed as to where we actually are. We want to forge ahead. You know, you're giving out mission statements saying we're going to position ourselves here in two or three years' time but they're actually looking at where you're establishing a baseline going 'That's different, what is this?' or 'How does this relate?' Or you're talking about ticking boxes: everybody has different boxes that must be ticked as well, so it's the connectivity of the environment that we're working within.

Doireann Ní Bhriain: Is there an issue around sharing, developing and communicating models of good experience?

Val Balance: Because everything you do is a one-off. Every project is unique. There is very little continuity, I've found.

Doireann Ní Bhriain: And why is that?

Val Ballance: Because everything is single, it is just a little thing that you do on the side.

Doireann Ní Bhriain: And if it were part of some greater plan?

Val Ballance: If there was a recognition that this thing exists in society which can be used for people's benefit then it would be used, I'm sure it would. But I think things are hampered by shoving out the money to the arts centres, for example. You know, capital funding is easy to give to something because you just give it and that's it. A commitment to keep it open for twenty-five years is another matter altogether.

Doireann Ní Bhriain: Is there a thing, though, about communicating? Do you hear the voice of community arts practice reflected strongly enough to indicate that things are not working and that there are things that you can do and if we don't hear it, why don't we hear it?

Declan Gorman: If we're talking specifically about capital development, we just don't hear the intelligent experience of artists. But there's another factor in this situation, and I don't want to go into the local politics of the town I work in, but, for instance, there are tensions in Drogheda at the moment between the traditional providers of the annual pantomime, which is a big entertainment of the town and has been for the past forty years and I respect it greatly, but they are a very powerful group of people, and their dream of a performance-art space in the town is utterly at odds with the vision that would be held by, let's say, a generation of practitioners, who have really created a new voice in the town over the last ten years from youth theatre, community music, from street pageantry and so on. So those tensions exist.

Emma Bowell: I'm actually interested in power, and the people you've described are a powerful group of people. It strikes me that there tends to be a shying away from the term radical. I mean, I think what we do is radical and I don't think people should shy away from that. I think what we're trying to do is to change the way things currently are, I really do. I know that there has to be a certain acceptance of things that are there and working as well, but I don't think we should ever be afraid of the fact that we are trying to change structures and that we're trying to open up.

Niall O'Baoill: Well the word radical means different things to people. For me it's about how one can develop a cultural confidence or a consciousness among people around you and by extension see what sort of thinking there is that can usefully inform the next step. Capturing and honouring that learning, becoming servant to it and all it insists upon, for me is the hallmark of true radicalism.

Emma Bowell: But it takes time for that to happen. It takes time for a particular community to work through that process, to talk about whether or not what we want is essential or isn't essential. And I think there's no political role there at the moment to allow that space and time to organically grow within a community.

Niall O'Baoill: But if that's the case, what choices are we left with in terms of how we invest our energy in practice?

Doireann Ní Bhriain: One of the things that I'd be curious about is what the reasons are now for the existence of community arts practice. Are they completely different to what they were twenty years ago, thirty years ago?

Declan Gorman: Well, we are the carriers of the torch. It's a fluid journey.

Doireann Ní Bhriain: I suppose what I'm asking is has the external environment utterly changed?

Declan Gorman: I think it has, and I think one of the significant aspects of the Civil Arts Inquiry and this particular discussion is that that line of continuity is actually availed of. But you know, I think that the point that Emma just made is absolutely accurate. There is no space in the hurried pace of major political and social change that is the norm now for long-term contemplative processes that might allow communities to involve themselves. Unfashionable as it may be, I've come to believe in the potential, if you learn how to use it, of the democratic process and one of the things that I have learned, just from bitter experiences of actually seeing the boats going out time and time again, is to not rush for the next boat but to actually get stuck in locally, work with other artists, work with the community who are around, work very carefully with your local arts officer around the possibility that you actually won't go for – say – this year's Culture 2000 funding but you might actually aim for it in 2005 because by the time 2005 comes up you might have actually cultivated a partner that you can really work with, and you might by then actually have winkled your way into the political consciousness of the local politicians who are likely to listen, etc., etc., who might then be ready.

I think part of the pressure that comes on the disempowered communities and the disempowered artists is the money that they will actually hang over you and say, there is an opportunity to go for funding next Tuesday and if you miss it you're going to miss the next one, and to have the courage to stand up and say, well we will miss it because there is no damn way we are going to be ready for it, and to know, no matter how much they tell you otherwise, it's not the last window. The first Arts Plan wasn't the last window, the second one wasn't the last and the third one wasn't the last one – you know things will continue to evolve.

Doireann Ní Bhriain: What I'd like to try and do in this next hour is bring things from the more general discussion that we've been having to a few more specific questions. For example, why are you working in this area?

Niall O'Baoill: Rotten childhoods.

Doireann Ní Bhriain: I mean, what's exciting about what you do, if there is anything exciting? Conor could you point to a couple of things that are really exciting and worth doing?

Conor Shields: Absolutely. I'll take one of the strands of activity that we do called Belfast Wheel, which takes twelve community groups right across the city of Belfast. We try to reflect the city of Belfast, and the make-up of the city as well, in those twelve groups. Through a community arts process, those twelve groups develop a piece of formal public art and then we have a companion piece that's sited in the city centre. The connectivity is what's important. I know it's a word that I've used before, but especially in terms of Belfast, where you are trying to deal with so many ideological separations, so many personal, physical separations and separations of age, you're giving those communities the opportunity to participate, knowing that another group is actually doing the same thing, that they're all working towards an end point where they come together, that they actually have something that's much greater than the sum of its parts. Through that process we're also giving twelve artists the opportunity to work in their discipline with a certain budget, – we won't get into money again – so that they can actually build something that truly represents what the community wants to say, wants to express. But also that they can engage in the most innovative practice that they can bring to it, so that you have a vibrant piece at the end of it that the community can come to look at. It's there, it's permanent, set in stone in the city centre. It's incredible! Knowing that that project is going so well has actually built momentum into the second project running now, where other communities have got involved. We want to be a part of that. And

St. Patricks Day festival, Dublin.
Photo: Derek Spiers/Report

artists are coming forward saying they want to be a part of that too. Success breeds success and opportunities are scarce. They want to see social benefit; they want to see real change; they want to develop dialogue; they want to be a part of a particular Belfast that is a changing city. It's in transformation, and any element of that momentum that is visible, that is tangible, you've got to push that. And for everybody, the wave of hope of renewal, of real transformation of our society from 1998 [the signing of the Good Friday Agreement], artists feel that as much as anybody else does, if not more so. And they want to propel that. They're coming to me all the time saying, 'I want to get involved, how do I get involved?' Artists are coming forward, looking at issues within the community, looking at activity that communities are crying out for. I'd also say that the quality of the work has produced the success that that strand has delivered.

Doireann Ní Bhriain: Why was the quality so high?

Conor Shields: Because the practitioners that were chosen were of a tremendously high quality. Their CVs spoke of commitment, of great knowledge, of tremendous sensitivity and an understanding of social issues and of what their role was in that engagement with the community group.

Lynne McCarthy: Can I go back to the notion of you guys saying that the whole thing is very complex and all the rest of it? I think at ground level it's not complex or it shouldn't be complex, that fundamentally it should be easy and it should be easy to engage in for an artist and the community. For me, I suppose, working as an artist, what I find fascinating about community arts is the way it compels me to leave behind the rules and structures that I have learnt, that I've been trained with. If I'm to apply those structures and tools to a community group they're not going to work, because it's of a specific time, a specific nature, a specific context. So when I engage with a community I find that I have to change my structures, and in changing my structures I find something completely new and completely refreshing and the same goes for the community, I would like to think. So in that sense, that's what drives me to work with communities.

Doireann Ní Bhriain: So it actually develops and changes your own practice.

Lynne McCarthy: Yeah, absolutely!

Doireann Ní Bhriain: Lynne, do you talk to other artists who are not involved in the kind of community practice that you are involved in?

Lynne McCarthy: Yeah. I come up against a stone wall if I do, really. I think there's a misconception or a miseducation as to what community arts is, with kind of insinuations of the amateur, which I really don't appreciate.

Doireann Ní Bhriain: And so is the issue of standards that you raised earlier, about people being put in situations that they're not prepared for, is that something that concerns you?

Lynne McCarthy: Absolutely, though, having said that, I'm looking for more training myself. I don't see myself as a professional community artist even though I would love to be one. I just don't see that there's enough training around.

Heather Floyd: There's very little training for artists. I think we have an expectation that we should be able to plonk an artist in a community and that the artist should be able to work collaboratively with a group in the way that community arts organisations would hope for. There is very little training for individual artists in that kind of work. A lot of artists coming out of art college want to work in the community but they don't know how.

Declan Gorman: When I was working in City Arts Centre in the early nineties, there was a project going on in Belfast in the area of community drama at that time. I remember crashing out on the floor of a flat where there were three young graduates who had all come out of college, two were from Belfast – they had come out of Queen's, if I can remember – and they were all working in the community. There was an abundance of work in the community, and I remember sitting there listening to the cynicism of the conversation about what they were doing and by the end being really, really worried about that. There was actually so much money being poured, pre-Belfast agreement days, into anything that brought people from different communities together that actors who basically couldn't afford to do what they really, really wanted to do, and more to the point, really, aspiring young directors who actually couldn't get work, were working with children and slagging the participants over tea at night. Now that was a very isolated example but it worried me.

Lynne McCarthy: It wouldn't be isolated because I've had the same experiences.

Niall O'Baoill: And I think it remains. I think there's various legitimate definitions of community, but if people broadly speaking want to create conditions under which they're exercising themselves artistically or aesthetically — at a local level, as children, special interests groups or on a larger geographic basis — I think there are particular responsibilities and certain structures that have to kick in at that level. But that accepted, the greatest impediment is the lack of a really creative conjunction between the terms community and art. For example, the innate conservatism and fear among students and the institutions in which they're trained and orientated has to be experienced to be believed. Not too long ago I was invited to lecture some of the NCAD fine-art students on the eve of their leaving college, and around the same time I gave a talk to students at the Gaiety School of Acting. The response of the NCAD students was one of shock and disbelief at what I was presenting and arguing. They thought I was exaggerating until such time as the weight of evidence become so clear, because I was using a lot of facts and reinforcing my views with practical examples. The course director was getting worried. He interjected and basically said, look, do you not think it's a terrible indictment on the part of the students that they are so ignorant of all that which you are presenting? I thought to myself and said as much, that whatever about the students it was certainly an indictment of the college. He left in a somewhat churlish humour but the students stayed on for a further two hours. Another example was the theatre school where, after a not dissimilar input, most came up and apologised to me, by and large to say, look it's great, I think it's amazing this area of work, but I'm sorry I can't do it, I can't do it. And they didn't even know what they couldn't do! They had already being fucked around both in relation to their ambitions and sense of self. In visual art colleges young impressionable people are being insisted upon to abstract everything, to intellectualise and explain everything before they even pick up a brush or to get to work or to draw or to do anything else like that, never mind meet or consider working in a community or collaborative setting. In the performing arts there is a corresponding set of unnecessary and absurd neurosis. I don't know if we truly recognise how relentless and wasteful this situation is in Ireland.

Heather Floyd: Our experience in the North is that many artists are engaged with community arts and that they're quite knowledgeable about it.

Declan Gorman: But I think the thing that Conor identified is actually critical, which is the intuitive thing. The sense of a society in change and that there is a critical mass of people who identify with the positive potential of a society that is actually rising from the shadows of the past and into something hopeful in the future and that's a very, very long journey.

Niall O'Baoill: Well, I think there's another side to it that relates to the level of cultural confidence within communities. Because there are inferiorities and tribalism around and I feel it falls to the leadership within those communities, geographic or communities of interest, to get over being stuck as well. Blue Drum recently finished a survey of community development projects nationally and I think that over 80 per cent of the projects said that they actually had arts practices as a core element of what they were doing. Now after that they were strapped in relation to resources, training and a whole lot of other things, but it was there. Among many communities, both urban and rural, there is a shared sense of trying to use the languages and capacities of the arts as a way of awakening a different type of a voice and as an incitement to journey and challenge what is actually at play within their community. But that community then has to create a particular dialectic with artists, because they too are indispensable.

Declan Gorman: And this is the enormous irony. I think that there is such a hunger that can be found across all kind of communities in Ireland. I wasn't aware of that particular survey but I would be conscious of it just from working on the ground in Co. Louth and in the border regions. Almost everywhere we go we are receiving invitations from locally based organisations or groups of people who have formed themselves. They want to make art, they want to create art and they have no interest in the old ways. There is a stratum of people and a stratum of organisations that actually want to connect with the arts in one way or another and part of that now is actually identifying artists who are motivated and competent to connect with that energy. Ten, fifteen years ago I thought that if you spent long enough working in a community as an artist, you could depart and leave behind you a tradition that would then be self-sustaining. To a certain extent that can happen, and I have seen some evidence of it. But I believe that the best community arts will ultimately flow from extended relationships between community artists or good arts organisations and it's about sensitivities within that relationship.

Doireann Ní Bhriain: And would that happen organically or do you need direction, research, ways of facilitating and putting those things together, making those connections happen?

Declan Gorman: I think the kind of brokerage that Conor and Heather have been describing in Belfast is very interesting.

Tony Sheehan: That brokerage is exactly what's needed, and there's that fundamental relationship-building. It's parity of esteem actually, it takes time. From the community there is a huge sense of goodwill but there's a need to have a mutual understanding of where their pressures are coming from. We live in a time when certainly if you practice in community arts, galleries will turn you down on the basis that they've decided that you are now, somehow amateur all of a sudden. There's a huge snobbery there. Community arts and practitioners of community arts lack a kind of validation.

Doireann Ní Bhriain: Has that been challenged Tony? How has that been challenged by artists?.

Tony Sheehan: Well, there are numerous examples of really well-established artists, who, when they did encounter that good will, that sense of wanting to collaborate, it was actually cathartic for them as artists. Artists who would be practising for thirty and forty years and who had never had the opportunity to work that directly.

Doireann Ní Bhriain: But what about on a wider scale?

Niall O'Baoill: I think no, and this is one of the reasons the City Arts Centre originated this Civil Arts Inquiry in which ideas about art and its various constituents that care about change might relate purposefully together over a sustained two-year period. On entering the new millennium community arts had already been floundering, exhausted through the lack of organisation, through European funny money spins, through whatever. We needed to pause and consider the bigger questions together

Augusto Boal visits Belfast, 1998.
Photo: Timeline

Doireann Ní Bhriain: But is there an art form called community arts?

Niall O'Baoill: I'd be interested how they see it in the north.

Heather Floyd: No, we wouldn't see community arts as an art form. We would see it as a process, as practice.

Niall O'Baoill: Well, I think it's cheeky, useful and provocative to be talking about community arts in those terms.

Emma Bowell: There is a dilemma, I mean, I know within the Cork Arts Development seminars people would break into the art-form groups but for people like ourselves, film-makers who are also community artists, there is a 'Do we go to the community arts table over there?' type question, you know.

Lynne McCarthy: So then is the problem of a lack of community art organisations devoted purely to community arts regardless of the art forms involved, rather than a lot of organisations devoted to different disciplines like film or theatre or whichever, and having their own outreaches.

Niall O'Baoill: There's no argument whatsoever there. I mean, again we have a problem facing the facts. The Arts Council would have commissioned studies on audiences and policy priorities over the years. The evidence is clear but nobody wants to talk about it, whether it was the *Economy of the Arts* report or *Audiences, Acquisitions and Amateurs* or *Performing Arts and the Public Purse*: all of these publications speak to the disproportionate investments in particular types of locations and particular types of art forms. They all show the appalling lack of communication as regards the arts in the broader society. They also attitudinally show that when the public are asked how they'd like to see the investment in the arts and where they'd like to see it going, that it's the inverse of what's actually going on at the moment. So in a sense there is a national dilemma. It is doubly extraordinary when you consider the paucity of arts organisations addressing this reality.

Doireann Ní Bhriain: Could you give an example of one that would be?

Niall O'Baoill: Well you've got CREATE and especially City Arts Centre at this juncture.

Doireann Ní Bhriain: In an art-form context, say a dance organisation or a film organisation or whatever.

Niall O'Baoill: I think what you get in the art forms, you get organisations that make choices around attaching themselves like limpets to things like education or a specific sense of festival or whatever like that, but not in the more open explorative sense in which they're looking at form being kind of shared or meant to address a particular culture or context, no.

Declan Gorman: We [Upstate] will not be pigeon-holed as a community arts organisation and we will not be pigeon-holed as a typical theatre company. Because what our starting point is, is that neither of those groups of people have a monopoly on creativity and a lot of what we're doing is actually the process of creating work, so it's actually encouraging people to conceive of work, to have the courage to enunciate their dreams. The anarchy of making the work actually can come from any source. Declan McGonagle has actually helped me to understand that the problem was about the means of distribution. The reason that we haven't heard of this practice or that we don't know about community arts and that there aren't famous community artists is that somebody else in the power structure is actually controlling the means of distribution. Whether it's the gallery owners or the agents who actually stop their young actors from going to work in community arts is they're worried that if they touch sort of education theatre it will be a negative for their professional careers.

Doireann Ní Bhriain: Or could it be that the young actors or the young artists haven't been shown what is possible?

Declan Gorman: But this is the question of distribution again. I know that my own practice was turned around and fired up a number of times over the years because, although Niall and I started out around the same time in the arts, Niall was working in the community field before I was, and when I met Niall and he showed me some documentation like video images, or brought me along to see good project work in action, my life changed, my own practice as an artist changed.

Doireann Ní Bhriain: So documentation, evaluation, all of those things. How important are they?

Niall O'Baoill: Evaluation really depends on where you're coming from. There is not a great tradition of evaluating from an arts perspective. In a community context things get evaluated all the time but for different reasons. More recently, however, communities are displaying enthusiasm around evaluating arts specific work and interventions and are developing new tools to do so. Regrettably, though, what I have found disheartening is when you do evaluate good participative practice and process it at a local level, and then move to present its findings as a distilled form of learning back to arts policy makers or whatever, they appear disinterested. Consequently I do feel documentary processes and evaluation are really necessary and need to be well conceived and built into the project from the outset. But I equally think that evaluation can be an empty and perfunctory experience. Personally I have little regard for evaluation where there is not some commitment to continuity. What I mean is there are many times when evaluation has been made mandatory. But to bring real meaning to evaluation there needs to be a next step. It's a little too clinical and scientific otherwise.

Counterbalance Dance Group, part of City Arts Centre's VSA programme, 1995

Declan Gorman: I think it's not whether to document and whether to evaluate, it's actually why and partly how.

Heather Floyd: There is a lack of consultation as well about what we would find useful for evaluation.

Niall O'Baoill: But we have no mechanism here in the Republic, despite the promise. The Arts Council's shift from being a simple grant-giving body into a purported developmental agency raised the bar, insofar as it advanced a series of plans and new models of investment through which they insisted that the organisations in receipt of such funding would be monitored and evaluated. The expected consequence being that a new critical rigour and means of addressing cultural values and the benefits of different models of arts provision might be significantly advanced. This has not happened and I am not alone in feeling very strongly that people are expected to take on far too much around the science of planning and compliance with new processes without their being adequate means of keeping the people that are insisting upon such strategies and ideas in any way accountable for them.

Wes Wilkie: It's really very important to evaluate from a management point of view. If you're going to learn from your experiences, you don't want to make the same mistakes again: you want to enhance the programme next time you run it or a variation of it.

Val Ballance: I often hear about something and I think, wow, it's fantastic, it's amazing and then I'll go and have a bit of a closer look at it and think, Jesus, is that it? Somebody would be just talking it up.

Lynne McCarthy: I don't know if I'm totally ignorant but I have never seen a really good model for evaluation. I know it would vary from organisation to organisation but I wouldn't be happy with the agendas hidden within the evaluations.

Val Ballance: It's very difficult. You know this thing of giving out forms to everybody that participated, you know mark on a scale of one to ten. It's nonsense, that. People don't even write down the truth half the time.

Doireann Ní Bhriain: There's always the question of how you evaluate art anyway. It's a complex area.

Val Ballance: Well, you're not evaluating art. This is all, as you said, a process. Community arts is not an art form – you can call it what you want but it's not.

Heather Floyd: There's all these evaluations going on about the country but nothing kind of concrete around collating it all and putting it all together and saying, this is the impact, these are the benefits, this is what happens to the community, this is what happens to the individual. There is again a lack of coherence and strategy around evaluation.

Doireann Ní Bhriain: Can we talk a bit before finishing about standards and quality, what their relevance is or how you'd measure them in the context of community arts practice, or whether you should be trying to do that at all?

Declan Gorman: I think the question of aesthetic standards is much more difficult. It's very difficult in art generally and I think we have tied ourselves up like a dish cloth and run out of ideas of how to evaluate community arts and the arts generally. I remember way back in the early nineties, there was, I think, an evaluation at the end of one of the CAFE community drama festivals. There was a line that became such a hackneyed cliché – and yet there was a grain of truth in it when I came back to it recently –and it was, 'If the process was good, the product will probably be good.' It doesn't always work out that way, you know, the process of preparing for a football match in Switzerland! [Laughing from table members.] I know that there was a terrible fear in community arts in Dublin in the past. Debating standards was seen either as an invasive contribution from people outside who had a vested interest in pushing a point of view that aesthetic standards were low. Or because there were far more important things to be done, women had to be liberated, communities had to be liberated and so on and so forth, so talk of the aesthetics standards was considered actually a heresy from within. I think we've moved on a huge distance from that and I think what we've done is we've developed a confidence as practitioners ourselves to actually acknowledge that the field that we're in is a new field. And like in any science, early experiments are going to be hit and miss – there is going to be good practice; there's going to be bad practice. If there is a great romantic drama performed in costume in the Gate Theatre or on the London West End stage, there are three hundred years of tradition that has been drawn from. If you are creating a new piece of graffiti art under a bridge somewhere with a group of young people who have no history of any kind, who are living in a wasteland housing estate that was a swamp before, there is no tradition, there are no roots. So what do you evaluate it against? You evaluate it against some other comparable achievement and the next aerosol programme will learn from the first one and then eventually maybe in ten years, there is actually a body of work, and like trends to compared with like.

Emma Bowell: No, in a sense this is really what I was trying to say at the start of the discussion in terms of developmental community arts. I realised as the discussion progressed, what I was trying to say about that was something altogether different from what a few people around the table thought that I was saying because of my use of the word developmental. In a sense I was talking about what we're talking about now, in terms of continuity, in terms of a project ending. We often would conduct film interviews with people at the end of a project and we would talk to people, and some fantastic work comes out of that, but you know if there is no possibility of continuing our project then, in a sense, it's like for what? It's a full stop. So when I was talking about developmental, I was talking about this sense of long term, of being able to actually move through a project. Maybe it might be a different group, the same group mightn't want to come back, but there's some sort of legacy that's been left behind. That's really what I was trying to get at.

Doireann Ní Bhriain: Talking about legacies being left behind, does anybody around the table feel this conversation has been useful in any way, or illuminating in any way or did you just talk about the same thing as you always talk about?

Conor Shields: It's been tremendous for me, coming from an organisation that sees itself, its geographical and social remit, as being bordered by the city of Belfast, to actually leave the city of Belfast and meet arts professionals who are doing the same work with the same level of commitment and dynamism right across Ireland. It's fantastic to respond to the same issues and the same problems, because if governments and policy makers aren't connected, we must be connected. We must make those connections because it's only through our ability to do that will we actually present ourselves to them in a way that they will more comprehensively know what the hell we're on about. I think it's been fantastic and I've enjoyed every minute of it and I think we should extend it by another three hours [laughing from table members].

Essayists' biographies

Chris Ball served as a journalist for a number of local newspapers in Northern Ireland, and edited an online information portal, before joining the Community Arts Forum in 2002. Lacking much in the way of artistic ability, Chris occasionally plays the banjo and guitar and currently sits on the board of Bruiser Theatre Company.

Will Chamberlain is the director of the Belfast Community Circus School, and he has lived in Ireland for over five years. He moved to Belfast from Switzerland to take up his current post. Will served as CAF chair for three years. A clown by trade, Will manages to juggle his roles of director of a community arts provider organisation, advocate for community arts and arts practitioner, with a deft hand.

Paula Clancy is director of tasc – a think tank for action on social change. She has written extensively on the cultural sector in Ireland. She was formerly the Head of the School of Business and Humanities in the DLIADT where she developed the BA in Arts and Media Management, the first such degree programme in Ireland. Prior to that she was deputy director of the Business Research Programme in UCD's Smurfit Graduate School of Business, where she was responsible for a number of research projects on the cultural sector in Ireland.

Susan Coughlan is a former arts development officer of the Arts Council, where she had responsibility for the development of policy and funding for arts centres, multidisciplinary arts festivals and community arts. Prior to this, she held project management and development posts with Wet Paint Arts, the National Youth Council of Ireland and the Centre for Adult and Community Education, Maynooth College. Currently, she is a lecturer on the H. Dip. in Community Arts Education at NCAD and an independent arts consultant.

Jo Egan is former co-chair of CAF. She is originally from Dublin and has worked as a community theatre artist for over twelve years in both Dublin and Belfast. She produced and co-directed *The Wedding Community Play* and has facilitated drama workshops in many parts of

Ireland. Until recently, she was development officer with the Creative Writers' Network. Her most recent piece of work is Director of the highly acclaimed community play *Time After Time*.

Sandy Fitzgerald has over thirty years' experience as a cultural practitioner and manager. Sandy has participated in many areas of cultural development in Ireland and abroad, working at local, national and international level. His experience includes founder member and director of City Arts Centre, 1973–2002; director of the Dublin Street Carnival, 1988–1991; founder member of CAFE (Creative Activity for Everyone); board member of the Royal Hospital National Cultural Centre (later to become the Irish Museum of Modern Art); executive committee member of Trans Europe Halles (a European network of Cultural Centres) and board member of the Dublin Film Festival. On leaving City Arts Centre in 2002 he became a partner in the international arts consultation group CultureWorks.

Heather Floyd has worked in the Community Arts Forum (CAF) for the past four years, first as training officer and subsequently as director. She came to CAF from a community education background, having worked in Shankill Women's Centre for eight years developing educational and cultural programmes.

Dr Anthony Grayling MA D.Phil. is reader in philosophy at Birkbeck College, University of London, and a supernumerary fellow of St Anne's College, Oxford. He has written and edited many books on philosophy and other subjects. Among his most recent are a biography of William Hazlitt and a collection of essays, but he is probably best known for his book *The Meaning of Things*. For several years he wrote the 'Last Word' column for the *Guardian* newspaper and is a regular reviewer for the *Literary Review* and the *Financial Times*. He also writes for the *Observer*, *Economist*, *Times Literary Supplement*, *Independent on Sunday* and *New Statesman*, and is a frequent broadcaster on BBC Radios 4, 3 and the World Service. He is a past chair of June Fourth, a human rights group concerned with China, and has been involved in UN human rights initiatives.

Rhona Henderson is a graduate of the National College of Art and Design (BA Hons in Fine Art) and Trinity College, Dublin (M.Phil. in Psychoanalytic Studies). For the last ten years she has worked as an artist on a broad range of community and collaborative art projects in Dublin. She has also worked in the formal and informal education sectors, for example as an artist educator at the Irish Museum of Modern Art and as a lecturer in Cultural and Critical Theory at the National College of Art and Design and Dun Laoghaire Institute of Art, Design and Technology.

Martin Lynch is a founding member of CAF and remained director of that organisation until he left in 2001 to concentrate on his writing career. Martin is a renowned northern Irish writer, famous for breaking down barriers by creating access to the theatre for working-class audiences by writing about issues relevant to their lives. His latest play, *The History of the Troubles (according to my da)* is currently on tour across Ireland and the UK.

Brian Maguire is one of Ireland's foremost visual artists. He is a painter who is known for his arts facilitation work in prisons and his championing of art and artists outside of the mainstream. He has worked and shown in the Americas and in Europe. He is represented by the Kerlin Gallery, Dublin. He was very involved in establishing the NCAD's Art Course in Portlaoise Prison. In 2000 he became the head of the Fine Art Faculty in the NCAD.

Declan McGonagle first came to prominence as the founding director of the Orchard Gallery in Derry. His innovative and groundbreaking work at the Orchard led him to the position of director of exhibitions at the ICA in London from 1984 to 1986, after which he returned to Derry to set up new exhibition and public art projects as well as education and community programmes for the City Council. In 1991 he was appointed the first director of the Irish Museum of Modern Art in Dublin. In 2002 he was contracted by City Arts Centre to head up a two-year re-visioning process for the Centre, entitled the Civil Arts Inquiry. Presently he is professor of Fine Art at the School of Art and Design, University of Ulster, in Belfast and director of INTERFACE, a new practice-based Research Centre, dealing with issues of art and context.

Gerri Moriarty is a drama worker, director and trainer. She has over 27 years' experience working with groups of all ages, backgrounds and abilities, to give voice to their concerns, dreams and aspirations through drama and performance. Over the past five years her work has included directing part of *The Wedding Community Play* and devising drama pieces with groups in Ethiopia and Eritrea. She also prepared the access part of the bid for Liverpool to be short-listed to become European Capital of Culture 2008. Gerri also works on evaluations and consultations for community arts projects.

Ailbhe Murphy is an artist living and working in Dublin. In 1991 she initiated the Unspoken Truths project and has continued to work in community contexts ever since, most recently as liaison artist for Breaking Ground, the Per Cent for Art programme in Ballymun. In 2003 Ailbhe was the first recipient of the Arts Council's Lar Cassidy Award for artists working in context. She is currently developing a cross-community city-wide collaborative project called Tower Songs. She is a board member of City Arts.

Fintan O'Toole is recognised as one of the most incisive Irish journalists of our time. Columnist and theatre critic for *The Irish Times*, he has published a wide range of books including *The Politics of Magic*; *No More Heroes*; *A Mass for Jesse James*; *Black Hole, Green Card*; and *After the Ball*.

Historical time line

The historical time line provided below, with short descriptions, is purely a help in tracing key moments of shift for community arts in Ireland and should not be read as definitive.

1932

- Stalin introduces 'Social Realism' and unionises the arts in the USSR.

    This had a profound effect on western artists, many of whom had aligned themselves to the left. In retrospect it was clearly part of the Communist regime's master plan of control but at the time it was interpreted differently. And it *was* different in that it gave all professional artists in the USSR the possibility of a minimum wage (provided they were party members) and established many community arts projects throughout Russia and its states, such as the 'agit-trains' – steam-driven arts centres that toured the country.

    In the West these new policies by the Soviet Union of 1932 created both a vision and a structure through which an artist could pursue his or her ideals within socialism. It brought the artist into the 'working-class' fold, legitimising the practice of the arts as part of the world-wide revolutionary struggle. Certainly, from the 1930s through to the 1970s, the perceived legitimising of 'artist as worker' by the USSR influenced alternative culture in the West, including community arts. It also inspired a building programme for cultural centres that saw almost every town, in not only Russia but in all of the USSR, have one such house.

1935

- Roosevelt's 'new deal' sees $46 million spent on commissioning work from unemployed artists (1935–1939).

When Franklin D. Roosevelt was elected president in 1933, he initiated a whole raft of progressive social policies to combat the great American depression that had followed from the Wall Street crash. This initiative was called 'The New Deal'. The arts were included in this New Deal, resulting in a staggering array of projects – for example, 2,566 public murals, 17,544 public sculptures, 108,899 paintings, eleven thousand theatre workers employed and new theatre shows that attract an audience of twelve million. Not only that, but a lot of these new companies, shows and artists were based in the community, in black areas such as Harlem in New York and in the rural areas of the Mid-West.

Like the USSR policies of 1932, the New Deal arts programme inspired many artists and opened the door for much greater participation in the arts, giving new perspectives and ways of working in a community context.

1940

- Committee for the Encouragement of Music and the Arts (CEMA) is established under the United Kingdom's 'emergency government' at the outbreak of the Second World War, a forerunner of the Arts Council of Great Britain (established in 1945).

    The CEMA had a very 'community arts' approach during the war years, with workshops, participation and equal access to the fore. The London Philharmonic and the London Symphony Orchestras gave concerts in factories; CEMA-employed musicians performed in air-raid shelters during the blitz; professional and amateur artists from all disciplines mixed and produced work for assembly lines, canteens and bombed-out areas; a mobile gallery brought works of art to hospitals and convalescent homes.

1951

- An Arts Act is passed into legislation by the Irish government, which leads to the formation of the Arts Council.

    The Arts Council/An Chomhairle Ealaíon is an autonomous body established to 'stimulate public interest in and promote the knowledge, appreciation and practice of the arts in the Republic of Ireland'. It grant aids individual professional artists through direct awards and bursaries and through Aosdána, the affiliation of creative artists. The Arts Council also supports multidisciplinary arts through activities and facilities such as arts centres, festivals and community arts.

    A point to note is that the Arts Act of 1951 does not mention the 'artist' anywhere in its definitions or functions. The sole emphasis is on stimulating public interest in the arts and assisting the public to know, appreciate and participate in the arts.

1962

- The Arts Council of Northern Ireland (ACNI) is established as the main distributor of arts funding in Northern Ireland, replacing the Council for the Encouragement of Music and the Arts (CEMA). ACNI became a company limited by guarantee in 1995.

1967

- The Blackie in Liverpool is established as the first community arts centre in Britain.

1968

- Fusion of art, youth culture and protest sparks world-wide agitation and consciousness raising.

    Almost ten years of a growing counterculturalism, fuelled by anti-Vietnam War protests, civil rights demonstrations, the assassination of Martin Luther King and repressive measures by the establishment, boil over resulting in ten thousand marchers battling with police in Paris, riots in Washington that bring armed National Guardsmen onto the streets and similar events in many other countries. Particular historical injustices and world events lead directly to civil rights activism in Ireland and riots in Northern Ireland.

A central part of this agitation and counterculturalism is freedom of expression and the arts as a liberating force for everyone.

- Welfare State International is founded.

   Welfare State International was one of the most successful touring theatre companies to emerge out of England in the 1960s. But more, its work was based on a marriage of ideology and creativity which was to inform the emerging community arts movement as this quote from their book 'Engineers of the Imagination' explains.

   'This long-term process of research-and-practice seeks to re-establish, away from the conventional building-based middlebrow/middle-class theatre, the popular theatre traditions of the working class.'

   Their success was an inspiration to many in Ireland.

1969

- Tax exemption for artists is declared in the 1969 Finance Bill and passed into Irish law.

1970

- Ciotog Drama Project is established in Waterford.

   This drama project, with its open and developmental approach, influenced and inspired a generation of people in Waterford and resulted in Waterford Arts for All and similar community arts initiatives.

1972

- *Pedagogy of the Oppressed* by Paolo Freire is published.

This book quickly became one of the defining texts for many working in the community arts field. It articulated arguments for such work and why it was important.

1973

- Grapevine (City Arts Centre) is founded.

  Grapevine grew out of a particular Dublin working-class experience, which was not related to any established arts movement or practice. Grapevine's birth was cultural in nature, emerging from class and personal struggles seeking to have a voice and a freedom promised by the radical developments of the 1960s. Founded as an alternative arts space in one room, the Centre moved three times over the next fifteen years, growing steadily in terms of programme and capacity, until it purchased its own building, a warehouse in the docklands, in 1988 and changed its name to City Arts Centre. Grapevine/City Arts Centre has traced and influenced community arts development in Ireland over a thirty-year history. In 2002 the Centre initiated the Civil Arts Enquiry, a strategic research initiative around issues of cultural production, distribution, participation and validation. While looking for new models of participatory civil culture in general, City Arts Centre was also looking to transform itself, responding to new challenges and changes in the cultural landscape of the new century. In 2004 the Centre published the results of the Civil Arts Enquiry and embarked on implementing these results.

1974

- The Arts Council of Great Britain establishes a Community Arts Panel.
- Wexford Arts Centre is founded.

  Wexford offered a new arts voice outside of Dublin

and signalled that change was afoot in Ireland as a whole.

- Albany Empire in London is founded.

   The Albany Empire is a community arts centre located in Deptford, London. Originally based in an old Victorian Theatre, which was demolished to make way for a road, the centre moved into a purpose-built building in 1984. One of the first of such buildings in these islands, the Albany Empire became something of a model and an inspiration for community groups in Ireland and Britain. The building itself comprised a café, theatre, bar, children–parent centre, workshop spaces, community shops and video/photography resource.

- Free International University is founded.

   The primary objective of the Free International University was to reactivate 'life values' through a creative interchange on the basis of equality between teachers and learners. In February 1974, after his return from his first lecture tour through the United States, entitled 'Energy Plan for the Western Man', Joseph Beúys and poet Heinrich Böll announced the Free International University for Creativity and Interdisciplinary Research (FIU). Offices of the Free International University were established across Europe and several branches continue to function to this day.

   Joseph Beúys (1921–1986) is quoted and mentioned at various times through this book. He was a visual artist who initiated and influenced many developments whereby art became a central protagonist in politics, the ecology movement, education and philosophy. An internationally renowned artist, Beúys was one of the pioneers of the concept of performance art and put forward many ideas that broke down the boundaries between art and cultural life in general. As the decades advanced, his commitment to political reform increased and he was involved in the founding of several activist groups: in 1967, the German Student Party, whose platform included world-wide disarmament and educational reform; in 1970, the Organisation for Direct Democracy by Referendum, which proposed increased political power for individuals; and the Free International University, which emphasised the creative potential in all human beings and advocated cross-pollination of ideas across disciplines. In 1979 he was one of five hundred founding members of the Green Party.

1975

- North City Centre Community Action Programme (NCCCAP) is established in Dublin's north inner city.

    Dublin's NCCCAP became a powerhouse of ideas and actions around innovative community development. From the beginning, in addition to its work in campaigning for better housing, social services and education for local people, the NCCCAP supported community arts and initiated a range of projects including the Lourdes arts and crafts centre and City Workshop drama project. In 1982 it ran the very successful 'Inner City, Looking On' festival. In 1991, the NCCCAP became a partner in establishing an arts facility in the old fire station in Buckingham Street and it is now resident as one of the organisations in that building.

1976

- First regional arts officer is appointed (Paul Funge – Mid-West Region).

    This move by the Arts Council represented a formal-isation of the acceptance of 'arts-as-development' rather than 'arts-as-separate' within society.

1978

- *Artists & People* by Sue Braden is published.

    This book is one of the few of its time that articulates arguments supporting community arts.

- Neighbourhood Open Workshops (NOW) is founded in Belfast.

  Neighbourhood Open Workshops began operations in the autumn of 1978 in Belfast. NOW was founded by a group of people working as volunteers on summer play schemes in Belfast for VSB (Voluntary Service Belfast). NOW, as well as being based in and being instrumental in developing the Crescent Arts Centre (as – at the time – Belfast's only 'neutral' community arts centre), also contributed to the establishment of CAFE as an Ireland-wide agency; conceived and set up the Play Resource Warehouse in Belfast; and was part of the consortium that set up the Old Museum Arts Centre. Also, NOW gave birth to Belfast Community Circus School. In addition, between 1982 and 1990, NOW ran workshops and classes in the Centre for Adult and Community Education, St Patrick's College, Maynooth, feeding in activities and findings from its work in Belfast. Other projects included: 1981 – 'A Weaving', tour of eighteen community venues North and South; 1983 – 'Jungle Bullion' in Belfast's Botanic Gardens staged by Welfare State International in collaboration with Neighbourhood Open Workshops.

- First Carnsore Point anti-nuclear festival is held.

  In 1977, the Irish government decided to instigate plans for building Ireland's first nuclear power plant in Carne, near Carnsore Point, Co. Wexford. Many people, both locally and nationally, were strongly opposed to nuclear power in Ireland and the idea of the free concerts/rallies in Carnsore Point was born. Entitled 'Get to the Point' (1978) and 'Back to the Point' (1979), with a final celebration in 1980, the concerts were a massive success and served to bring to public notice the whole question of nuclear power. Musicians, performers, visual artists, dancers and a host of helpers donated their time and energy in order that the festivals were as successful as they were. At the end of the seventies, the government decided that a nuclear power station was not viable for a country the size of Ireland. Today, Ireland remains nuclear-free.

1979

- Temporary Youth Employment Scheme allocates its first arts grants.

    The TYES, a Department of Education initiative funded by the government's Youth Employment Levy, begins funding arts projects under its manager Tony Ó Dálaigh. Shortly after its establishment, TYES becomes Teamwork. This scheme, growing and developing over the coming years as part of the Youth Employment Agency, sets a precedent for arts funding that continues on through ANCO (the training council) and FÁS.

- *Theatre of the Oppressed* by Augusto Boal is published.

    The Brazilian writer and theatre director uses drama as a means of empowering people. His theories and methods are widely used by community arts groups.

- Shelton Trust, a national organisation for community arts, is founded in England.

- Co-operation North (later known as Co-operation Ireland) is founded.

- Waterford Arts for All is founded

    Waterford Arts for All came about through the work of the Combat Poverty Agency. The aim of the group was to break down barriers to the arts, particularly for young people. Run as a democratic organisation, with open meetings at least once a month, their work covered many events throughout the year, including an annual arts festival. One of the main objectives of the group was to establish an arts centre in Waterford and this was finally realised with the opening of Garter Lane arts centre in 1985.

1980

- City Workshop is established in Dublin's north inner city.

    City Workshop was a groundbreaking drama project set

up under one of the NCCCAP's many community initiatives. The aim of City Workshop was to show that a community arts project could work, not as art for the people but as art by the people. Funded under a Teamwork scheme, participants were employed on a full-time basis and drawn from the local inner city community. In all, the project lasted for three years and resulted in three original productions based on themes relevant to Dublin's north inner city area and its history. The workshop was led by Peter Sheridan and it achieved much success, including critical acclaim for its productions.

- Community arts becomes a separate heading for Arts Council funding.
- Waterford Arts for All is founded.

  Waterford Arts for All came about through the work of Waterford Combat Poverty in 1979. The aim of the group was to break down barriers to the arts and to have fun, while, at the same time, tackling youth unemployment. Run as a democratic organisation, with open meetings at least once a month, their work covered many events throughout the year, including an annual arts festival. One of the main objectives of the group was to establish an arts centre in Waterford and this was finally realised with the opening of Garter Lane arts centre in 1985.

1982

- 'The Arts In Schools' by the Arts Council is published.
- 'Inner City, Looking On' Festival takes place.

  This festival was organised by the NCCCAP as a cultural statement and to highlight issues affecting the communities of Dublin's north inner city at that time. It was also a celebration, the first to profile these communities in any significant and positive way. The festival included all forms of expression and community life and spilled out from the main venues of the

Diamond and Mountjoy Square to stage events along the Quays and on the river Liffey itself.

- Moving Theatre is founded in Dublin.

  Founded by Annie Kilmartin, Moving Theatre brought live entertainment to Dublin audiences, performing in community centres, women's clubs, libraries and prisons. Moving Theatre's aim was to devise plays about issues that touched the hearts of its audience, providing entertainment for people who were not regular theatre-goers and offering them an alternative to bingo and the pub. Moving Theatre's workshop programme MADCAP (Moving Arts and Drama Community Action Programme) was established to provide opportunities for creative activity and to encourage the development of new art forms. The programme ran parallel to the work of the theatre company and in collaboration with play-schools, youth groups, senior citizens and community environmental projects.

1983

- Seminar on the place and role of creative activity takes place in the community, North Star Hotel, Dublin.

  Organised by City Workshop, this was the first recorded meeting in Ireland to discuss the type of work becoming known as community arts.

- CAFE is founded.

  Creative Activity for Everyone (CAFE) was founded as an umbrella group for community arts in Ireland. At that time it stated its main objective as 'community and individual development with creative activity as a means to that end'. Over the years CAFE took on a wide range of activities, including holding the first community arts conference, the setting up of the first community arts database, the publication of a funding handbook and the organising of the first community arts workers course. In 2003, CAFE changed its name to CREATE.

- *Engineers of the Imagination* by Welfare State International is published.

  This book became the main reference book for many community artists.
- Aosdána is inaugurated by the Arts Council.

1984

- First national community arts seminar is organised by CAFE, North Star Hotel (April).
- Wet Paint Arts is founded.

  Wet Paint was a ground-breaking arts initiative, concerned with developing models of relevant arts experience for young people.
- *Community, Art and the State* by Owen Kelly is published in England.

  This work created fierce debate in the community arts sector because of its unequivocal Marxist stance.
- Belfast Community Circus is founded.

1985

- First County Arts Officer is appointed (County Clare).
- ACE (Arts Community Education) scheme is launched by the Arts Council in partnership with Gulbenkian.

  Running from 1985 to 1989, ACE was an action research programme established by the Arts Council (Republic of Ireland) with the support of the Gulbenkian Foundation to examine the practice of community arts in Ireland. The methodology employed was to make a nationwide call for applicants to participate in the ACE programme, a selection of which would be funded to realise their projects. The monitoring and final evaluation of these projects would make up case studies to help the Arts Council (and any other interested parties) in their understanding of community arts. Six projects were chosen out of a total of 104 submissions: Cork

Teachers Centre (An Education Workshop), City Vision (Look at My Hands), ACE Committee (Poetry Project), Macnas (The Big Game), CAFE (Information Network Project), Fatima Development Group (Environmental Project). *Art and the Ordinary – The ACE Report* was published in 1989.

- 'Another Standard – Culture & Democracy' conference takes place in Sheffield organised by the Shelton Trust. CAFE is represented.
- *Another Standard – Culture and Democracy, the Manifesto* is published by the Shelton Trust.
- CAFE initiates the first community arts worker course.
- 'Art and Social Change in Ireland' conference takes place in Central Hall, Rosemary Street, Belfast, from 21–23 March, organised by Art and Research Exchange (ARE), Creative Activity for Everyone (CAFE), Neighbourhood Open Workshops (NOW) and Workers' Educational Association (WEA).
- Anglo-Irish agreement is published.
- Macnas is established in Galway.

   Macnas became Ireland's foremost street theatre company but their surrounding activities of training in all areas of pageantry, producing original stage work and inviting innovative circus and physical theatre companies from abroad had a huge impact on this area of work in Ireland.

- Social Employment Scheme is launched by FÁS giving rise to hundreds of community arts projects.

1986

- First 'cultural agreement' is reached between the Arts Council and a local authority (Limerick).
- Combat Poverty Agency is established.

   The Combat Poverty Agency is an Irish state agency that works as an advisory body to the government. The aim of the Agency is to promote a more just and inclusive society by working for the prevention and elimination of poverty and social exclusion. The Agency pursues this aim through the four main functions set out in the Combat Poverty Agency Act: policy advice; project support and innovation; research and public education. Under various headings, since its establishment, the Combat Poverty Agency has funded community arts programmes as part of its strategy.

- GLC (Greater London Council) is abolished.

  Between 1981 and 1986, the GLC funding policy with regard to community arts had been a strong example for Irish community arts groups (up to £9 million in a year for community arts projects) and when it was disbanded by Margaret Thatcher, a vital source of contact, support and leadership for community arts in general went with it.
- CAFE publishes the first Funding Handbook.

1987

- The North-West Musicians' Collective is established, which later became the Nerve Centre – Derry.
- Irish government White Paper on the arts *Access and Participation* is published.
- First allocation from the National Lottery in the Republic to the arts amounts to £8 million.

1988

- Féile an Phobail / West Belfast Festival is established.
- FÁS is established.

  FÁS (The Training and Employment Authority) becomes the new authority for 'back to work' training, replacing the Youth Employment Agency, ANCO and the National Manpower Service. Its stated aim is to provide training to help meet national objectives. It is responsible for apprenticeship, non-apprenticeship skills training and in-company industrial training and it introduced a range of training programmes to carry out its mandate, such as the Social Employment Scheme and Community Employment.

- Balcony Bells is founded.

  The Balcony Bells was a community theatre group established by women living in and around Sheriff Street in Dublin's north inner city.

1989

- The ACE (Arts Community Education) report (Ciarán Benson) is published by the Arts Council.
- 'The Stone Chair', Belfast's first large-scale community play, is produced at the Grand Opera House.
- 'Parade of Innocence' takes place in Dublin.

  This was an arts event around the issue of innocent Irish people in English jails because of miscarriages of justice.
- City Arts Centre becomes the affiliate organisation for the American arts and disability foundation, Very Special Arts, later to become the independent organisation Arts and Disability Ireland.

1990

- Art Squads is founded by Artists Association of Ireland and Sculptors Society and funded by FÁS.
- Arts Council introduces the Artist in the Community scheme.
- Nerve Centre is established in Derry to promote youth culture.

  The Nerve Centre in Derry is an award-winning arts and technology resource for youth culture and creativity. It is fully equipped for every aspect of multi-media production and digital technologies. The centre pursues an integrated strategy combining cultural and educational objectives with social and economic goals.

1991

- 'Unspoken Truths' exhibition opens in the Irish Museum of Modern Art (IMMA).
- City Arts Centre, under its Very Special Arts wing, holds its first Young Playwrights Programme, producing the winning play

Seconds Out, by students at St Francis' Training Centre in Cork, at the Abbey Theatre.

- National Arts Workers Course is established.

  The National Arts Workers Course was established by CAFE, the first full-time, accredited community arts training programme in the Republic of Ireland. This was a course for experienced community arts workers with the aim of enhancing their skills and ability once back in their respective communities. The course received its accreditation as an extra-mural diploma from St Patrick's College, Maynooth.

1992

- Verbal Arts Centre, Derry, is established.
- Community Employment Development Programme (CEDP) is launched by FÁS in the twelve Programme for Economic and Social Progress areas.
- Open Arts is formed in Belfast.

  Open Arts exists to encourage disabled people to participate in the arts. It seeks to help disabled people to create their own art by improving accessibility and creating equal opportunities to participate in the arts. Activities include drama, creative writing, visual arts, photography, music and dance. Open Arts participated in the Special Olympics opening ceremony in 2003.

- First festival of community and youth theatre takes place in City Arts Centre.
- The Playhouse Community Arts Resource Centre in Derry is opened.

  The Playhouse opened to serve the people of the diverse communities of the north west by providing an environment in which people could express and develop their creative abilities. It adopts a multi-cultural, multidisciplinary approach to the arts and houses a range of community based arts projects. The Playhouse is a multi-media venue with a fully equipped two-hundred-seat theatre, a dance studio, a gallery and training rooms.

- Beat Initiative is set up in Belfast.

  The Beat Initiative was established in east Belfast in 1992 as a creative mix of arts, media, business and community work practice. Based around a yearly street carnival, the Belfast Carnival Parade, the Beat Initiative aims to promote quality arts access, engagement and production with a wide programme of workshops, events and multi-arts collaborations. The organisation is currently exploring the possibility of developing an innovative carnival arts training course.

1993

- Community Arts Forum (CAF) is founded in Northern Ireland. CAF is the umbrella and developmental body for community arts in Northern Ireland. CAF aims to develop the sector and all its constituent parts through a programme of training, information, research, publications, advice, support, advocacy and networking.
- First Arts & Health conference – organised by City Arts Centre in partnership with the Healthy Cities Project – takes place.
- 'Celebrating Difference' exhibition (arts and disability, disability arts) opens in City Arts Centre and goes on tour until the end of 1994.
- First Department of Arts, Culture and the Gaeltacht is established by the Irish government with Michael D. Higgins as its first Minister.
- Community arts pilot scheme is established by CAFE and Combat Poverty Agency.

1994

- Republican and Loyalist cease-fire is declared in Northern Ireland.
- First Arts & Disability conference, Royal Hospital, Kilmainham is organised by City Arts Centre in partnership with the National Rehabilitation Board (NRB).
- Community Employment (CE) is launched by FÁS (replacing SES, CEDP and Teamwork).

- Arts & Disability Forum is formed in Northern Ireland.
- 'Big Bang' festival, Dublin, is produced by Wet Paint Arts and City Arts Centre. This was the largest coming together of community music in Ireland to date.

1995

- WheelWorks is formed in Belfast.

    WheelWorks was established to provide artistic and creative opportunities to young people across Northern Ireland, offering a wide range of services including facilitators for visual arts, music, drama, dance and multi-media arts projects, resources which make projects happen, training for projects working with young people, advice and a consultancy service.
- A *Strategy for Equality* report is delivered to government by the Commission on the Status of People with Disabilities. It contains a substantial section on arts and culture.
- 'Arts and the Community' conference, Maynooth College is organised by City Arts Centre in partnership with CAFE and Combat Poverty Agency (June).
- The Arts Council publishes its first strategic Arts Plan.

1997

- Large street carnival in Belfast is organised by the Beat Initiative as a community celebration for the whole city.

1998

- *Vital Signs*, mapping community arts in Belfast, is published by Comedia.
- Good Friday Agreement is endorsed overwhelmingly by a majority of Irish voters north and south of the border.

1999

- Greater East Belfast Community Arts Network is formed.
- New Belfast Community Arts Initiative is formed.
- *The Wedding Community Play* takes Belfast Festival at Queens by storm.

2000

- 'Eleven Acres-Ten Steps' regeneration document is launched by Fatima Mansions, Dublin.
- The St Patrick's Day parade is re-vamped into a festival with community participation.
- Northern Ireland community arts sector organises protest to DCAL to raise awareness around arts funding distribution within Northern Ireland.

2001

- 'Community Arts: The Next Five Years' conference is organised by CAFE and CAF in Maynooth College.

2002

- NCAD (National College of Art and Design) introduces Higher Diploma in Community Arts.
- City Arts Centre launches the 'Civil Arts Inquiry'.
- The Department of Arts, Heritage, the Gaeltacht and the Islands is restructured, making the arts simply a section within in the Department of Arts, Sport and Tourism.
Ireland's first community dance conference takes place in the Waterside Theatre in Derry organised by CAF, Dance Northern Ireland and the Waterside Development Trust as part of the 'Gathering' festival.

2003

- 'Good, Better, Best' arts and disability conference at Craigavon Civic Centre is organised by CAF, Open Arts, Adapt Northern Ireland and the Arts and Disability Forum.
- The first all-Ireland community arts journal, *Contexts,* is published by CAFE/CREATE.

2004

- *An Outburst of Frankness* is published.